Contents

Preface

In the thirty-three years since publication of the first edition, the field of learning theory has (predictably) demonstrated both stability and change. Hull's theory, then the dominant contender among a group of competing "grand theories," has passed from the contemporary scene. Supporters of Skinner's "nontheory" have risen from the status of embattled radicals to a position of near dominance and then sunk again, in spite of many empirical successes, to the status of embattled conservatives, if not reactionaries. Cognitive approaches, so long rejected by the mainstream, have become the mainstream. Both biology and computer science have become increasingly relevant to learning theory, and mathematics has retained its relevance as well. Grand theories may seem less grand than they used to, given the more recent popularity of smaller models, but the creation and justification of both large and small theories goes vigorously on.

These changes present a problem for the author of a book such as this. Ideally the theories given most prominence would be those that are at the cutting edge of scientific psychology, that have the most practical applications to offer, and that are most accessible to typical students. In the early years of American learning theory, to a considerable extent the same theories satisfied all three of these criteria. By 1963, when the first edition appeared, this was already less true, and it is still less true in 1996. In addition, the history of earlier theories—no longer active but still relevant and heuristically useful—has of course grown longer. Difficult choices are therefore required as to which theories to include.

The goal of both the continuity and the changes in this edition is to provide a brief, accessible introduction to theories of learning, including the logic of what they try to accomplish, their historical development, their present status, and the usefulness of their applications. The book does not attempt to be a comprehensive treatment of the psychology of learning. Rather, it can be used as the core text (with supplements) in a theory-oriented learning course, as one of several readings in a general course on learning (or learning and motivation), as the learning part of an advanced course in educational psychology or in history and systems of psychology, or in various other ways.

In this edition I have increased the emphasis on accessibility. The most noticeable result is that coverage of mathematical theories has been reduced from a chapter to a section, in which the general characteristics of mathematical models are briefly discussed, but without consideration of any specific model. In addition, treatment of the specifics of Hull's theory has been further reduced, without shortening the discussion of that theory's central place both in the logic of theory construction and in the development of interdisciplinary applications. In order to achieve clearer focus on fewer theories, Lewin's theory has been deleted, and the resulting extra space has been used to provide more explanations and illustrations elsewhere in the book.

The contrast between connectionist and cognitive theories remains central to the book, as it has been since the first edition, but with a considerable increase in the treatment of cognitive approaches. Whereas in previous editions the applications that were considered came largely from connectionist theories, this edition includes a number of applications of cognitive theories. These additions include cognitive behavioral therapy, Seligman's work on explanatory styles, and Ausubel's use of advance organizers in education. Rescorla's cognitive interpretation of classical conditioning has also been added. Moreover, the cognitive revolution is treated more explicitly than in the previous edition, with extensive consideration of when, how, and why it happened.

As in earlier editions, the focus remains on long-term learning rather than short-term information processing. However, retention as distinguished from acquisition—that is, the explicit consideration of memory—is no longer treated separately, but only incorporated with other topics when specifically relevant. Motivation, however, still receives chapter-length treatment. Biology receives more emphasis in the context of species-specific learning patterns as evolutionary adaptations, and also in the context of individual differences, including how heredity and cultural learning interact in the development of each person's individuality. However, I decided that another aspect of biology, namely the physiology and biochemistry of learning, for all its current importance to learning, is too technical for this book.

I have kept the treatment of computers both as a key factor in the development of cognitive theory and as a possible basis for integrating connectionist and cognitive models, since these issues can be treated in a largely nontechnical way. Indeed, Anderson's ACT theory, which can be seen as a current attempt to do with computer-based cognitive theory what Hull tried to do with connectionist theory, has been expanded with a detailed example. The one exception to the increased emphasis on accessibility is the chapter on the new connectionism, which I have retained for its integrative potential, but it can be omitted by instructors who find that potential insufficient to justify the effort.

I want to thank the following reviewers for their valuable comments on the manuscript:

James Calkins
Drexel University

John Rosenbach
SUNY Albany

Peter Toscano
University of Massachusetts

Kevin Vinson
Loyola College

I was helped by their suggestions, heartened by their encouragement, and stimulated by their diversity. I hope the resulting sixth edition is both an improvement over the previous edition and a continuation of what has been valuable in the book's thirty-three-year life.

WINFRED F. HILL

Chapter
1

How Psychologists
Study Learning

T heoretical systems for the interpretation of learning have grown up along with the experimental study of learning, and to understand one it is necessary to understand the other. Although the experimental study of learning to a large extent grew out of everyday problems, particularly problems in education, it soon became involved with theoretical issues and with experiments appropriate for dealing with them. This theoretical involvement proceeded to such an extent that the original problems became barely recognizable. It is therefore worthwhile to take a long look at the interrelations between theory, research, and applications in the field of learning before undertaking a detailed survey of different theoretical systems.

The reader should be warned at the outset that psychologists use the term *learning* more broadly than it is used in popular speech. Although it is almost impossible to give an exact definition of learning that all psychologists will accept, we can at least note certain phenomena to which the term is or is not applied. In psychological usage, what is learned need not be "correct" or adaptive (we learn bad habits as well as good), need not be conscious or deliberate (one of the advantages of coaching in a skill is that it makes us aware of mistakes we have unconsciously learned to make), and need not involve any overt act (attitudes and emotions can be learned as well as knowledge and skills). Reactions as diverse as driving a car, remembering a pleasant vacation, believing in democracy, and disliking one's boss all represent the results of learning.

How does learning take place? What factors determine what we will learn and how rapidly we will learn it? Innumerable people are in situations in which it would be useful to have answers to these questions. We think at once of students looking for better methods of study, of teachers wanting to improve their classroom techniques, and of people in industry seeking better ways of training new workers. We may also consider the parent looking for the best way of raising children, the counselor trying to improve a client's emotional and social adjustment, the animal trainer preparing seeing-eye dogs for their work, and the advertiser attempting to develop a consumer's preference for a client's product. In all of these cases, knowledge about the learning process represents power.

The above practical needs are not the only reasons for wanting to know more about learning. People have always been curious about themselves, have always wanted to know more about what "makes them tick." Since learning is such an important factor in what we are and do, a greater understanding of the learning process would go far toward increasing self-knowledge. Consequently, people are motivated to study learning, not only by the practical benefits to be gained but also by curiosity about themselves and how they came to be as they are.

LEARNING IN SCHOOL

Let's begin by looking at a setting in which learning is the primary focus: the school. Children in school face a bewilderingly complex learning situation. It is complex from their point of view; it is even more so from the point of view of the psychologist who bravely attempts to analyze it. The children are influenced in countless ways by the varied aspects of the classroom situation. They learn much from the teacher, including many things not prescribed in the curriculum and some things of which neither teacher nor pupils are aware. They also learn from books, from fellow students, and from the physical arrangements of the school. Part of what they learn is measurable as specific knowledge and skills, while another part involves changes, some very subtle but a few quite dramatic, in attitudes, emotions, social behavior, and a variety of other reactions. The psychologist's job is to analyze such complex situations into their component parts and to try to understand the principles of learning and motivation involved.

Let us consider some incidents in the school day of a particular sixth-grader, Alex B. We meet Alex first as he is studying a vocabulary list in his reading book. His teacher (a trifle old-fashioned) has instructed the class to learn to spell these words. He is thus confronted with a list of 12 words for which he must learn to give the correct written form when presented with the spoken form. However, in studying from his book he faces a slightly different task, since only the written form is before him and he must provide the spoken version himself, but without saying it aloud. He goes through the list, pronouncing and spelling the words to himself, but finds his attention wandering. He looks out the window and remembers how much he enjoyed the previous weekend. Snapping back to the spelling book, he continues dutifully to the end of the list. Then he tries covering all but the first letter of each word with his hand in an attempt to spell the word to himself. At *r* he proceeds cautiously, trying to remember the rule for *i* and *e*. Finally he decides on "receive," moves his hand away, and relaxes a bit as he finds his guess confirmed. At *s* he spells to himself, without hesitation, "seperate," then frowns as he sees his mistake. He stares for a moment at the *ar*, trying to fix it in his memory, then continues through the list. Halfway through, he finds himself unable to remember a word from the first letter.

Annoyed, he looks at the word and then concentrates heavily on trying to remember it. Two words later, the same thing happens again. He looks at the word, wonders why it should be hard to remember, and begins to feel discouraged. He stares at the picture on the wall of Washington crossing the Delaware, and imagines himself leading such an expedition. Catching the teacher's eye, he returns quickly to his book and finishes the list. He spells the last word confidently as "cematary," only to find "cemetery" staring back at him from the page. Puzzled, he looks back and forth from *separate* to *cemetery* and thinks, "I hate spelling."

We see Alex next at recess running excitedly out to join a softball game. He begins the game in the outfield. As the batter hits a ground ball in his direction, he starts running, his speed and direction adjusted to make his path intercept that of the ball. As he nears the ball he bends over, puts his hands in front of it, and closes them at just the right moment to catch the ball. He then looks up, notes the position of the runner, and throws the ball in the direction of first base, his arm motion just forceful enough to carry the ball to the first baseman. This whole sequence of coordinated, purposeful behavior occurs rapidly, almost automatically, with no evidence of thought or verbal self-instruction. Watching him, the teacher is impressed by how much Alex has improved at softball since she has known him.

During the game, Alex calls frequently, "Wait'll I get to bat!" and "When am I up?" Finally his turn comes. He pounds the plate and shouts, "Put it over!" When the pitcher throws the ball, Alex takes a mighty swing at it, and misses. He looks chagrined, but shouts, "Let's have another!" Again he swings and misses. This time he frowns and says nothing. He stands more rigidly at the plate, his teeth clenched. His swing at the third pitch is more tense, less free, and again he misses. He throws the bat down and stalks away. At his next turn in the outfield, he does no shouting, and his fielding is less coordinated. When recess ends, he returns quietly to the classroom, ignoring the chatter around him. He seems relieved that recess is over.

Later we see Alex during his math lesson. The class has been learning how to find the areas of rectangles. Now the teacher raises the problem of how to find the area of a triangle. She draws a right triangle with a 4-inch side and 3-inch side on the blackboard and asks the students what the area is. Alex likes math and enjoys learning how to solve new problems, so he eagerly tries to figure this one out. He tries to apply the rule for rectangles, but cannot see how to do it. Then the teacher draws two more lines, making a rectangle with the hypotenuse of the triangle as its diagonal. Alex stares at this for a moment, then grins and excitedly holds up his hand. "The area is 6. The whole rectangle is 12, and there are two triangles, and each triangle is half of the rectangle!" The teacher smiles. "Very good. The area is half of 4 times 3. Math makes a lot of sense when you figure it out like that." Alex basks in his success, pleased both with the teacher's approval and with his triumph over the impersonal challenge of the problem.

We leave Alex now, happy that a rather frustrating day for him has ended with success. However, the challenge to a psychologist to analyze Alex's experiences lasts long after the incidents are over. In fact, the narrative of Alex's day might be used as a hidden-picture puzzle: "How many aspects of learning can you find illustrated in these incidents?" Consider, for example, the similarities and differences among the three situations in which we saw Alex. All involved learning, motivation, goal-directed behavior, and success or failure. All could be analyzed in terms of the responses that Alex made to various stimuli in his environment, and also in terms of the way he perceived the environment. All occurred in social situations and against a background of norms and values shared (though not completely) by Alex, his teacher, and his fellow students. However, the three situations differed in the principal kinds of learning involved (verbal memorization of the spelling list, motor skill on the softball field, and logical insight in the math problem). The situations also differed in the emotional learning that occurred and in some of the subsidiary principles. In each situation we may ask what factors contributed to Alex's successes and failures. How much did his difficulty in spelling *cemetery,* for example, depend on the word itself, on its position in the list, on the fact that *separate* came earlier in the same lesson, on distractions in the room at that moment, or on a variety of other facts about Alex, the lesson, and the general situation? There are endless possibilities for the psychologist to analyze in these three everyday situations.

However, such analysis assumes that we already know a great deal about the principles of learning. In cases where a number of factors might have influenced Alex's behavior, we cannot make worthwhile guesses about how important each was unless we have information about how important each has been in other similar situations. For example, we cannot judge whether the word *cemetery* itself or the situation in which Alex encountered it contributed more to his error unless we know something about the relative importance of words and their context in other cases of memorization. It is to provide such information about the regularities in behavior that psychologists do experimental studies. If we learn from such studies that certain situations cause special difficulty in memorizing, we are in a much better position both to explain Alex's errors and to find ways of helping him.

LEARNING IN THE LABORATORY

Let us now look at some typical laboratory learning situations. As compared with Alex's experiences, some of these may appear artificial or trivial. This difference is the price we pay in order to have situations in which we can manipulate certain variables, hold others constant, and measure precisely the resultant changes in behavior. We will see many relations between the complex situations in which Alex learned and these simpler, better-controlled laboratory learning situations.

Two Complex Learning Situations

In the first laboratory situation, as in Alex's math lesson, the learner (commonly called the subject) is presented with a problem for which he or she must find a solution. A traditional problem for use with college students requires the subject to tie together two strings hanging from the ceiling. The strings are so far apart that when one is held, the student cannot reach the other, which is why this otherwise easy task constitutes a problem. The only equipment available to help with the job is a pair of pliers. Can the student find a way of tying the strings together? (There need not be an actual room with two strings; problem and solution can all be worked with pencil and paper.)

What commonly happens in this situation is that the subject tries a variety of approaches, all unsuccessful. The pliers might be used as an extension of the arm to reach the second string, but they are too short. It might be possible to cut a piece off one of the strings with the pliers and tie it to the other, but the two strings could still not be brought together. Finally, the thought of swinging the strings occurs to most people. Given this lead, the solution usually comes quickly: tie the pliers to one of the strings, start the string swinging as a pendulum, then run over to the other string, bring it as close as possible to the one that is swinging, and catch the swinging one at the closest point of its arc. Since the subject is now holding both strings, he or she can easily tie them together.

How does this laboratory problem differ from the geometric problem that Alex solved in the classroom? In principle, there is very little difference. Both have simple solutions drawing on the solver's past experience, but both are difficult because they require the use of this past experience in new ways. The solution in each case usually involves a period of futile search followed by a flash of insight. A hint, such as the two extra lines the teacher drew, or the word *pendulum* in the two-string problem, often results in quick solution of the problem. The ability to tie the strings or compute the area of the triangle not only appears suddenly but is also very well retained compared with much other learned material.

The important difference is not between the two problems but between the classroom and the laboratory. In the classroom, on the one hand, we do not know how soon (if at all) Alex would have solved the problem without the teacher's hint, or why Alex rather than another student solved it first, or how many other students would have found the solution if Alex had not beaten them to it, or how the presence of other students helped or hindered him. In the laboratory, on the other hand, all of these questions can be systematically studied. The problem can be presented to subjects singly or in groups, with hints at predetermined points, and each person's time to solution (and mistaken "solutions") can be recorded. This laboratory situation makes it possible to investigate two sets of factors—those in the situation and those in the individual—that contribute to this learning.

Another laboratory example, closer to the popular image of a learning situation, involves rote memorization. The items to be memorized are commonly either words or *trigrams* (three-letter sequences that do not make a word), but they may be sentences or longer passages of connected material. The task may be to learn a series of them in order (as would be the case in learning a series of instructions), or to remember as many items as possible regardless of order (as for remembering a number of jobs that need to be done), or to learn a number of pairs of items with one member of the pair always given as the response to the other (comparable to learning a foreign language vocabulary), or any of various other possibilities. Usually the rate at which the items are delivered to the learner is controlled by the experimenter, such as by presenting them on the screen of a computer terminal.

The contrast between such a learning task and Alex's spelling lesson again lies largely in the precision of control that the laboratory setup permits. On the one hand, Alex could approach the words to be learned in any order and divide his time among them in way he chose. Moreover, he had to study from a book, even though the test of his mastery would consist of writing the words in response to oral dictation. This difference forced him to devise techniques of practice that would as nearly as possible match the test procedure. Finally, he was subjected to the distractions of the classroom situation. The laboratory subject, on the other hand, commonly sees the items in a predetermined order and for constant amounts of time in a small room with a minimum of distractions. Often the subject is automatically tested on each item each time through the list, so there is a continuous record of mastery of each item at each stage in the learning process. This record makes possible separate analyses of different stages of learning, different parts of the list, and different individual items.

Two Simpler Learning Situations

Both the problem-solving and the rote-learning situations in the laboratory represent refinements of learning situations found in the classroom and elsewhere in everyday life outside the laboratory. However, many psychological experimenters analyze these and other examples of learning (e.g., Alex's learning of the motor skills involved in fielding a softball) into simpler components and then study these components separately. Rather than working with complex patterns of responses such as Alex learned, they study changes in the frequency or magnitude or speed of a single response. Their object is not to study everyday kinds of learning under better-controlled conditions, but to study the underlying components of everyday learning in order to get a better understanding of what learning is. Such understanding, it is hoped, can then be used to predict learning in a great variety of more complex situations. This approach is comparable to that in other sciences, in which complex chemical substances are analyzed into their component elements or the speed of a falling object is studied as a function of the distance it has fallen, without regard to whether the object is a mailbag, a skydiver before the parachute opens, or a hydrogen bomb.

Since research of this sort attempts to reduce learning to its assumed simplest essentials, animals have often been found to be more satisfactory subjects than humans. Animals lack the complexities of language and cultural traditions, their background of previous experience is both simpler and (at least if they are reared in the laboratory) less variable than that of humans, and their heredity as well as their rearing can to a considerable extent be controlled. All these factors make it easier to study one aspect of the animal's learning processes at a time while holding others constant. For example, if we want to study the rate at which a dog learns to flex its leg to avoid an electric shock, we probably do not have to worry about the dog's interpretation of the purpose of the experiment or about its concern with behaving bravely, politely, or rationally, all of which would be factors if we were studying the same behavior in humans. This is not to say that humans cannot usefully be studied in such situations, for they often are; but it points out why for certain purposes animals often are preferred.

The above discussion implies that it does not make much difference what species we study—that the basic laws of learning are the same in rats, dogs, pigeons, monkeys, and humans. Learning theorists have indeed commonly made that assumption. The emphasis here is on the word *basic*. No one doubts that there are differences in the way different species learn, but it is often assumed that there are common underlying principles that apply to a wide range of species, principles from which we can deduce the detailed patterns of learning in different species. More is said about this assumption in Chapter 14, but for the present it is enough to note how important the assumption has been in learning theory over the years. We will see many examples of its application in the chapters that follow.

One simple animal response that has been extensively studied is the pecking response in pigeons. A lighted disk is displayed on the side of the box in which the pigeon is confined. The disk is referred to as a *key*, since like a telegraph key it closes an electrical circuit to record the pigeon's response, and the whole apparatus is known as a Skinner box, in honor of the theorist we will consider in Chapter 6. If a hungry pigeon is occasionally rewarded with food for pecking the key, it will peck it at a high rate. This pecking rate is quite sensitive to changes in level of hunger, frequency of food reward, and other variables. It can thus be used to investigate many of the phenomena of simple learning.

The low rate at which the pigeon pecks before food is introduced is called the *operant* (or *baseline*) *rate*. When food is first presented as soon as the pigeon pecks the key, the rate of pecking rises. In technical terms, this change indicates that the food reinforces the pecking, or that it is a *reinforcer*. If some but not all pecks are followed by food, the particular pattern used (e.g., food after every tenth peck, or after one peck each minute) is known as the *schedule of reinforcement*. If pecking is no longer followed by food, the rate drops. This decline in rate resulting from the removal of the reinforcer is known as *extinction*. If after extinction takes place there is an interval of time during which the pigeon does not have access to the key, and then the key is presented again, the pecking rate is likely to be higher than it was at the end of extinction. This increase in rate is called, naturally enough, *spontaneous recovery*. If a key that the pigeon has been reinforced for pecking is replaced by another key of a different color, the pigeon will peck at this key also, though not as much as at the original one. This tendency to respond to stimuli other than the one used in training is known as *generalization*. If, however, the two keys are presented alternately, with pecking at one reinforced and pecking at the other nonreinforced (extinguished), the pigeon will learn to peck the reinforced key at a high rate and the nonreinforced key very little. We then say that a *discrimination* between the keys has been formed.

Many aspects of the above learning phenomena have been studied experimentally. How does the rate of pecking vary with the amount of food given, the schedule of reinforcement, or the delay between peck and food? How does spontaneous recovery vary with the time interval between extinction and test, or generalization vary with the difference in color between the two keys? Will making a pigeon more hungry increase or decrease its ability to form a discrimination? Questions like this may be studied, not only with regard to the rate of key pecking in pigeons, but also with regard to many other forms of behavior in a variety of species.

These learning phenomena, established in experimental studies, can be applied (though often with some modification) to complex learning in everyday life. Though we did not see Alex over a long enough period of time to observe the effects of reinforcement and extinction in his behavior, we can note a number of cases in which these processes were probably occurring for him. On the one hand, his statement about the area of the triangle was reinforced by the teacher's praise, his techniques of fielding the softball by the approval of his fellow players, and his correct spellings by seeing those spellings confirmed by the printed words. On the other hand, his incorrect spellings, his batting techniques, and his confident manner with regard to batting were not reinforced and hence presumably underwent some extinction. The disappearance of his confident shouting after he struck out might be taken as evidence of extinction. If the shouting reappeared at his next softball game, this renewal could be interpreted as spontaneous recovery. The problem of spelling *separate* with an *ar* and *cemetery* with an *er* clearly involved making a discrimination between two similar situations, and it might also be interpreted as extinguishing the tendency to spell phonetically.

Not only can we identify these learning processes operating in everyday life; we can also make predictions from learning experiments to everyday learning situations. For example, it is commonly found in experiments that a delay between the response and the reinforcer results in poorer performance of the learned response. From this finding we could make predictions about the efficacy of different teaching methods. If Alex had taken a spelling quiz on one day but had not found out which words he got right until the papers were handed back the next day, he probably would have learned less spelling than he did with his book, because of the delay in reinforcement. However, it is possible that the opposite might be true, either because correctness on a graded test is more reinforcing than correctness on a private self-test, or because writing from dictation is a better way of studying spelling, or for a variety of other reasons. This example demonstrates both the usefulness of laboratory study in making suggestions about everyday learning and the danger in taking such suggestions uncritically.

A fourth example of laboratory learning, and one even less like the ordinary picture of a learning situation, occurs in experiments on *classical conditioning*. The first of these, and still the most famous, were those in which the Russian physiologist Ivan Pavlov, who will be considered in Chapter 3, used the procedure to train dogs to salivate to a new stimulus. Another version of this procedure (less famous than Pavlov's salivating dogs, but more popular in American labs) is the conditioning of the eye-blink reflex in humans and in rabbits. If people who are watching a dim light see the light grow somewhat brighter, they ordinarily do not blink their eyes in response to this stimulus. If, however, they are hit in the eye by a mild puff of air, they do blink. The conditioning procedure consists in pairing these two stimuli, with the brightening of the light coming a fraction of a second before the puff of air. Each time this sequence occurs, the subject blinks in response to the air puff. Presently, however, the subject begins to blink as soon as the light changes, before the puff comes. Since the changing light now produces a blinking response which it formerly did not produce, learning is said to have taken place. In this setup the puff, which already produced blinking, is called the *unconditioned stimulus,* and blinking to the puff is the *unconditioned response.* The increase in brightness of the light is called the *conditioned stimulus,* and the learned response of blinking to it is the *conditioned response.* The whole learning sequence is known as *conditioning.* The same principles of reinforcement, extinction, spontaneous recovery, generalization, and discrimination that were illustrated by the pigeon pecking a key can also be demonstrated in classical conditioning situations.

The distinctive characteristic of this kind of learning is that the conditioned stimulus elicits a response after the learning experience that only the unconditioned stimulus elicited before. (Because some authorities use the term *conditioning* rather broadly, this specific kind is often referred to as either classical conditioning or Pavlovian conditioning.) Since classical conditioning does not involve learning new responses, solving problems, or carrying out goal-directed activity, it seems at first glance to be of little importance compared with the other forms of learning discussed so far. Some theorists have concurred in this judgment, regarding classical conditioning as nothing more than a laboratory curiosity. Others, as we shall see, have regarded it as being of central importance. One viewpoint is that its importance is mainly for understanding the learning of emotional reactions, such as preferences for certain tastes or fears of certain objects or situations. When Alex experienced failures at spelling and at batting, he reacted with discouragement and anger. These can be considered unconditioned responses to the unconditioned stimulus of failure. When he said, "I hate spelling," this opinion may have indicated that conditioning was taking place, with the spelling lesson as the conditioned stimulus and discouragement and anger as the conditioned response. This interpretation makes classical conditioning of emotional responses crucial to our learning of attitudes toward all the people, objects, and situations we encounter in our lives.

Advantages of Laboratory Study

The preceding examples should have helped to indicate the relationships between the sorts of learning situations studied in the laboratory and those of most interest to educators and to others directly concerned with the problems of learning in everyday life. However, it may be well to discuss certain aspects of the relationships more explicitly. Two main points need to be considered: (1) what psychologists gain by studying learning under the somewhat artificial conditions of the laboratory, and (2) what difficulties are involved in applying the results to other, nonlaboratory situations.

There are two main ways in which psychologists gain by taking questions about learning into the laboratory. One of these pertains to measurement. The laboratory situation permits experimenters to measure the subject's behavior more adequately than is usually possible outside the laboratory. They can keep an accurate record of how long it takes a subject to memorize certain material or to solve a given problem, of how many and what kinds of errors a subject makes, and of the successive stages by which mastery is reached. This improved measurement is valuable for three reasons. First, it gives a more complete picture of the learning process. Details are recorded that otherwise would be overlooked or quickly forgotten. Second, it protects researchers from the mistake of noticing and remembering only what they expect. Thus a teacher who is convinced that a certain new method of teaching long division will work better than the old method may clearly remember striking successes with the new method, while overlooking the failures as unimportant exceptions. It is possible, of course, that in this case the failures *are* unimportant exceptions, but whether or not they are should be decided by careful consideration, not by spur-of-the-moment intuition. If both successes and failures are recorded as they occur, and if extenuating circumstances are noted for the successes as well as for the failures, the effect of teaching with the new method can be more objectively evaluated. Third, apart from such systematic biases as this teacher has, careful measurement also protects researchers against all the unsystematic errors of observation and memory that are likely to occur when research is carried on as part of everyday work. Thus measurement in the laboratory will probably be more thorough, more precise, and more objective than measurement in comparable situations elsewhere. Although in principle it is possible to achieve equally good measurement outside the laboratory, in practice it is usually much harder to do so.

The other gain from studying learning in the lab is control. Essentially, this gain is associated with our ability to study one thing at a time. When we control a variable, we hold it constant so that it will not interfere with our studying another variable. Suppose, for example, that we want to find out whether it is easier to learn spelling when words that are likely to cause confusion because of similar letter sequences (e.g., *separate* and *cemetery*) are in the same lesson or in different lessons. We can study this problem by preparing two sets of lessons, one according to each principle, and using them with two sets of students. However, we must see to it that the two sets of students do not differ in intelligence, interest in spelling, previous experience with these words, or motivation to do well in their studies. We must also see that the groups are taught by teachers who do not differ in teaching ability or in enthusiasm. In other words, we must control intelligence, motivation, and all other variables except arrangement of the words in the spelling lessons. Only then can we be confident that any difference we find in mastery of the spelling lessons is due to arrangement of the words rather than to some other difference between the two sets of students or between the ways they are taught. Because the practical demands of the classroom make it difficult to obtain such control, or even to know whether one has obtained it, it is valuable to have laboratories specially arranged for doing well-controlled experiments.

Though laboratory studies of learning provide great advantages in measurement and in control, we must not suppose that they provide easy answers to questions about the practical management of learning. Because they typically study single variables out of their usual context, laboratory experiments can seldom give direct answers to questions about how these variables work together in that context. For example, it has been established in a number of experiments that larger reinforcers lead to better performance in a learning situation. Does it follow that the more lavishly a teacher praises students for their successes, the better the students will do their work? Perhaps, but there are various reasons that this result might not follow. The students might become so used to this effusive praise that it would soon be no more reinforcing to them than mild praise would be to other students. Or, perhaps, those who failed to win the praise might be all the more frustrated because the praise they missed was so desirable, a consequence that might result in disappointment and anger becoming conditioned as responses to the stimuli of the whole situation. Moreover, neither the reinforcers nor the learning tasks used in the laboratory are likely to be the same ones used in the classroom (in fact, many of the studies on reinforcement magnitude were done with animals); this kind of difference will probably make the outcomes different in degree, and possibly in kind. Finally, even if the subjects, tasks, and reinforcers are all similar in the laboratory and in the classroom, the difference between working alone in an unfamiliar situation (the laboratory) and working in a familiar group situation (the classroom) may produce considerable differences in behavior. For all these reasons we would be rash to generalize directly and confidently from the laboratory studies to the classroom application. However, the laboratory studies, in addition to providing basic knowledge about the processes of learning, suggest many possible applications to the classroom and to other applied settings.

Chapter
2

The Nature
of Learning Theories

Researchers in the field of learning, like those in any other branch of science, are concerned with discovering scientific *laws*. All the experimental procedures we have examined are directed toward such discovery. A law is a statement about the conditions under which certain things occur. Some laws are highly precise and accurate, as in the physicist's statement that the period of a pendulum is proportional to the square root of its length. Other laws are much less precise and much more subject to error, as when the amateur weather prophet maintains, "Red sky at night, sailor's delight; red sky in the morning, sailor take warning." In both cases, however, we are being told that certain events occur under certain conditions. Given those conditions, we can predict that these events will occur. The prediction need not always be correct, so long as it is correct often enough to be useful. If bad weather occurs 75 percent of the time when the morning sky is red and only 20 percent of the time when the morning sky is gray, the amateur weather prophet has a useful law, even though not a wholly accurate one, for predicting the weather.

VARIABLES AND LAWS

All laws state a relationship between a *dependent variable* and one or more *independent variables*. A variable is any measurable characteristic, whether of a person, a situation, or anything else. A dependent variable is one about which we make a prediction; an independent variable is one we use to make the prediction. In the above examples, the length of the pendulum and the color of the sky were independent variables, while the period of the pendulum (the time it takes to make its complete swing) and the weather were dependent variables. In a study of learning, the dependent variable is some aspect of the learner's performance, while the independent variables may be any characteristics of the learner, the task, or the situation.

In some cases these variables and the laws relating them to one another involve merely the presence or absence of something. This is true with the weather prediction law. Red in the evening indicates good weather and red in the morning bad weather; that is all we are told. Does it matter whether the red is pale or deep? Will the bad weather be a drizzle or a hurricane? The law does not tell us. In other words, it deals with *qualitative* information only, information about the *kinds* of events that occur. In other cases, however, degrees of the independent variable are related to degrees of the dependent variable. The physicist's law tells us how much of a change in pendulum length will produce how much of a change in period. This, then, is a *quantitative* law, one that gives information about *amounts* of things, about the degree to which certain events occur. On the one hand, in learning, the statement that removal of a reinforcer produces extinction is a qualitative law, since it refers only to whether or not reinforcement is removed and whether or not extinction occurs. On the other hand, the statement that a larger reward results in a higher level of performance is quantitative, since it deals with different amounts of reward and different levels of performance. Both qualitative and quantitative laws are found in all branches of science, but in general the more highly developed sciences tend to have more quantitative laws, resulting in more precise predictions.

Independent variables also differ in another respect. Some independent variables can be directly varied by an experimenter, who can arrange the independent variable in a certain way and then see what happens to the dependent variable. For example, a physicist can change the length of a pendulum in order to see how this difference affects the rate at which the pendulum swings. Likewise, a psychologist can stop reinforcing a pigeon for pecking a key and watch what happens to the rate of pecking. Such a study, in which the independent variable is manipulated by the researcher, is called an *experiment.* If the experiment is properly controlled, we can conclude definitely that the changes in the independent variable caused the changes in the dependent variable.

There are other independent variables, however, that cannot be manipulated by an experimenter. The weather prophet cannot make the sky red in order to see what will happen to the weather. One has to wait until the sky gets red by itself and then watch for changes in the weather. This is still a perfectly valid scientific study, but it is not an experiment, for the researcher does not manipulate the independent variable. A similar example in learning would be a study of memorization rate in people of varying IQs. Here IQ would be the independent variable and rate of learning the dependent variable. The researchers could not change a person's IQ; they could only choose subjects who already had different IQs and then compare learning rates.

A difficulty with such nonexperimental studies is that we can seldom be sure just what is causing what. We would not be likely to say that red in the evening sky caused good weather; presumably some atmospheric condition caused both. The red sky was merely an indicator of good weather, not its cause. If it turned out that people with high IQs were faster memorizers (which might or might not be the case, depending on the particular memory task), we might be tempted to say that high IQ caused faster memorizing. However, perhaps it would be just as reasonable to say that high memorizing ability was the cause and high IQ the effect. In other words, people with higher memorizing ability would tend to learn more in a given period of time and therefore gradually to develop a high IQ. So, although these nonexperimental studies do give us laws that are valuable for prediction, they are definitely inferior for telling us what causes what. For this and other reasons, experimental studies are preferable whenever it is possible to do them, and the great majority of psychological studies of learning are experiments.

As we have seen, scientific laws may differ in several ways. They may indicate simply that when something happens, something else will happen, or they may relate the amount of something to the amount of something else. They may be based on experiments or on nonexperimental observations. They may be very precise or they may allow for a large amount of error. In all cases, however, they state a relationship between an independent and a dependent variable in such a way as to make possible prediction from the independent to the dependent variable. These laws are the primary focus of science in general and hence of the psychology of learning in particular.

ABSTRACTION

Scientific laws are statements about the way the world operates, and like all statements they involve abstractions. Whenever we apply words to things and events, we ignore a great deal of what is there in order to focus attention on what this particular thing or event has in common with others. For example, when we call something a car, we are ignoring its make, model, year, and color in order to emphasize the features it has in common with other cars. In other words, we are abstracting its "car-ness" from all the other characteristics of the particular battered brown 8-year-old two-door Ford. The same is true when we use the term *discrimination* to describe the behavior both of a pigeon learning whether to peck the right or the left key and of a pupil learning whether to use *ar* or *er* in spelling a word. Again, we are dealing with an abstract concept, ignoring most aspects of the two situations in order to concentrate on one thing that they have in common.

Since some degree of abstraction is inescapable, any statement, however concretely "factual," is an abstract formulation that tells only a part of the truth. To say "Columbus crossed the ocean blue in 1492" is to give only the barest outline of that momentous event. Even to say "Jane Doe dropped a copy of *A Tale of Two Cities* from her school desk to the floor in the middle of an arithmetic lesson in Room 6 on the morning of March 17" is to give only a minute fraction of the detail that could have been observed. For all their tremendous value, words are only pale shadows of the things they represent.

This process of abstraction goes on in all description and in all thought. Every intellectual activity involves the organization and simplification of "reality" as it is presented to our senses. This statement is true whether we consider simple perceptions or complex thoughts, and whether we look at science, art, sports, business, or any other area of human interest. Imagine, for example, what a broadcast of a football game would sound like if it were presented by a society editor, or by the proud parent of one of the players, or by a foreigner studying American customs. The society editor might concentrate on the uniforms and the family backgrounds of the players; the proud parent might report only what his or her own child was doing; and the foreigner might be much more interested in the cheers and card stunts than in the progress of the game. Each of these three descriptions could be perfectly true and valid as far as it went, but what football fan would accept it as an adequate report of the game? Any description, including that of the professional sportscaster, deals with only some aspects of the "real game," reflecting not only what "really happened" but also the interests and biases and vocabulary of the reporter.

In effect, there is no such thing as pure reality; there is only reality as described or interpreted or reacted to by someone. Some descriptions are more accurate or more detailed than others, but no description is complete. Even if someone were ambitious enough to collect descriptions of a football game from everyone who was there, check them with other kinds of evidence, spend years sifting and combining these accounts, and give a final report of the game many volumes long, there would still be details that were omitted. The report would still be only an abstract, even though a very detailed one, of what happened at the game. In any case, no one would read the report, since each possible reader would be interested in those aspects of the game that the reader considered interesting or important, not in the most detailed account that human patience and ingenuity could devise. Hence any useful report of the game would involve far more abstraction and organization and simplification than our imaginary multivolume monstrosity of a description.

This process of abstraction is carried even further in scientific laws than in many other kinds of statements. In history, biography, and literature, as well as in everyday speech, we are often concerned with describing an event in as much rich detail as time and the limitations of language permit. Our several imaginary broadcasts of the football game, different as they were, were nevertheless all trying for such completeness within the limits of the reporters' interests. In science, however, we always are concerned with picking out certain aspects of the situation to be related to other aspects. In relating the period of a pendulum to its length, the physicist need not be concerned with what the pendulum is made of or with whether it is a clock pendulum, a plumb bob, or a museum display. Similarly, the psychologist's statement that removal of the reinforcer reduces the frequency of the response applies whether the reinforcer is food or praise and whether the response is pecking a key or studying spelling. The laws connecting independent and dependent variables are not descriptions of any particular event—they are statements about the conditions under which certain kinds of events occur. Scientific laws are not concerned specifically with the red sky in Chicago on June 10 or with the pendulum of Mary Jones's grandfather clock, but with all red skies or all pendulums. Some laws may be quite narrow in the range of phenomena to which they refer, but even the narrowest always refers to collections of certain kinds of events, never merely to a single unique event.

The above does not mean, of course, that scientists never try to explain why a single particular event occurred. Meteorologists tell us why it rained today; geologists tell us why a particular cliff face is layered; psychologists tell us why a certain student got a particular question wrong on one occasion even though he had got it right on a previous occasion. However, in order for these explanations to be anything more than wild guesses, they must be based on general laws about the operation of weather or rock formations or memory performance, laws about the conditions under which certain kinds of events occur. The research that scientists do is intended to establish these general laws, which they can then use to predict and to explain specific events.

The Value of Scientific Laws

Scientific laws serve two main purposes. One purpose is practical—to provide the means of predicting and controlling events. Simply being able to predict what will happen and thus take measures to deal with it is of considerable value. Such prediction is what keeps the weather bureau and the various investment advisory services in business. (As these examples show, prediction doesn't have to be perfect in order to be useful.)

It is even more useful to be able to control events. An independent variable that we can manipulate gives us some degree of control over the dependent variable. This fact is the meaning of the saying that "knowledge is power." Only if we have a law about the conditions under which certain kinds of events happen can we set up the necessary conditions for one such event to happen when we want it to. It is not necessary, of course, for the law to be formally stated; much of our practical knowledge is very casual. However, the more complete and accurate our formulation of the law is, the better able we are to control the world around us.

Scientific laws also have a less utilitarian value. Since earliest times, people have sought to understand the world in which they lived. From the child trying to find out what makes the watch tick to the cosmologist trying to find out what makes the universe tick, people constantly are asking, "What is it?" and "How does it work?" and "Why?" No practical benefits are required to justify this curiosity; to gain the knowledge is benefit enough in itself. This benefit is the basis of pure science, the search for fundamental knowledge about the world.

Both of these purposes of science are exemplified in the study of the psychology of learning. The laws of learning are of crucial importance to education, industrial, military, and other forms of training, child rearing, psychotherapy, and a variety of other practical areas of work. They are also basic to an understanding of how individuals and societies come to be as they are, of how knowledge is obtained—indeed, of how people acquire their unique humanness.

Hence for both reasons an increase in our knowledge of the laws of learning is much to be desired.

WHAT ARE LEARNING THEORIES?

Researchers are rarely satisfied, however, merely to collect more and more laws about learning or anything else. To satisfy our desire for understanding, knowledge must be organized. An encyclopedia full of laws relating each of a vast number of independent variables to each of a vast number of dependent variables might give its owner the emotional satisfaction of having a great deal of knowledge available, but it would not provide the intellectual satisfaction of understanding the topics involved. Such satisfaction requires more general knowledge than that provided by this imaginary encyclopedia of laws. Even for practical purposes, such an encyclo-pedia would be cumbersome. It would be more convenient to have general princi-ples from which the specific laws could be deduced. So, although the establishing of laws is in one sense the most basic activity of science, it is not the end of scien-tific activity. Much of the researcher's effort is dedicated toward establishing more general principles or interpretations. This effort takes the researcher into the realm of scientific theory.

We have already seen that description represents some abstraction and orga-nization and simplification of the events being described, and that the statement of laws represents a higher level of abstraction. With theory we come to a still higher level of abstraction. It differs in degree but not in kind from the lower levels. It is a serious mistake to think of a realm of theory that is separate and different from the realm of fact. When people speak of "facts," they are referring sometimes to descriptions of single events ("It is a fact that John W. Hinckley, Jr., shot President Reagan in 1981") and sometimes to laws ("It is a fact that hydrogen and oxygen will combine with each other to form water"). As we have seen, both descriptions and laws represent organizations and simplifications of what is "really there" according to the language and the biases and the objectives of whoever is describing the event or stating the law. Theory exemplifies the same processes, but in still greater degree. It would be reasonable to say either that facts represent one kind of theo-ry or that theories represent one kind of fact, but most reasonable to say that fact and theory represent different degrees of what is basically a single process.

What is a theory? This is not an easy question to answer, partly because there are a number of different opinions about what a theory should be like and what functions it should serve. It is really only through studying different theories—not-ing their similarities and differences and the purposes their creators had in mind—that we can get a general understanding of what theories are. In a sense, therefore, the rest of this book is an attempt to answer this question. In this chapter we can hope to get only a rough and general overview.

In the broadest sense, a theory is a systematic interpretation of an area of knowledge. In the psychology of learning, *system* or *systematic interpretation* is probably a better term than *theory*, for *theory* sometimes is used in a narrower sense to refer to a kind of formal logical system. However, in this book *theory, system,* and *systematic interpretation* will be treated as synonyms.

Three Functions of Theory

A theory of learning usually consists of three different but closely related functions. First, it is an approach to the area of knowledge, a way of analyzing and talking about and doing research on learning. It represents the researcher's point of view about what aspects of learning are most worth studying, what independent variables should be manipulated and what dependent variables studied, what research techniques should be employed, and what language should be used to describe the findings. It focuses the researcher's attention on certain topics and helps the person to decide which of all the possible abstractions will be most useful. Thus theory serves as a guide and a source of stimulation for research and for scientific thought.

Second, a theory of learning is an attempt to summarize a large amount of knowledge about the laws of learning in a fairly small space. In this process of summarization, some exactness and detail are likely to be lost. In such precise and well-developed sciences as physics and chemistry, theories do quite well in summarizing laws so that the same exact predictions can be made from the theories as from the much more detailed laws. Psychology, to date, has been less successful in finding such theories. Theories of learning, in attempting to summarize large amounts of knowledge, lose completeness and precision. They are simplifications or skeletal outlines of the material with which they deal. As such, they represent a gain in breadth, in organization, and in simplicity, but also a loss in accuracy of detail.

Third, a theory of learning is a creative attempt to explain what learning is and why it works as it does. The laws give us the "how" of learning; the theories attempt to give us the "why." Thus they seek to provide that basic understanding which is one of the goals, not alone of science, but of all forms of scholarship. Theories represent people's best efforts to determine the underlying structure of the world in which they live.

Intervening Variables

In most cases, theorists have sought this underlying structure in entities that were not visible to the observer. Theorists in the field of chemistry, for example, assumed the existence of molecules long before anyone had ever seen a molecule under the microscope. They did so because the laws of chemistry formed a simpler and more logical pattern if all substances were assumed to be made up of molecules. The laws of chemistry did not themselves deal with molecules, but with substances that could be seen and touched and weighed. The molecules were in effect invented by the theorists as an explanation for the laws. This invention was a creative guess that has received more and more support from later evidence and has contributed immensely to the development of chemistry.

Let us consider a corresponding example, though admittedly a less striking one, from the psychology of learning. A person might be deprived of water for a period of time, or be on a daily ration of water below the normal intake, or have a chance to drink only for a limited time once a day, or have to eat a lot of dry food without water available, or have a hypertonic salt solution pumped directly into the stomach. The extent to which any one of these things happened (e.g., how much the water ration was reduced or how concentrated the salt solution was) would be an independent variable. We would find that each of these independent variables was related in much the same way to each of several dependent variables. As any of these independent variables increased, the subject would probably become more restless, would drink more water when it was available, would work harder to get to a drinking fountain, and would complain more about being thirsty. Pairing each of these five independent variables with each of the four dependent variables would give us a total of 20 laws. However, all 20 laws are closely related in that all have something to do with thirst. We can, therefore, reduce the 20 laws to 9 laws by saying that each of the 5 independent variables produces a state of thirst (5 laws) and that this thirst in turn produces changes in the 4 dependent variables (another 4 laws). By including this state of thirst, we have more than cut in half the number of laws required to describe the relationships involved.

So far this act of theoretical simplification is no more than what the average person does. It is so commonplace, indeed, that it is easy to overlook its importance. To see its importance, we must remember that no one has ever seen or touched or weighed thirst. We have each felt it in ourselves, but in anyone else we can only infer it. We have to infer other people's thirst from what has happened to them (the independent variables) or from what they do (the dependent variables). If they tell us they are thirsty, their statement is only one of the possible dependent variables, and not necessarily the most reliable. When a 3-year-old boy who has been put to bed for the night gets out of bed for the fourth time and this time tells his mother that he is thirsty, the mother is understandably more likely to trust other evidence than what the child says. Anyone who thinks it is possible to differentiate sharply between theory and fact should consider how much theory there is in the simple "factual" statement "He is thirsty."

The psychologist's use of the concept *thirst* differs from the layperson's in two respects. One is in precision. The psychologist, not satisfied with saying that certain manipulations will produce thirst and thirst will produce certain behaviors, goes on to determine what degrees of the independent variables are related to what degrees of thirst and what degrees of thirst are related to what increases in the dependent variables. Thus the psychologist's use of the concept *thirst* allows for more complete and accurate detail than the layperson's.

The other difference is that the psychologist is likely to go further in relating this concept to others. Many theorists of learning have been struck with the similarities between hunger, thirst, pain, and a variety of other such hypothetical states (hypothetical because none of them can be directly observed). All of these tend to produce both increases in certain forms of activity and physiological changes characteristic of stress. Moreover, the termination of any of these states is reinforcing. They have therefore often been classified together as *drives*. The concept of drive provides a higher level of theoretical integration, bringing together far more laws than the separate concepts of hunger, thirst, pain, and the like.

Theoretical concepts of the sort we have been discussing are often called *intervening variables*. This name (from the Latin for "come between") reflects their place in the theoretical structure, coming between the independent and the dependent variables, forming a link that joins them together, and serving to explain how the independent variables produce changes in the dependent variables. These intervening variables are states or conditions of the individual that are inferred from observations. These states or conditions are of various kinds. *Habits, beliefs*, and *motives* are different kinds of intervening variables that are important in various theories of learning.

By this time you may be asking, "Are these intervening variables really there, waiting to be discovered, or are they invented by theorists as a matter of convenience?" In other words, is the theorist more like an explorer, discovering hidden truths, or more like an artist, creating views of the world that suit his or her own purposes? If the discussion so far has been vague on this question, it is because theorists by no means agree on the matter. Undoubtedly both discovery and creation enter into theory, as indeed into all scientific work. A theory must lead to accurate predictions, must be consistent with well-established laws; otherwise it is worthless. This requirement sets limits on the theorist's creative freedom. However, the same laws can be interpreted in different ways, and these interpretations are not waiting around to be discovered—they must be created by an interpreter. Perhaps the theorist is less like either an explorer or an artist than like an architect, limited by materials and by the demands of the job, but still working with originality and imagination to produce a new, useful, and beautiful structure.

This is admittedly not a very adequate answer to the question of whether the intervening variables are "really there." Some theorists talk as though the variables are really there and others as though it is merely convenient to pretend that they are there. It has been suggested that there should be two different terms, one for those variables that theorists think they have discovered and the other for those that they think they have invented. Fortunately, we can leave this issue to the philosophers and concern ourselves only with the part that intervening variables play in the various theories we will be studying.

In any case, the element of creativity in theory construction explains why there are many theories of learning. All theorists try to find ways of structuring reality that will be useful and meaningful to themselves. The differences among the resulting theories reflect partly the differences in the topics that various theorists find most interesting to work with, and partly the differences in the kinds of systematic structures that different theorists consider worth producing. All, however, reflect the efforts of thoughtful humans to interpret the phenomena of learning in coherent and intellectually satisfying ways.

Kinds of Learning Theories

Theories of learning can be classified in a number of ways. For our purposes, one difference is particularly outstanding: the difference between the *connectionist* and the *cognitive* theories. Connectionist interpretations of learning, however much they may differ among themselves, agree that what we learn are connections between stimuli and responses. A response may be any item of behavior. A stimulus (plural, stimuli) is a little harder to define, and not all theorists define it in exactly the same way. We may think of a stimulus as a change in the environment, or as an input of energy to the organism, or as a sensation. In any case, it must be something that happens that tends to affect behavior. Connectionist theorists typically assume that all responses are elicited by stimuli. The connections that get formed between stimuli and responses are intervening variables of a simple kind, usually called *stimulus-response bonds* or *habits*. Connectionist theories concentrate on the responses that occur, on the stimuli (and perhaps other conditions) that elicit them, and on the ways that these relationships between stimuli and responses change with experience.

Cognitive interpretations are concerned with more complex intervening variables called cognitions. These are perceptions or attitudes or beliefs that individuals have about their environment. In cognitive theories, learning is the study of the ways in which cognitions are modified by experience and in which they work together to influence behavior.

Common sense makes use of both kinds of interpretations. When discussing simple reactions or more complex physical skills, we are likely to say, "I guess it's just a bad habit I've learned," or "With all that practice, her reactions have become very fast and smooth." These are connectionist interpretations. When discussing matters that involve words or deliberate decisions, we often say things like "He has acquired a lot of knowledge on that subject," or "You'll have to learn that people don't like to be treated that way," or "Now I really understand geometry!" These interpretations are all cognitive.

Whether a given psychologist will prefer a connectionist or a cognitive theory of learning depends partly on the kind of learning in which that person is most interested. A specialist in the study of conditioning may find a connectionist interpretation better suited to his or her needs, while a specialist in problem solving may find a cognitive interpretation more useful. However, specialists tend to believe that the theory they prefer is best, not only for their own field of study, but for the whole psychology of learning. This tendency reflects a desire for unity and simplicity that is one of the reasons theories are developed in the first place. As a result, some people adopt general cognitive theories of learning and others adopt general connectionist ones.

The distinction between connectionist and cognitive theories is not, of course, an all-or-nothing matter; there are numerous middle positions and combinations. Nevertheless, the distinction forms a convenient and useful basis for classifying the interpretations of learning that we will be investigating here. We will look first at a number of connectionist theories, since that is the kind of theory that was originally most popular with psychologists of learning in the United States. Next we will consider some cognitive theories, since this kind of theory has become increasingly popular in recent years and now largely dominates the field. In the process we will note numerous differences among different theories in each of these two main categories, as well as various attempts to combine the best of both. After that we will look at some special topics and problems in learning theory, and, finally, speculate a bit on the possible future of learning theory. It is hoped that this survey will indicate what learning theories are, what they try to accomplish, how successful they are, and what they can contribute to our understanding of the learning process.

Chapter
3

Three Early Connnectionist Theories

*H*uman interest in psychology has a long history. At least since the time of the ancient Greeks, philosophers have been speculating about topics that are now considered part of psychology. How do we think and feel and learn and know and make decisions and act on them? Attempts to answer these questions make up a considerable part of the history of philosophy. It was not until the nineteenth century, however, that attempts were made to study these topics experimentally. The first psychological laboratory was founded by Wilhelm Wundt in Germany in 1879. Although research in psychology had been going on before then, this date is widely regarded as marking the point at which modern scientific psychology was placed on a definite institutional footing.

Wundt and his colleagues in early scientific psychology, like the philosophers from whom they drew much of their inspiration, were largely interested in conscious experience. They wanted to understand human sensations and thoughts and feelings. They wanted to take the continuous flux of conscious awareness and analyze it into its basic components. Are memory images the same as sensations? Are feelings a special kind of sensation or are they something really different? How is the intensity of a sensation related to the intensity of the physical stimulus that produces it? These were the sorts of questions that the early experimental psychologists studied.

This kind of psychology, developed in Germany, became to a great extent the standard for the rest of Europe and for America. The research in psychological laboratories and the discussion in psychology textbooks were based principally on this approach. Its acceptance, however, was never complete. In both Russia and the United States there were always strong trends toward the study of objective behavior as well as the study of conscious experience, and interest in what people did as well as in what they thought and felt. These trends gave rise to two major traditions of studying behavior, one Russian and one American, to which we now turn.

PAVLOVIAN CONDITIONING

In 1904, Ivan P. Pavlov (1849–1936) won the Nobel Prize in physiology and medicine for his work on digestion. To do this research, he had to perform a difficult operation, opening a fistula in the wall of a dog's stomach. He noticed that the stomach secretions he was studying were first triggered not by food reaching the stomach but by the chewing or even just the sight of food, and he began to find this anticipatory secretion the most interesting aspect of the digestive process. To study it, he focused on a different part of digestion, the secretions of the salivary glands, which could be measured through a much simpler operation: placing a duct in a dog's salivary gland. When Pavlov presented food to a dog with such a duct in its cheek, drops of saliva fell into a beaker, where they could easily be counted. Soon these drops of saliva began to appear in response not only to food but also to a variety of other stimuli in the lab. At the time, the standard way of explaining this extra salivation was to say merely that these other stimuli had become associated with food. Pavlov decided that this was not an exact enough answer, and devoted the rest of his long life to studying the process in precise detail. Through this new line of research (Pavlov 1960), he became even more famous as the father of conditioning.

We saw the basic elements of conditioning in Chapter 1. The experimenter starts with a stimulus (the unconditioned stimulus) that will reliably elicit a specific response (the unconditioned response). In Pavlov's research, the unconditioned stimulus was meat and the unconditioned response salivation. What was to become the conditioned stimulus could be any of a great variety of stimuli: a bell, a ticking metronome, a triangle drawn on a large card, and so on. If this stimulus was presented repeatedly just before the meat, it too came to elicit salivation, the conditioned response, and it thus became a conditioned stimulus. Since the term *conditioning* came to be applied quite broadly, this particular kind of conditioning, being the first studied, came to be called *classical conditioning* (Hilgard & Marquis 1940). More recently, as it has become increasingly common to name everything from diseases to measuring units after people, classical conditioning has come to be often called Pavlovian conditioning. Though Pavlov should share some of the credit with such other Russian pioneer researchers as I. M. Sechenov (1965) and V. M. Bekhterev (1994), his work was clearly of central importance and deserving of the tribute.

The terms *unconditioned stimulus* and *conditioned stimulus* may seem a bit odd, considering what they mean. It is now generally agreed that these terms are poor translations of the Russian words that Pavlov used. What is meant is that the meat is an unconditional stimulus (not conditional on any previous training), while the bell (or whatever stimulus precedes the meat) is a conditional stimulus for salivation—conditional on having been paired with the meat. By a clumsiness in translation, then, generations of English-speaking psychologists have been saddled with the strange terms *conditioned* and *unconditioned.* Though a few writers now use *conditional* and *unconditional,* most writers stick with long-standing tradition and use the less appropriate but more familiar terms.

Finally, we should emphasize that, although Pavlov's own studies mostly used food as the unconditioned stimulus, there was no such limitation either in his theory or in other research on Pavlovian conditioning. As we saw in Chapter 1, unpleasant (or *noxious*) stimuli have been used as unconditioned stimuli as much as have pleasant ones. Indeed, for practical applications, noxious unconditioned stimuli may well be the more important kind. Our dislikes and fears, even more than our likes, are quite likely due to classical conditioning with noxious unconditioned stimuli. Examples range from dislike of a food because eating it was followed by illness to being afraid of a person who attacked you or of horses after being thrown by one. This sort of conditioning will be discussed at various points later in this book.

Excitation and Inhibition

Since Pavlov was a physiologist, it was natural that he should try to explain conditioning in physiological terms. He suggested that the laws of conditioning could be explained by the joint action of two main processes in the brain: excitation and inhibition. *Excitation* is a process of arousal, one that tends to make responses happen, whereas *inhibition* is a process of suppression, one that tends to prevent responses from occurring. Excitation and inhibition therefore operate in opposition to each other. Of the two, excitation plays a much greater part in producing conditioning, but inhibition is needed to explain many of the specific ways in which conditioning works.

Let us consider a specific example of conditioning, in which a bell as the conditioned stimulus is presented to the dog just before meat is presented as the unconditioned stimulus. Both of these stimuli produce excitation in the cerebral cortex of the brain, each at a particular spot in the cortex appropriate to that stimulus. Since the food is something important to the dog's survival, whereas the bell is a biologically less important stimulus, the excitation produced by the food is the stronger of the two.

According to Pavlov, excitation is then drawn from the location on the cortex where the bell is represented to the location where the food is represented. This effect occurs because of two general tendencies. One is the tendency for weaker excitation to be drawn toward the location of stronger excitation. The other is the tendency for excitation that occurs first to be drawn toward the location of excitation that occurs slightly later. Each time the bell is presented just before the food, the excitation from the conditioned stimulus is drawn to the location of the excitation from the unconditioned stimulus, and as a result the connection between these two regions in the cortex gets stronger. After a number of presentations of the bell immediately before the food, excitation will move from the "bell" location to the "food" location even if on a given occasion no food is presented.

Once this movement on the cortex has occurred, what will happen if the bell is sounded but no food is presented? Excitation will occur not only at the place on the cortex appropriate for the conditioned stimulus, but also at the place where the unconditioned stimulus is represented. This excitation, in turn, will produce a response similar to the unconditioned response. However, the excitation at that point on the cortex is weaker than if it had been produced directly by the unconditioned stimulus, so the response is also weaker than the unconditioned response would have been. This weaker version of the unconditioned response, produced by the conditioned stimulus rather than by the unconditioned stimulus, is of course the conditioned response.

The process by which excitation from the conditioned stimulus is drawn to the location of the unconditioned stimulus is not the only way in which excitation moves around on the cortex. Excitation also has an automatic tendency to *irradiate*—that is, to spread out from its original focus in all directions over the surface of the cortex. The closer any spot on the cortex is to the center of excitation from the conditioned stimulus, the more quickly and strongly the excitation from the conditioned stimulus will irradiate to that point. When it does, that point also shares in the conditioning, forming a connection (though to a lesser degree) with the cortical site for the unconditioned stimulus.

Because of the way the cortex is organized, points that are close together on the cortex are typically the sites for similar stimuli. For example, a bell of similar tone to the conditioned stimulus will be represented closest to the conditioned stimulus on the cortex; a bell of a different tone will be represented farther away, and a buzzer still farther. The similar bell therefore receives the most irradiated excitation from the conditioned stimulus, the different bell less, and the buzzer still less. As a result, the similar bell has the greatest tendency to produce the same effect as the conditioned stimulus (namely, the conditioned response), whereas the other stimuli do so to progressively lesser degrees. This results in the phenomenon of generalization described in Chapter 1.

So far we have looked only at excitation. This is appropriate, since excitation has to come first; for the most part inhibition does not occur alone. Instead, it appears where there is excitation but then no unconditioned stimulus occurs. One such case is *extinction*. If the bell continued to be presented repeatedly without ever again being followed by the food, inhibition would build up at the cortical site of the conditioned stimulus and weaken the conditioned response.

Another example is *inhibition of delay*, which builds up when there is a substantial delay between the beginning of the conditioned stimulus and the beginning of the unconditioned stimulus. At first, the conditioned response tends to occur as soon as the conditioned stimulus is presented, but after a good deal of training it does not come until shortly before the unconditioned stimulus is due to arrive. This increasing delay in the conditioned response is attributed by Pavlov to the gradual buildup of inhibition of delay.

A third example involves *discrimination training*. If the original bell continued to be followed by food, but a similar bell was also repeatedly sounded without being followed by food, the generalized response to the similar bell would become less and less, indicating that a discrimination between the two bells had been formed. This would result from a buildup of inhibition at the cortical site of the bell that was not followed by food.

Though inhibition and excitation produce opposite effects, the two processes are alike in various other respects. For example, inhibition as well as excitation irradiates over the surface of the cortex. According to Pavlov, the interaction between the two processes explains most of what goes on in conditioning.

We should note that none of these ideas of Pavlov's was based on direct physiological information. The irradiation of excitation and inhibition over the surface of the cortex and the drawing of excitation or inhibition from one place on the cortex to another were speculations based on studies of conditioning. Physiologists now know a good deal more than Pavlov did about the ways in which individual neurons excite and inhibit one another; this knowledge has not confirmed Pavlov in detail. The particular excitatory and inhibitory processes that he described remain as they were then: speculations about physiology based only on observations of behavior.

Applications and Implications

Pavlov believed that the principles of conditioning could be used to explain a variety of phenomena. In particular, he related these principles to personality, considering that one of the most fundamental differences among dogs—and among humans—is the balance between excitation and inhibition. Excitatory personalities tend toward too much unrestrained activity ("When in doubt, do something, do anything!"), whereas inhibitory personalities tend toward unresponsiveness ("When in doubt, the safest thing to do is nothing.")

Finally, Pavlov considered conflict between excitation and inhibition to be the basis of neurosis. Consider the case of dogs that had learned a discrimination between a circle and an ellipse. After they had learned, on further trials the ellipse was gradually changed in shape to resemble more and more closely a circle, so that it was harder and harder to make the discrimination. Eventually the task became impossible and the discrimination broke down completely. How did the dogs behave in this situation? Pavlov noted that excitatory dogs would respond to both stimuli, inhibitory dogs to neither. Moreover, this failure to discriminate was not just a calm adoption of the same response to both stimuli. Rather, the dogs barked, tried to leave the experimental room, and generally appeared anxious, frustrated, and upset. These symptoms seemed so similar to those of humans in difficult conflict situations that Pavlov labeled the syndrome "experimental neurosis."

Pavlov's work earned him tremendous prestige in Russia. Remarkably, this prestige held during both the czarist regime in which he began his work and the Communist regime that followed it, even though his own reaction to the new Soviet government was far from enthusiastic. Various aspects of Pavlov's system probably helped to make him popular with the Soviet government: his emphasis on reducing "higher mental processes" to conditioning appealed to Communist materialism, and his emphasis on learning was consistent with the Communist philosophy that we are all products of our various environments. Pavlov's system became so much a "state system" that citation of Pavlov in an article became almost as much a symbol of loyalty as citation of Karl Marx. Though a good deal has been added to Pavlov's system by other eastern European psychologists and physiologists, his basic ideas remain unchanged.

Many of the later additions to Pavlov's system have involved discoveries as to what can serve as unconditioned and conditioned stimuli and responses. One example is *interoceptive conditioning*, in which either the conditioned or the unconditioned stimulus, or both, is presented directly to one of the internal organs. The responses that get conditioned by such interoceptive stimulation are also responses of the internal organs or their blood supplies. For example, cold water as the unconditioned stimulus can make the blood vessels in the wall of the stomach constrict, and this unconditioned response can then be trained as a conditioned response to some conditioned stimulus. Such conditioning brings unconscious bodily processes, such as changes in the blood supply to the stomach, under the control of a conditioned stimulus. Sometimes the conditioned stimulus is a word spoken by the person. In that case the person can, by saying that word, bring the response under voluntary control. Interoceptive conditioning thus offers a way of making various unconscious bodily processes voluntary.

The use of words as stimuli introduces another application: *semantic conditioning*, the conditioning of meaning. Later in his career Pavlov noted the importance of words as conditioned stimuli. Whereas bells and lights and other such conditioned stimuli make up a first signaling system, language, he said, becomes a second signaling system. It is, of course, a complicated system, but it is based on semantic conditioning, in which words serve as conditioned stimuli. However, it is not just the words as sounds that become conditioned stimuli, but their meanings.

This relationship of language to conditioning has been demonstrated by a simple experiment (Razran 1961). A boy was conditioned to salivate when he heard the Russian word for "good" or "well" as the conditioned stimulus (S+), while the word for "bad" or "badly" was non-reinforced (an S−). The boy was then tested with a variety of sentences that did not contain either word but that had definite positive or negative connotations, and was found to salivate much more to the positive than to the negative ones. He produced the most drops of saliva to "The enemy army was defeated and annihilated" and the fewest to "The pupil was fresh to the teacher." In addition to what this experiment tells us about conditioning, it gives us an interesting look at the value system of the former Soviet Union!

In the Western world, Pavlov's work was received with a good deal of enthusiasm. Americans, in particular, were ready for the idea of conditioning. However, it was primarily the idea that Americans adopted, rather than the details of either research or theory. The empirical findings of Pavlov's research were widely quoted but little studied: some Americans studied the conditioning of the eye-blink reflex or the galvanic skin response, but not of salivation, and the majority of researchers on animal learning did not study classical conditioning at all. As for Pavlov's theory, even those Westerners who admired Pavlov's pioneering research tended to dismiss it. The irradiation of excitation and inhibition was inferred almost entirely from behavior, rather than from any direct study of the brain, and did not seem to most Westerners to be a very useful theory anyway. Thus, outside of eastern Europe,

Pavlov was widely admired as a pioneer, widely cited, and widely followed in general outline, but many of the details of his system were largely neglected nonetheless. Only fairly recently have psychologists in the West begun to look more carefully at the details of his system. They have since confirmed some of his findings, challenged others, and found still others hard to check because the research reports were so brief and so casually written. Though Pavlov's theories are still not much admired in the West, those of some of his followers have turned out to resemble those of some Westerners, developed independently. Pavlov's influence has, however, survived the mixture of adulation, contradiction, and partial neglect that he has received, so that he remains one of the great pioneers in the psychology of learning.

WATSON'S BEHAVIORISM

About the same time that Pavlov was working in Russia, the trend toward the study of objective behavior in American psychology was bringing it more and more into conflict with the German tradition. Pressure increased to break the traditional mold and to develop a psychology that was frankly oriented toward objective behavior and practical usefulness. To varying degrees, psychologists were taking up the cry "Enough of studying what people think and feel; let's begin studying what people do!" This movement found its most vocal spokesperson in John B. Watson (1878–1958). It was through his vigorous attacks on traditional psychology and his attempts to build a radically different system that American theoretical psychology came into its own.

In 1903 Watson received the first Ph.D. in psychology granted by the University of Chicago. His dissertation was a study of maze learning by rats, and this concern with animal behavior was typical of his early interests. He was impressed by the fact that in studying animal behavior it is possible to dispense with consciousness and simply study what the animal does. Why, he asked, can't we do the same with humans? Behavior is real and objective and practical, while consciousness belongs to a realm of vague subjectivity. Let us abolish consciousness from our discussions and study behavior! Watson's professors at Chicago agreed with many of his objections to traditional psychology, but considered his solution too radical. Perhaps they thought that, like many young rebels, he would become more conservative with age and responsibility. In Watson's case, however, this change did not occur. After joining the faculty at Johns Hopkins University in 1908, he became all the more convinced that his extreme position was the answer to psychology's problems. A few years later (1913), Watson published the first formal statement of his position, an article entitled "Psychology as the Behaviorist Views It," and the psychological revolution known as behaviorism was under way.

The reason for the label *behaviorism* is clear enough. Watson was interested only in behavior, not in conscious experience. Human behavior was to be studied as objectively as was the behavior of machines. Consciousness was not objective; therefore it was not scientifically valid and could not be meaningfully studied. And by *behavior* Watson meant nothing more abstruse than the movements of muscles. What is speech? Movements of the muscles of the throat. What is thought? Subvocal speech, that is, talking silently to oneself. What are feeling and emotion? Movements of the muscles of the gut. Thus did Watson dispose of mentalism in favor of a purely objective science of behavior.

It is easy to satirize such a position. (Estes, e.g., has suggested that a behaviorist might change the familiar motto from "Think!" to "Behave!" and finally to "Twitch!") But we must not overlook the tremendous importance of this position for the development of modern psychological science. Though much objective study of behavior antedated Watson, he stands out as the great popularizer, the man who turned this sort of study into a widespread movement and philosophy.

Watson's demolition of existing ideas extended not only to consciousness but to many supposedly innate characteristics of humans. He denied that we are born with any particular mental abilities or traits or motives or predispositions. All we inherit is our bodies and a few reflexes; differences in ability and in personality are simply differences in learned behavior. Thus Watson was a strong exponent of environment as against heredity in the familiar nature-nurture controversy. What we are (except for clearly anatomical differences) depends entirely on what we have learned. And since new learning can at least modify and perhaps completely override previous learning, this contention meant that human nature, either in general or in a particular person, was greatly subject to change. There was practically no limit to what a person, properly conditioned, might become. As Watson expressed it in his most famous quote:

> Give me a dozen healthy infants, well-formed, and my own specified world to bring them up in and I'll guarantee to take any one at random and train him to become any type of specialist I might select—doctor, lawyer, artist, merchant-chief and, yes, even beggar-man and thief, regardless of his talents, penchants, tendencies, abilities, vocations, and race of his ancestors. (Watson 1966, p. 104)

This blending of objectivity with faith in the power of learning swept American psychology and captured the popular imagination. Combined with some more specific ideas about learning, it had great implications for child rearing, education, advertising, and social organization. When we consider how well Watson's ideas fitted in with the American belief in equality of opportunity, emphasis on unemotional practicality, and faith in progress, it is no surprise that behaviorism came to occupy the center of the American psychological stage.

We cannot, of course, picture Watson as suddenly presenting behaviorism and having it promptly and universally adopted. When Watson published "Psychology as the Behaviorist Views It," the trends to objectivity and to environmentalism were already under way. Moreover, Watson owed many of his ideas to sources as diverse as the philosophy of John Locke in England and the new physiological psychology of Pavlov in Russia. Finally, alternative points of view continued to be defended, and Watson faced much opposition. Nevertheless, there was a marked change in American psychology during this period, and Watson was the keynote speaker around whom any discussion of the change is likely to center. He gave behaviorism its name, its loudest voice, and its sense of mission.

Watson's Interpretation of Learning

What, then, was Watson's interpretation of learning? To begin with, he said, we are born with certain stimulus-response connections called reflexes. Examples are sneezing in response to an irritation of the nose and the knee-jerk reflex in response to a sharp tap on the knee. These reflexes, according to Watson, are the entire behavioral repertoire that we inherit. However, we can build a multiplicity of new stimulus-response connections through learning. Some of this learning occurs according to the process of conditioning that Pavlov described. If a new stimulus occurs along with the original (unconditioned) stimulus for the reflex, after several such pairings the new stimulus alone will produce the response. This conditioning process makes it possible for each response in the original repertoire of reflexes to be elicited by a great variety of new stimuli in addition to the ones that originally elicited it. This, according to Watson, is how we learn to respond to new situations.

Such conditioning, however, is only part of the learning process. We must not only learn to respond to new situations; we must also learn new responses. Sneezes, knee jerks, and the like would not carry us very far in dealing with complex situations. How can complex new habits be learned? The answer, according to Watson, is by building up a series of reflexes. Walking, for example, is a sequence of many responses: putting the weight on one foot, swinging the other foot forward, bringing it down, thrusting the weight forward from one foot to the other, and so forth. All these responses occurring in proper order constitute the skilled performance of walking. The building up of such a sequence is possible because each response produces muscular sensations that become stimuli for the next response. Thus new and complex behavior is acquired through the serial combination of simple reflexes.

What determines which particular reflexes will get organized into what particular sequence? Watson's simple answer is that we learn to do by doing: what we do is what we learn. Obviously, however, we do not learn everything that we do equally well, so to be more specific, Watson relies on two principles: *frequency* and *recency*. The principle of frequency states that the more frequently we have made a given response to a given stimulus, the more likely we are to make that response to that stimulus again. Similarly, the principle of recency states that the more recently we have made a given response to a given stimulus, the more likely we are to make it again.

Watson illustrates these principles with the example of a 3-year-old boy learning to open a puzzle box with candy inside. The boy turns the box around, pounds it on the floor, and makes a variety of other useless responses. Finally, by chance, he presses a button on the box, which is the one response that will release the lid so he can open the box and obtain the candy. Since the box is now open and the candy obtained, the child is no longer in the presence of the stimuli that kept him working at the box. The last response made in the presence of those stimuli was the response of pressing the button. The next time his father or mother puts candy in the box and closes the lid, the child will go through much the same sequence of trial and error as before. However, by chance, he will try some new responses and leave out some of those from last time. Again, however, the last response he makes will be that of pressing the button, since that is the one that changes the stimulus situation. Every time he works with the box, pressing the button occurs, whereas other responses may or may not. Thus, in the long run, button pushing gains a lead in frequency. Since it is always the last response, it always has a lead in recency. As a result, button pushing occurs sooner and sooner on successive experiences with the box. Since button pushing solves the problem, other responses have less and less chance to occur on successive experiences with the box. Button pushing as a response to the stimulus of the closed box has been learned.

This illustration shows only how a single response, pressing a button, is learned. The problem might, however, have required the child to make a series of several successive responses to open the box, with each response changing the situation so that the next response could be made. Pressing the button, for example, might have opened an outer lid and revealed a lever that had to be moved sideways in order to open the inner lid. In this case, both button pushing and lever moving would be learned in the same way, since each would change the stimulus and thus become the last response to the old stimulus. Such a series of responses could be extended indefinitely.

Why, then, does one particular response rather than others occur to the stimulus at a given place in a complex sequence? Watson's answer is that during learning many different responses occur to the stimulus, but that through the process described above, most of them drop out. The response that changes the situation gains in frequency and recency until it comes to occur as soon as the stimulus is presented. That particular stimulus-response unit in the sequence is then complete.

All these statements about the learning of new responses are left rather undeveloped in Watson's treatment. How are conditioning, the principle of frequency, and the principle of recency related to one another? How does the fact that the learner may at first make some wrong response much more often than the right one, yet still eventually learn the right one, fit in with the principle of frequency? Watson does not tell us. He was confident that complex learning could be explained by simple principles, but his attempted explanations were tentative and were never organized into a clear and consistent theory.

One thing that is clear, however, is Watson's lack of interest in reinforcement, in reward and punishment as causes of learning. Indeed, he regards such concepts as too subjective for a really behavioristic interpretation of learning. Instead, he maintains, we learn a connection between a stimulus and a response simply because the two occur together, that is, in *contiguity*. Watson is therefore referred to as a *contiguity theorist*—one who believes that contiguity alone, without reinforcement, is sufficient to produce learning.

Special Kinds of Learning

What about the learning of emotional reactions? Here Watson makes a concession to heredity, beyond what he has already made by recognizing the existence of innate reflexes, since he recognizes three innate patterns of emotional reaction. In principle, these reaction patterns are the same as reflexes, for we can state what movements (including those of the internal organs) they involve and what stimuli will produce them. However, they are more complicated than what is usually meant by a reflex. The three emotional reaction patterns may for convenience be labeled as fear, rage, and love. We must note, however, says Watson, that these labels refer to patterns of movement, not to conscious feelings. If we bang a gong close to a child, and he or she starts to cry, we may describe this event by saying that the stimulus of a loud noise has produced the emotion of fear. However, we are simply giving a name to the behavior we see, not commenting on the child's feelings.

Emotional learning involves the conditioning of these three patterns of emotional response, interpreted as three complex unconditioned responses, to new stimuli. The above example of innate fear was taken from a famous experiment of Watson's, one that can also be used to illustrate conditioned fear. Little Albert, aged 11 months, was permitted to play with a white rat, which he did happily and with no sign of fear. A metal bar was then hit with a hammer close behind him. He started and fell sideways. This sudden loud noise was repeated a number of times just as the rat was presented to him, and each time he reacted in the same way, sometimes also whimpering. These responses indicate that the noise was an unconditioned stimulus for the emotion of fear. After this training, the rat was presented without the noise. Albert fell over, cried, and crawled away from the rat as fast as he could. This change indicates that through the training procedure the rat had become a conditioned stimulus for fear. According to Watson, such conditioned and unconditioned responses account for all our emotions.

What about the acquisition of knowledge? Can conditioning be used to explain how we learn, for example, the facts of history? Certainly, says Watson, for this knowledge consists simply of saying certain words, aloud or to ourselves. The response sequence involved in saying "William the Conqueror defeated Harold the Saxon at Hastings in 1066" is in principle no different from that involved in walking across a room. A question such as "How did the Norman Conquest occur?" elicits the statement, which is itself a sequence of words with each word a conditioned stimulus for the next one. Acquiring knowledge is a process of learning to give the proper sequence of words in response to a question or other conditioned stimulus.

All of our behavior, says Watson, tends to involve the whole body. When we think, we may pace the floor or furrow our brows. We announce our opinions with smiles or waves of the arm as well as with words. We cannot really say, therefore, that thinking is made up simply of vocal or subvocal responses. They are the dominant but by no means the only responses involved. Everything we think, feel, say, or do involves, to varying degrees, the activity of the entire body. This is perhaps the most fundamental credo of behaviorism.

Evaluation of Watson

Watson's great contribution to the development of psychology was his rejection of the distinction between body and mind and his emphasis on the study of objective behavior. This battle was so effectively won that most of the learning theory in

America, at least through the 1950s, was behavioristic in the broad sense of the term. Since then more of the field has gone in directions that are no longer commonly called behavioristic, but that still reflect the legacy of behaviorism.

In this book we will see a number of theoretical systems that represent different variations on the behaviorist theme. All of them have in common a concern with objective behavior, a strong interest in animal studies, a preference for stimulus-response analysis, and a concentration on learning as the central topic in psychology. This fact makes Watson in some ways the intellectual father or grandfather of a large portion of the systems we will be considering here.

Watson, however, was much less thorough than he might have been in dealing with the detailed problems of learning. In his eagerness to build an objective psychology, he was somewhat cavalier with the matter of logical thoroughness. Perhaps if he had worked on his theory longer he would have extended his system to deal with some of these problems. More likely, however, his zeal for freeing psychology from subjectivism and belief in innate tendencies was incompatible with laborious theoretical completeness. In any case, he left the academic world in 1920 as a result of a sensational (for its day) divorce scandal and, though continuing to write about behaviorism for a short time afterward, devoted most of his later life to the applied psychology of advertising. Watson is now admired mainly for his philosophical trailblazing rather than for his detailed system building. It has remained for others to try to build, within the behavioristic framework, a more complete theory of learning.

THORNDIKE'S EARLY CONNECTIONISM

One idea that is noticeably absent from Watson's theory is the concept of reinforcement. The tendency of rewards to increase a given response, and of nonrewards to produce extinction, is not part of his thinking (or, should we say, of his verbal behavior?). However, many of those who agreed with his emphasis on the objective analysis of behavior disagreed with that omission. They felt that the question of which responses will be learned could best be answered by looking at the rewarding or punishing consequences that each response produced.

The idea that pleasure and pain as consequences of our acts are important determiners of behavior has a distinguished history in psychology. It forms the basis of the theory of psychological hedonism that was developed by the English philosopher Jeremy Bentham in the eighteenth century and adopted by a number of other British philosophers. According to this view, we all do those things that give us pleasure and avoid those that give us pain. However, it remained for Edward L. Thorndike (1874–1949) to make a similar, more behavioristic view central to the psychology of learning.

Thorndike was a pioneer in experimental animal psychology. Instead of relying on stories about the intelligent feats of this or that animal, he took animals into the laboratory, presented them with standardized problems, and made careful observations of how they solved the problems. His monograph "Animal Intelligence" (1898) is one of the classics in the field. His most widely quoted studies

involved cats in a problem box. A hungry cat was confined in a cage with a tempting morsel of fish outside. The cat could open the door by pulling a loop of string
hanging inside the cage. Usually a cat went through a long process of walking
around, clawing the sides of the cage, and other responses before it pulled the loop
of string and was able to leave the cage. On successive tests in the cage, the cats
took shorter and shorter times to pull the string. However, this improvement was
very gradual. Even after several experiences of opening the door by pulling the
string, on a given trial a cat would still spend considerable time in other behavior
before pulling the string. This led Thorndike to conclude that the cat's learning to
pull the string involved not an "intelligent" understanding of a relation between
string pulling and door opening but a gradual "stamping in" of the stimulus-
response connection between seeing the string and pulling it.

At the time Thorndike published these studies, they were radical in two
respects: their careful observation of animal behavior under controlled conditions
and their concern with the gradual strengthening of stimulus-response bonds.
They were Thorndike's answer to the argument about whether animals solve problems by reasoning or by instinct. By neither, said Thorndike, but rather by the
gradual learning of the correct response.

The most noteworthy point is that, whereas Watson was a contiguity theorist,
Thorndike was a reinforcement theorist. Watson's laws of frequency and recency
state that stimulus-response bonds are strengthened simply by the response occurring in the presence of the stimulus. Thorndike did not completely reject this view,
which he summarized as the *law of exercise*. His primary law of learning, however,
was the *law of effect*. This stated that the stamping in of stimulus-response connections depended not simply on the fact that the stimulus and response occurred
together but on the effects that followed the response. If a stimulus was followed
by a response and then by a *satisfier*, the stimulus-response connection was
strengthened. If, however, a stimulus was followed by a response and then by an
annoyer, the stimulus-response connection was weakened. Thus satisfying and
annoying effects of responses determined whether the stimulus-response connections would be stamped in or stamped out.

The terms *satisfier* and *annoyer* sound startlingly subjective for a theory concerned with the mechanical stamping in and stamping out of stimulus-response
bonds. This language of satisfiers and annoyers is much more like that of the hedo-
nistic philosophers than like Watson's. Thorndike was indeed criticized by behaviorists for this way of talking about learning. Actually, however, he defined the two
terms in a quite objective way:

> By a satisfying state of affairs is meant one which the animal does nothing to avoid, of-
> ten doing things which maintain or renew it. By an annoying state of affairs is meant
> one which the animal does nothing to preserve, often doing things which put an end to
> it. (Thorndike 1913, p. 2)

Thorndike says nothing here about the animal's feelings, only about what the animal
does. Thus he adheres to the concern of behaviorism with what organisms do. His
language may sound subjective, but his meaning is as objective as Watson's. Working at the height of the behaviorist movement, Thorndike had his disagreements

with its extreme supporters, but actually he and they were close together in inter-ests and objectives. In the broader sense of the term, Thorndike was certainly him-self a behaviorist.

Later in his career, Thorndike modified the law of effect to make satisfiers much more important than annoyers. Reward, he decided, strengthens connec-tions, but punishment does not directly weaken them. If punishment is effective in weakening the tendency to do something, it is primarily because it makes behavior more variable and thus gives some new response a chance to be rewarded. He based this change in interpretation on a variety of animal and human research, including analysis of biographical information (Thorndike, 1935). Though the issue is complex and the evidence he cited is not conclusive, his view that reward and punishment act in somewhat different ways has been widely accepted among psy-chologists. With this modification, the law of effect became the now familiar statement (but not so familiar when Thorndike presented it) that satisfying conse-quences serve to reinforce stimulus-response bonds.

Thorndike was a man of practical interests, and he took a special interest in the psychology of education. For many years he served on the faculty of Teachers Col-lege, Columbia University. Throughout his professional life, his studies on the "pure" psychology of learning with both human and animal subjects were inter-spersed with studies on the applied psychology of education. His emphasis on specificity in learning and on the mechanical stamping in of stimulus-response connections has been both praised and condemned by educators over the years. (It is to him, indeed, that we owe the term *connectionism.*) For our purposes, howev-er, these aspects of Thorndike's work are too similar to Watson's to require further comment here. Thorndike was no less a pioneer of objective psychology than Wat-son; indeed, his original contributions were quite likely more important than Wat-son's. However, our concern here is that he incorporated within his objective psychology of learning the law of effect, and thus became the first real reinforce-ment theorist.

Thorndike's view of learning—that it involves the formation of stimulus-response bonds through the operation of reinforcement—became the dominant view in American learning theory. Not only did the majority of learning theorists hold some version of this view until well beyond the middle of the twentieth cen-tury; even those who held other views found that much of their energy went into disagreeing with Thorndike's approach. As Edward Tolman later wrote (1938), one might agree with Thorndike or disagree with him or try to improve on him in var-ious ways, but he remained the starting point for any discussion of learning. As we will see, much of Chapters 5, 6, and 7 is concerned with attempts by other theorists to improve on Thorndike's work while maintaining its basic ideas.

Chapter
4

Guthrie's Contiguity Interpretation of Learning

*O*f those who continued in the behaviorist tradition, the one who remained closest to Watson's original position was Edwin R. Guthrie (1886–1959). From 1914 until his retirement in 1956, Guthrie was a professor at the University of Washington. He never studied with Watson, and his graduate education was more in philosophy than in psychology. Nevertheless, his interpretation of learning sounds much like what Watson's might have been if he had had another decade to work on the topic. His definitive work, *The Psychology of Learning*, was published in 1935 and revised in 1952, and his final theoretical statement was published in 1959. Thus, though his university teaching career began only 10 years later than Watson's, Guthrie was of an intellectually younger generation. He belongs, not with the pioneers of American learning theory, but with the generation that came next and followed up on those pioneering ideas.

Among theories of learning, Guthrie's is one of the easiest to read but nonetheless hard to discuss. It is easy to read because he wrote in an informal style, making his points with homely anecdotes rather than with technical terms and mathematical equations. It is hard to discuss or write about because his casual presentation contains the germ of a highly technical deductive theory of learning. Reading Guthrie is like reading an exciting novel that contains a difficult allegory. That is, he can be read on an easy or a hard level. At the heart of his system is one basic principle of learning. Interpreted loosely, this principle is a source both of entertaining interpretations of learning and of valuable advice about the management of learning situations. Interpreted rigorously, it becomes the basis of a profound theory. This theory, so deceptively simple at first glance but so maddeningly complex on closer investigation, stands as a challenge to students of learning. Has Guthrie actually succeeded in summing up the whole field of learning in one key statement?

ONE BASIC PRINCIPLE OF LEARNING

Guthrie's basic principle of learning is similar to the conditioning principle that was basic for Watson, but it is stated in a still more general form. Guthrie says: "A combination of stimuli which has accompanied a movement will on its recurrence tend to be followed by that movement" (1960, p. 23). The principle may be paraphrased as, "If you do something in a given situation, the next time you are in that situation you will tend to do the same thing again." This principle is more general than the principle of classical conditioning in that it says nothing about an unconditioned stimulus. It says only that if a response accompanies a given stimulus once, it is likely to follow that stimulus again. In classical conditioning, the response occurs with the (conditioned) stimulus during training because the unconditioned stimulus elicits it. This sequence of course fulfills Guthrie's conditions for learning. However, it does not matter to Guthrie whether the response is elicited during training by an unconditioned stimulus or in some other way. As long as the (conditioned) stimulus and the response occur together, learning will occur.

Amplification of the Principle

In claiming to sum up the whole field of learning in that one statement, Guthrie was inevitably challenging others to find inadequacies in the summary, and psychologists were quick to answer the challenge. The first difficulty with this principle is that a person often does many different things in the same situation. Which one will occur next time? This challenge is no problem for Guthrie; he simply replies, "The last one." A man struggling with a mechanical puzzle tries many responses. If he finally makes the correct response, he will tend to make this same response when next confronted with the puzzle. We say, then, that he has learned how to do the puzzle. Suppose, however, that he finally gives up and puts the puzzle aside unsolved. The next time he sees the puzzle he will tend to do what he did last—namely, put it aside. In that case we do not say that he has learned how to do the puzzle, but he has still learned something. In both cases he was presented with a combination of stimuli from the puzzle. In each case there was a movement that removed the stimuli. To the observer, one of these movements represented success and the other failure, but to Guthrie they both represented responses that removed the stimuli of the unsolved puzzle and that therefore became more likely to occur again. In both cases a response was learned, and in both cases the last response that the learner made to the stimuli was the one that was learned.

This aspect of Guthrie's system sounds much like Watson's principle of recency, since the last thing that occurred in a situation is the one that will occur again. However, Guthrie does not use Watson's other principle, frequency. Whereas for Watson a stimulus-response connection is something that varies in strength and grows stronger with practice, for Guthrie it is an all-or-nothing bond. The connection is either present or absent, with no intermediate variation in strength. Hence the conditioning of a movement to a combination of stimuli takes place completely in one experience, and further practice adds nothing to the strength of the connection.

At first glance this assumption seems contrary to well-known laws of learning. While practice may not make perfect, it usually does produce gradual improvement. How can Guthrie say that all the improvement takes place in a single experience? We must beware, replies Guthrie, of treating a "movement" as the same thing as an act or an accomplishment. Guthrie is referring in his principle of learning to specific small movements of particular muscles. It takes many such movements working together to make up a skilled act. Moreover, competent performance involves not just one but many skilled acts, each in response to a particular combination of stimuli. Hence learning how to do something involves learning an enormous number of specific stimulus-movement connections. Improvement in the skill is gradual even though the learning of each tiny part occurs suddenly.

Consider a particular skill, such as riding a bicycle. For each possible position of the bicycle, a different motion is required in order to keep it upright. Each of these motions, in turn, is made up of movements of the arms, torso, and legs. A particular movement of the left arm to help correct a particular kind and degree of tilt may be learned in one experience, but it certainly does not follow that the whole skill of balancing the bicycle will be learned so quickly. If we also consider all the other aspects of bicycle riding, the distinction between learning a movement and gradually mastering a skill becomes evident. This illustration does not show that Guthrie is necessarily correct when he says that a movement is learned in one trial, but it does make his interpretation more plausible.

This explanation, however, introduces some ambiguity into Guthrie's theory. In many cases "the last thing one did in a situation" refers to an act, such as lighting a cigarette or making a remark. These, however, are skilled performances made up of many specific movements. Why does Guthrie treat them as if they were single movements that could be conditioned in one trial? Presumably what is needed here is an analysis in terms of hierarchies of complexity. Lighting a match is a skill made up of many stimulus-movement connections that must be conditioned. However, once learned, this whole act may behave like a single movement in that it can be conditioned as such to combinations of stimuli. Guthrie does not concern himself with this relationship, but applies his principle of learning sometimes to movements and sometimes to acts, depending on the point he wants to make. Fortunately, this ambiguity is unimportant in most situations.

Is Reinforcement Necessary?

The aspect of Guthrie's theory that has been most attacked is his lack of concern with success and failure, with learning to do the "right" thing. Whatever one did last in the situation, right or wrong, is what one will do again. Guthrie makes no use of the concept of reinforcement. He does not say that we learn to make those responses that work, or that obtain reward. Whether or not something we do becomes learned as a response to the situation depends only on whether it changes the situation into a different situation, so that it becomes the last thing done in the old situation. Success has this result, since a solution changes a problem situation into a situation without a problem. Thus the successful act is the last one that occurs in the problem situation, and it will tend to occur if the problem is present-ed again. However, if we can somehow escape from the situation without solving the problem, the escape response will be learned. Inefficient methods may be learned and retained as well as efficient ones, since both get us out of the situation. Mistakes may be repeated over and over again. We learn, not by success or by rein-forcement, but simply by doing.

A number of testable predictions follow from this position. As an example, consider a hungry rat that can obtain food by pressing a lever. The rat learns to press the lever more and more rapidly. According to Guthrie, the rat learns because the food changes the situation through its effect on hunger and on the sen-sations in the mouth. Thus pressing the lever becomes the last thing the animal did in the old situation, and it becomes increasingly likely to occur. Suppose instead of getting food after each pressing of the lever the rat was simply taken out of the box as soon as it pressed the lever. This would change the situation even more than food did, so the rat should be even more likely to press the lever at the next oppor-tunity than if it had been fed. This experiment has been done, and the results did not confirm the prediction (Seward 1942). The rats receiving food showed far more lever pressing than those removed from the box, contrary to what would be expected from Guthrie's theory. This experiment and others like it cast doubt on Guthrie's view that reward has nothing to do with learning.

It may be, however, that our interpretation of this experiment is not altogeth-er fair to Guthrie. Although the food produced less change in the total stimulus combination than did removal from the box, the food did produce a marked change in certain particularly important stimuli. These were the *maintaining stim-uli*—those stimuli that kept the rat active in the situation. In this particular case the maintaining stimuli were those resulting from food deprivation—in other words, the stimuli of hunger. In other situations they might be the stimuli of thirst or pain or sexual arousal or anger or fear. At some places in his writings Guthrie suggests that it is changes in the maintaining stimuli that are crucial for learning. If a response removes the maintaining stimuli, by definition it solves the problem and thus becomes the last response in the problem situation. If it fails to remove the maintaining stimuli, then no matter what other changes it may produce it cannot be the last response in the problem situation. By this interpretation, we can see why food might be expected in Guthrie's theory to produce more learning than removal from the box.

However, this interpretation also raises other problems. In some cases responses are learned that do not remove the maintaining stimuli. A softball play-er learns those responses that produce successful batting and fielding, even though a base hit or a good catch does not reduce the competitive excitement that pro-vides the maintaining stimuli for playing. A rat in a maze learns the correct turn at each choice point, even though only the last turn is followed by any change in the maintaining stimuli. In both cases, however, the response does change the overall stimulus combination, so that it is in one sense the last response in the situation. Thus we are faced with the problem that sometimes only changes in the maintain-ing stimuli are crucial, while at other times changes in other stimuli are important. How do we know which times are which? Guthrie does not tell us. By sometimes considering all stimuli and sometimes considering only maintaining stimuli Guthrie can explain any case of learning after it has occurred, but he cannot do so well at predicting what learning will take place.

By now it should be clear why Guthrie's system is difficult to treat as a formal logical theory. When are we talking about movements and when about acts? When should we look at all stimulus changes and when only at changes in the maintaining stimuli? Because he concentrates on presenting simple, entertaining interpretations of learning, Guthrie never gives clear answers to these awkward questions. As a result, his theory, which at first glance seemed so direct and precise, turns out to be discouragingly vague. His attempt to reduce all learning to one basic principle is, in any precise sense, inadequate.

His loose, anecdotal approach reflects the fact that Guthrie was interested more in the undergraduate teaching of psychology than in detailed research. He himself produced only one major experiment bearing on his theory, a demonstration of the stereotyped behavior of cats in escaping from a cage (Guthrie & Horton 1946), which we will encounter again in Chapter 14. Perhaps because of this lack of emphasis on research he has had many sympathizers but few active followers. There has never been a long and active tradition of research within the framework of Guthrie's theory (though various of his followers did make some starts toward one, and he influenced the statistical learning models that are considered in Chapter 5). However, many psychologists have found that once they stop treating Guthrie's system as a formal theory and concentrate on its informal implications, its basic principle of learning turns out to be quite useful. In any situation, says Guthrie, if you want to know what an individual will learn, look at what he or she does. What the person does, right or wrong, is what he or she will learn. As an informal source of advice, this suggestion turns our attention to aspects of learning that we would otherwise be very likely to neglect. We can best appreciate Guthrie's contribution by looking at his discussions of some practical learning situations.

BREAKING HABITS

Perhaps the best known of Guthrie's applications are his three methods for changing a bad habit. All three methods depend on finding out what stimuli evoke the undesirable response and then finding a way of making some other response occur in the presence of those stimuli. This other response should then occur again the next time the stimuli are presented. The emphasis is on the exact stimulus and the exact response that are connected. Guthrie gives the example of a 10-year-old girl who, whenever she came in the door of her house, threw her hat and coat on the floor. Time and again her mother scolded her and made her go back and hang them up, but to no avail. Finally, the mother realized that the stimulus for the girl to hang up her wraps was the mother's nagging. The next time the girl threw down her wraps, her mother insisted that she put them on again, go outside, come in the door again, and hang up her coat and hat at once. After a few trials of this procedure the girl learned to hang up her wraps. The desired response had been attached to the stimuli of coming in the door, and the habit of throwing down the wraps had thus been replaced by the habit of hanging them up. This procedure worked where the previous nagging had failed because this time the mother saw to it that the girl hung up her wraps in the presence of the particular stimuli (those resulting from having just come through the door) that had previously led to the response of throwing the wraps down.

How does one get the desired response to occur in the presence of those stimuli that have been eliciting only an undesired response? Guthrie's first method, which may be called the *threshold* method, involves presenting the stimuli so faintly or weakly that the undesirable response does not occur. (Such faint stimuli are said to be below the threshold intensity that is necessary for the response to occur, hence the name.) Whatever response the individual makes to these weak stimuli, in place of the undesirable response, is the response that is likely to occur next time. Next time the stimuli can be made a little stronger, and because of the experience with the original very weak stimuli, the undesirable response will still not occur. The stimuli continue to be increased in strength gradually from trial to trial, and it is the new response (whatever it is) instead of the old, undesirable response, that occurs each time. Eventually the stimuli can be presented at full strength without eliciting the undesired response.

You will notice that Guthrie is not much interested in what the new response is; he is just interested in getting rid of the old one. This method is useful mainly for emotional responses involving anger, fear, and the like. (In those cases, the new response can be any behavior that is not emotional; usually it will just be standing or sitting quietly and unemotionally. Guthrie gives the example of the old cavalry method of training saddle horses. If an untrained horse is saddled and ridden, it will buck wildly. This reaction can be avoided by employing the method of thresholds to replace the bucking response with a response of standing quietly. First a blanket is put on the horse's back. This pressure on its back is the sort of stimulus that induces bucking, but the blanket alone is too weak a stimulus to have this effect. After some experience with the blanket the horse is saddled. Prior to experience with the blanket, the saddle might have produced bucking, but now it does not. Eventually, after the horse's experience with the saddle, a rider can mount without producing bucking, though the horse would certainly have bucked if it had been mounted before the training with blanket and saddle. The experience of not bucking while successively heavier weights were placed on its back has eventually resulted in the horse's standing still even for the weight of a rider.

The second method may be called the method of *fatigue*. The response to be eliminated is elicited again and again, until the individual is so tired that he or she stops making the response and does something else (if only resting) instead. This other response is then the one likely to occur when the stimuli are presented again. Here too Guthrie used an example of a disobedient girl, though we are not told whether it is the same one who would not hang up her clothes. This girl had a habit of lighting matches. After scolding and punishment failed, her worried mother finally eliminated the habit by making the girl light a whole box of matches in quick succession. Long after the girl was thoroughly tired of lighting matches, her mother insisted that she continue. Eventually the girl began actively resisting, throwing the box of matches down and pushing it away. These new responses, incompatible with match lighting, then became attached to the stimuli from the matchbox. As a result, the next time she had a chance to light matches, the girl showed no inclination to do so, and her dangerous habit was cured.

This method illustrates in extreme degree Guthrie's reliance on his version of Watson's law of recency (doing again what one did last in a given situation) and his rejection of Watson's law of frequency. The girl had lighted matches more frequently at the end of this experience than at the beginning, but the last thing she did was to push the matchbox away. Pushing it away was therefore what she tended to do when she next encountered a matchbox.

In the third method, which we may call the method of *incompatible stimuli*, the stimuli for the undesired response are presented along with other stimuli that can be counted on to produce a different, incompatible response. The original stimuli then become attached to the new response. Guthrie illustrated this method with the case of a college student who could not study because of distracting noises. She solved this problem by spending a period of time reading absorbing mystery novels instead of studying. These stories held her attention so well that she ignored the distracting noises. The stimuli of noise thus occurred along with the responses of reading and became attached to these responses. When she then changed back (however reluctantly) from reading mysteries to reading textbooks, she found that the noises no longer distracted her, for they were now attached to reading responses instead of listening responses.

It is noteworthy that there is no reference to punishment in any of these methods. Someone might suggest that it was punishing for the disobedient girl in one example to go out of the house, come in again, and hang up her clothes, and also punishing for the girl in the other example to light so many matches at once. True, says Guthrie, but remember that other forms of punishment had previously failed. The important question is not whether these experiences were punishing but what they led the individuals to do. Inflicting pain on someone, says Guthrie, cannot be expected to change bad habits if the pain does not occur in the presence of the stimuli that produce the behavior. Scolding a child after her clothes were already on the floor, or slapping a child after she had finished lighting matches, would be irrelevant to the habits in question. Only when the punishment resulted in a new response to the same stimuli, incompatible with the old response, was it effective. Moreover, as the threshold method indicates, absence of punishment may be just as good a way of producing new responses as is punishment.

This attitude is characteristic of Guthrie's interpretation of punishment. Always look at what punishment makes the individual do. If punishment succeeds in changing the punished habit, it is because it elicits behavior incompatible with it. If punishment fails, it is because the behavior elicited by the punishment is not incompatible with the punished behavior. Thus, if you want to stop a dog from chasing cars, slapping its nose as it runs is likely to work, whereas slapping the dog's rear is not. The two blows may be equally painful, but the one on the nose tends to make the dog stop and jump backward, whereas the one on the rear tends to make it continue forward all the more vigorously. Hence the blow on the nose, by eliciting behavior incompatible with running after the car, makes this nonrunning more likely to occur next time. The blow on the rear has no such effect; it may even strengthen the chasing. Punishment works, when it does work, not because it hurts the individual but because it changes the response to certain stimuli.

If we wanted to use these methods of Guthrie's as cure-alls for bad habits, we would immediately encounter a problem. In order to obtain different behavior from an individual, we have to change the stimuli in some way. For the little girl, coming in the door and taking off her wraps was not the same when she had just been sent out the door by her mother as when she had just come in after a long time outside. For the army horse, not bucking to a blanket was different from not bucking to a rider. There was a considerable difference between the stimulus situation when lighting a fiftieth match under a mother's prodding and when lighting a first match for fun. Now, when the original stimulus situation is restored, how do we know whether the two situations are enough alike so that the last response in one will occur in the other? For example, will the dog that jumped back when presented with the stimulus of moving-car-plus-blow-on-the-nose also jump back when presented with moving-car-alone? The answer in all these cases seems to be: Try it and see. This difficulty weakens the general usefulness of Guthrie's advice, not to mention the problem of relating the advice clearly to the theory. However, we can scarcely expect to get advice that will work infallibly in every situation without any ingenuity on the part of the person taking it. Guthrie's interpretation of punishment and his methods for changing habits are valuable tools for interpreting situations as well as useful suggestions for dealing with them. A theorist who can give us this much need not be ashamed of his practical contributions.

SOME SPECIAL TOPICS

Guthrie's emphasis on responses to stimuli and the ways of changing them shows up in other contexts, too. What of extinction? Since Guthrie does not talk about reinforcement, he cannot talk about extinction as resulting from the removal of reinforcement. Instead, he says that extinction is simply learning to do something else. The response was learned because it changed the stimulus situation into a different one, thus becoming the last thing that was done in the original situation. If, now, the learned response no longer produces this change, the individual will go on doing various things in the situation until some other response does change the situation. That new response will then be the one that tends to occur next time. If this new response consistently terminates the situation, it will replace the old response. If, however, there is no longer any consistency in what response will terminate the situation, behavior will be variable from time to time. No particular new response will be learned, but the old response will still be replaced by new responses—in this case, many new ones. If a dog has learned to get out of the yard by crawling through a hole in the fence, and if this hole is now mended, the dog may or may not discover some other mode of escape. In any case, however, the response of going to the place where the hole was will be replaced by some other response or combination of responses.

Forgetting

Guthrie's interpretation of forgetting is similar. Habits do not weaken with disuse; they are replaced by other habits. This principle applies fully as well to memories and skills as to specific acts. If we forget the German vocabulary we have learned, it is because the English words that serve as stimuli have become attached to other responses than the German words. If we lose our skill at horseback riding, it is because we have practiced other, competing responses in situations that were somewhat similar to being on horseback (such as being on a bicycle). In most cases the details of the relearning process are obscure, and it would be difficult to predict with accuracy how much of some knowledge or skill we would forget under a given set of circumstances. However, this interpretation of forgetting does provide a good starting point for studying the factors that influence forgetting.

Forgetting, like acquisition, is usually gradual because of the many specific stimulus-response connections that make up a complex habit. If the correct responses have been attached to many different stimuli, it will take longer for new responses to get attached to all these stimuli. Hence it is possible to make one definite prediction from Guthrie's interpretation of forgetting. We can predict that a habit will be better retained if it has been practiced in a number of different situations (i.e., in the presence of a number of different stimulus combinations). In the course of forgetting, new responses may replace the old, correct one quickly in any of these situations, but the old response will still be conditioned to many other stimulus combinations. On another occasion when the stimulus combination is different, the old response is likely to reappear. Forgetting, like learning, is specific to the situation, and what is forgotten in one situation may well be remembered in another. The "forgotten" response to the changed stimulus will occur only, however, if the response in question was originally learned to a variety of different stimulus combinations. Hence we can increase the resistance of a habit to forgetting (including those verbal habits that we call knowledge) not only by practicing it more but by practicing it in a variety of situations.

Making the Subjective Objective

The impression conveyed by most of Guthrie's writing is that human behavior is a very mechanistic matter. Behavior is rigidly controlled by stimuli, and changes in the stimulus-response connections follow simple mechanical laws. However, Guthrie has been more receptive than Watson to such concepts as desire and purpose. He recognizes that much behavior has a goal-directed character. Rather than ignore this, as Watson was inclined to do, he attempts to interpret it in rigorously physical terms.

What does it mean to say that someone has a desire, a purpose, or an intention to do something? Guthrie recognizes four components: (1) a complex of maintaining stimuli that keeps the organism active; (2) something that blocks any simple, direct action that would remove the maintaining stimuli at once; (3) muscular readiness to make certain responses; and (4) muscular readiness for the consequences of this action. Consider a person in a burning building who has the intention of jumping to safety. In this case the four components are as follows: (1) heat from the fire, choking sensations from the smoke, and fear; (2) the fire and the height that block the person from simply running away; (3) the tensing of muscles for the jump; and (4) the preparation of the body for the shock of the fall. These four components, says Guthrie, are all that we need to describe an intention.

If someone had suggested to Guthrie that intention is something mental, over and above these four physical components, he might have replied with his story about a strange murder case. A man resolved to shoot his neighbor, and he hid outside the neighbor's house with a rifle pointed at the door and his finger on the trigger. While sitting there, he began to think better of his plan. He was about to get up and go away when the neighbor came out the door. The man pulled the trigger and the neighbor fell. At his trial, the question arose as to whether or not he fired intentionally. According to Guthrie, this is a meaningless question. Because of the words that the man spoke subvocally to himself, part of his muscular readiness for action had changed, in that he had started to brace himself to get up and go away. However, the muscular readiness of his finger to pull the trigger had not changed. There was no one intention, only a variety of bodily adjustments that did or did not prepare him to shoot.

What is attention? It encompasses a variety of responses that orient the sense receptors toward certain stimuli, as in looking or listening. There may even be scanning, involving searching movements that end when a certain stimulus is perceived. This formulation of attention makes it possible for Guthrie to reword his basic principle of learning as follows: "What is being noticed becomes a signal for what is being done" (1959, p. 186).

In all these interpretations, Guthrie is insisting that the processes involved, though they may be called by subjective terms, refer to objective physical movements. They may be hard to observe, but they are there just as surely as any other movements. Guthrie particularly emphasizes the role of *movement-produced stimuli*, the sensations produced by our own movements. These play an important part in thought, purpose, the coordination of sequences of behavior, and responses to stimuli that are no longer present. For example, the combination of stimuli from feeling ourselves make a certain movement serves to produce our next movement. Likewise, we are able to respond to a stimulus that is no longer present (such as an object that has disappeared behind something) by moving part of our body in relation to where the object is, thereby producing stimuli that guide us toward the object though we cannot see it. Though these movement-produced stimuli often function like intervening variables in Guthrie's system (since they are often impractical to observe directly), he hesitates to call them intervening variables, since for him they are just as objectively present as the independent and the dependent variables.

Guthrie's final theoretical statement (1959), written shortly before his death, is both more technical and more tentative than most of his earlier work. He seems to be trying to clarify both his own ideas and his relationships to other theorists. In this statement he is concerned both with the concept of attention and with the formal structure of his theory. However, it is likely that Guthrie will be remembered not so much for his attempts, successful or not, at formal theory building as for his informal contributions to our thinking about the learning process.

In trying to understand or to control any learning situation, Guthrie reminds us to look at the particular response that is being made and the particular stimuli that are eliciting it. He warns us not to rely on vague exhortations, not to look for magic in the administration of rewards and punishments, but to concentrate on eliciting particular patterns of behavior in particular situations. Though he tends to draw his examples largely from child rearing and animal training, Guthrie has much that is useful to offer adult human learners as well.

College students often complain that they know the material they have studied but that they somehow cannot present it on examinations. A familiarity with Guthrie's thinking would lead one to say, "If the behavior you want to produce is the behavior of writing essays about certain topics, practice writing essays, and practice in a situation as close as possible to that of an exam." In a similar example in military training, studies of combat effectiveness resulted in training situations being made more and more like combat. As a result, infantry trainees spend less time practicing exact marksmanship with bull's-eye targets on the known-distance range and more time practicing rough-and-ready marksmanship with silhouette targets that pop up to confront the trainees as they advance. Similarly, more of first aid training is given in realistic simulations of accident scenes, complete with "blood," groans, and bystanders giving bad advice. Though we cannot say that these examples represent Guthrie's direct influence on the applied psychology of learning, we can say that Guthrie, perhaps more than any other major theorist, has emphasized the importance of such precise analysis of stimuli and responses. Guthrie's approach can stand one in good stead in many learning situations.

GUTHRIE AND WATSON AS CONTIGUITY THEORISTS

Watson and Guthrie of course have in common all the characteristics of behaviorism in the general sense of that term. In addition, there is one respect in which the two of them differ from the majority of other behavioristic theorists—namely, they do not regard learning as depending on reinforcement. Watson ridiculed the idea that reward could determine what was learned, regarding it as a magical notion unfit for a scientific explanation. Guthrie similarly avoided making any reference to the reinforcing effects of rewards. In their systems, learning is assumed to depend only on the contiguity of stimulus and response, in other words, on the fact that they occur together. Hence Watson and Guthrie are called *contiguity theorists.*

In taking this position, Watson and Guthrie stand in contrast to another group of connectionist behavioristic theorists known as *reinforcement theorists.* The latter group is just as dedicated to objectivity and just as much attached to the stimulus-response language in describing learning. Its proponents do not, however, see any objection to recognizing the reinforcing effect of reward in their theories; in fact, they consider this effect essential to the analysis of learning. We have already seen that Thorndike was a great early exponent of this view. For some decades it was the dominant approach in American learning theory, and it will occupy us for the next three chapters.

Chapter
5

Hull's Formal Theory Building

*T*he most ambitious of all the connectionist learning theories is that of Clark L. Hull (1884–1952). Long a professor at Yale, Hull was the most influential learning theorist of his time. He was a behaviorist, but far more sophisticated than Watson in the philosophy of science. He began college as a pre-engineering student, and something of the engineer's outlook is evident in his desire to construct an elaborate, formal, precise structure of psychological theory. In him we see the full logical flowering of the connectionist reinforcement tradition.

THE POSTULATIONAL METHOD OF THEORY CONSTRUCTION

Hull's concept of the ideal theory was a logical structure of postulates and theorems, similar to Euclid's geometry. The postulates would be statements about various aspects of behavior. They would not be laws taken directly from experiments, but more general statements about the basic processes involved. Like the postulates of geometry, they would not themselves be proved but would be taken as the starting points for proofs. From these postulates, a great variety of other statements, called theorems, could be logically derived. Each theorem could be proved by arguing logically from some combination of postulates. These theorems would be in the form of laws of behavior.

So far, such a theory is simply a logical creation. No mention has been made about whether its statements are true or false, only about how they hang together logically. When a theorem is proved, all this means is that if the postulates are true, the theorem must also be true. In order for the theory to have any value as a description of the real world, it is necessary to compare the theorems with actual laws of behavior as determined by experiments. In other words, after the theorist has determined by logic that the theorems follow from the postulates, he or she must then determine by experiment whether they are true. If they are, the whole theory is supported; if not, the theory is weakened and requires revision.

To anyone not acquainted with the philosophy of science, this approach may seem backward. The theorists start with postulates that may or may not be true. They then prove logically that if the postulates are true, certain theorems must also be true. Next, they determine by experiments whether each theorem is in fact true. Finally, they use the truth or falsity of the theorems to argue indirectly about the truth or falsity of the postulates. If a theorem turns out to be false, they know that at least one of the postulates from which the theorem was proved must also be false, since it led logically to a false conclusion. In consequence, some postulate (the theorists may not yet know which one) must be changed so that the theorems that follow from it will be true. If, instead, all the theorems turn out to be true, this verification increases their confidence that all the postulates are true. However, they can never be absolutely sure that the postulates are true, since false postulates can sometimes lead to true theorems. As more and more theorems turn out to be true, they become more confident that the postulates are true, but there is still the possibility that eventually a theorem derived from the postulates will turn out to be false.

Although this theoretical approach may sound both complicated and strange, it is actually rather similar to what we do in many familiar situations. Consider a teacher who is concerned about the poor performance of a certain student, one who has a high IQ. She suspects that the difficulty may reflect two factors in the student's personality: (1) a fear of competition, and (2) a tendency to react to fear (whatever its source) by "freezing up" and being unable to act effectively. These guesses are the equivalent of postulates. Each of them may be either true or false, and both would need to be true to explain the student's difficulty. How would one determine whether or not they are true?

To test these postulates, the teacher must first figure out how a student who has this fear and this reaction to fear would behave in certain situations. This is the process of deducing theorems from postulates. Thus, if the teacher's "postulates" about the student are true, it should also be true that (1) the student will do better on test items if they are presented to him casually in conversation rather than as part of a test; (2) if given an opportunity to compete for a prize, he will refuse; and (3) if offered a chance to give a talk to the class on some topic that interests him, he will accept. The teacher may try each of these approaches and see what happens. These, then, are three experiments, each designed to test one of the teacher's "theorems." If in each case the student does what the teacher predicted, her confidence in her interpretation (i.e., in her "postulates") will increase. She cannot, however, rule out the possibility that all of his behavior is really due to some other combination of factors, and that eventually he will do something that does not fit at all with her interpretation. She can become more and more confident that her interpretation is correct, but she can never be absolutely sure of it.

If it turned out that her first two predictions were confirmed, but the third was not, she would know that her "postulates" were not entirely correct. She might decide, since he refused to address the class even when no competition was involved, that his fear was not merely of competition but of any situation in which he faced the possibility of failure or disapproval. She could then look for new situations in which to test this revised "postulate." In this way her interpretation of his behavior would be a self-correcting process of making and testing assumptions.

The teacher's thinking in this example and Hull's thinking in constructing a scientific theory are, of course, markedly different in scope and in logical formality. These are differences of degree, however, rather than of kind. The teacher was concerned with very narrow interpretations, involving the behavior of a single student, whereas Hull was concerned with very broad ones, involving the whole range of human and animal behavior. In addition, Hull wrote down his postulates in detailed form and tested the theorems in controlled experiments, whereas the teacher merely developed hunches and tested them in a rough-and-ready fashion. Nevertheless, the two cases are basically similar enough to show the kind of reasoning that Hull followed in building his theory.

It should be clear from the above that Hull did not regard his theory as a final statement about the nature of learning. Rather, it was intended as a tentative formulation, always subject to revision to bring it in line with new data. This tentativeness was a necessary characteristic of the kind of system he wanted to build. A set of postulates from which many laws of behavior are supposed to follow by strictly logical deduction has more chances of being wrong than does an informal system that makes fewer or less exact predictions. Watson's and Guthrie's theories, for example, are informal enough to leave considerable doubt as to just what they would predict in a particular situation. Hull, in contrast, intended to create a theory specific enough so that it would be easy to see when it was contrary to the evidence. A theory of this sort is practically certain to be wrong in some respects when it is first formulated; hence it must be open to change as errors are discovered.

THE THEORY

It was Hull's plan to write three books expounding his theory. The first was to present and explain the postulate system. This appeared in 1943 as *Principles of Behavior.* The second book was to contain detailed derivations of individual behavior in a variety of situations. This was published in 1952 as *A Behavior System.* It contains 133 theorems with their derivations from the postulates and the evidence bearing on their correctness as laws of behavior. The topics with which these theorems deal are as diverse as discrimination learning, locomotion in space, and the acquisition of values. As might be expected, this system of postulates and theorems is much more complicated and technical than any of the other systems we have examined so far.

An invalid during the last few years of his life, Hull was barely able to finish this second major book. In the preface, he expressed his regret that the third book in the series, which was to present derivations of behavior in social interactions, would never be written. Four months later he died. Although his trilogy thus remains incomplete, it gives us a good picture both of the grandness of Hull's conception and of the many respects in which the actual system fell short of his aspirations. It is possible that if Hull had lived longer and had been in better health during his last years, many of the shortcomings of his theory would have been corrected. As it is, we must judge both his successes and his failures by his works as they stand.

The Four-Stage Analysis

Like most theorists, Hull wanted to develop a system for predicting the dependent variables of behavior from various independent variables. Recognizing the variety of independent and dependent variables with which he had to deal, he tried to simplify the task of prediction by introducing intervening variables. We saw in Chapter 2 how the use of such intervening variables (e.g., thirst) makes it possible to summarize a great many details with a small number of concepts. Hull organized his intervening variables into a four-stage predictive scheme. The first stage consisted of the independent variables from which he was predicting, the fourth stage consisted of the dependent variables to which he was predicting, and the second and third stages were made up of intervening variables connecting them. Knowing the values (amounts or degrees) of the independent variables, he could compute the values of the intervening variables at stage 2. From these he could in turn compute the value of the intervening variable at stage 3, and from that finally predict the values of the dependent variables. The general outline of this elaborate scheme is given in Figure 5.1, which may serve as a guide to the explanation below.

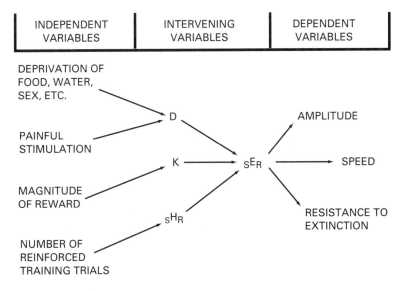

Figure 5.1   A schematic representation of a simplified version of Hull's system. The independent variables influence the intervening variables, which in turn influence the dependent variables. D = drive; K = incentive motivation; $_sH_R$ = habit strength; $_sE_R$ = excitatory potential.

The independent variables include all those that can be directly manipulated by an experimenter. These may be summarized briefly, since they are discussed in more detail in connection with the intervening variables. Some of the independent variables refer to the stimulation the learner is receiving at the moment, such as the brightness of a signal light or the intensity of an electric shock. Others refer to immediately preceding events, such as the number of hours since the learner's last meal or the amount of muscular effort recently put forth. Still others refer to previous experience in the same learning situation, such as the number of times the subject has previously made the response to be learned or the magnitude of the reward received the last time the response was made. The number of such independent variables that could be mentioned is endless; the important thing for our understanding of Hull is the way that he has organized them in his system.

The second stage of the analysis introduces intervening variables. These are hypothetical states of the organism that cannot be observed but that are assumed to be directly controlled by the independent variables. The two most prominent ones are *habit strength* and *drive*. Habit strength refers to the strength of the learned connection between a stimulus and a response, a connection built up through reinforced practice. Drive is an activating state of the organism, and a reduction in drive serves as a reward.

Since Hull was a connectionist theorist, habit strength is a key concept in his system. It is the strength of the bond connecting a stimulus with a response. To indicate the nature of this connection, habit strength is abbreviated $_sH_R$ (pronounced S H R), with the *H* standing for habit and the *S* and *R* subscripts standing for the stimulus and the response that the habit connects. This habit is a permanent connection, which can increase but cannot decrease in strength. All long-term learning involves the formation and strengthening of habits. Each time a response occurs in the presence of a stimulus and is quickly followed by reinforcement, the habit strength of this stimulus-response connection increases. In this postulate, Hull resembles all other reinforcement theorists. His system goes on to say that all reinforcement involves a reduction in the strength of a drive. The rate at which habit strength builds up with successive reinforced responses (given by an equation in another postulate) follows the well-known "law of diminishing returns," so that each successive reinforced response contributes less to $_sH_R$ than the previous one. Eventually a point is reached at which additional reinforced responses contribute very little more to habit strength.

Drive is a temporary state of the organism, produced by deprivation of something the body needs or by painful stimulation. There are many different specific drive conditions, of which hunger, thirst, and pain are typical examples. Drives have two different functions. For one thing, each drive condition, such as hunger or thirst, produces a characteristic strong drive stimulus. This stimulus indicates the particular need from which the body is suffering. A rapid reduction in this drive stimulus is reinforcing. As a result, any response that occurs just before a reduction in a drive stimulus tends to be learned as a response to whatever stimuli are present. (We have already seen this relationship in connection with the postulate about the building up of habit strength.) The other function of drives is an activating or energizing one. All drive conditions combine to make up the total drive level of the organism. This total drive (abbreviated D) serves to raise the individual's activity level. This activating effect of D can be seen both in an increased level of general body activity and in the increased vigor with which all learned habits are performed. In all these respects, Hull's D shows resemblances to Guthrie's maintaining stimuli.

Hull was also concerned with the size of the reward used as a reinforcer. We are all familiar with the law that people tend to work harder for a larger reward than for a smaller one. In other words, the level of performance is commonly higher when a larger reward is given after the response occurs. How should this law be handled by the theory? In his earlier book, Hull (1943) treated the magnitude of the reward as one aspect of reinforcement. The larger the reward, the greater the reduction in drive, and hence the greater the increase in habit strength. However, this treatment proved not to be satisfactory. Experiments showed that changes in the magnitude of the reward produced very rapid changes in the level of performance, much faster than the slow growth of habit strength could explain. This difference was particularly difficult for Hull to explain when the change was from a larger to a smaller reward. If the reward was made smaller and performance became poorer, this result seemed to mean that the habit strength had become less. Yet habit strength involved a permanent bond, one that became stronger with reinforced practice but never became weaker. Here was a striking example of a discrepancy between theory and experiment. How would Hull deal with it?

Hull's answer, in the later versions of his theory, was to introduce a third intervening variable at the second stage of the analysis. Along with habit strength and drive he added *incentive motivation* (abbreviated K). The magnitude of the reward, in the new version, affects only K, not habit strength. The level of K depends on the size of the reward (e.g., the amount of food) in the few immediately preceding trials. When the size of the reward is increased, at whatever stage of practice, K increases, and when the reward is decreased, K decreases. Incentive motivation thus refers, as the name implies, to the motivating effect of the incentive that is provided for making the response. The distinction between incentive motivation and reinforcement is subtle, since both depend on the reward, but the difference is nonetheless important. In order for a habit to increase in strength, the response must be followed by a reward that reduces a drive stimulus. The size of the reward makes no difference to the rate at which habit strength is built up; any reinforcement is as good as any other. The size of the reward does, however, affect the level of incentive motivation. Large rewards make for higher values of K, smaller rewards for lower values. When a rat learns to run down an alley for food, we see a gradual increase in its speed, an increase resulting from reinforced practice. However, over and above this slow increase in speed, we can increase or decrease the speed rapidly by changing the size of the food pellet we give at the end of each run. In the same way, it may be possible to increase a worker's output immediately by offering more pay for each item produced (thus increasing K), whereas it would take much longer to increase output by training the person in better work methods (increasing habit strength).

These three intervening variables—$_sH_R$, D, and K—work together to produce another intervening variable, which constitutes the third stage of the analysis. This is called *excitatory potential* and refers to the total tendency to make a given response to a given stimulus. It is abbreviated $_sE_R$, according to the same principle as $_sH_R$. It is equal to the product of the three other intervening variables; in other words, $_sE_R = {_sH_R} \times D \times K$. This equation means that the tendency to make a given response to a given stimulus depends on a habit built up through reinforced practice ($_sH_R$) and on two motivational factors, one depending on an internal state (D) and the other on an external incentive (K). For everyday purposes, we might refer to the $_sH_R$ for a given response as "having the skill to do it," to the K as "expecting a gain from doing it," and to D as "wanting the thing that is to be gained." Hull, however, would not use this terminology, as he would consider it too vague for the precise and objective science of behavior that he wanted to promote. For Hull, $_sH_R$, D, and K are defined by the operations that produce them (reinforced practice for $_sH_R$, deprivation or painful stimulation for D, nutritive substance for K), not by any vague, everyday names that we might choose to give them.

The fourth and final stage of Hull's analysis is made up of the dependent variables, the aspects of behavior that can actually be observed and measured. Hull relates three of these to excitatory potential ($_sE_R$): (1) the amplitude or size of the response, (2) the speed of the response, and (3) the total number of responses that will occur, after reinforcement is removed, before extinction is complete. As $_sE_R$ increases, amplitude, speed, and number of responses to complete extinction all increase.

In principle, it should be possible to use this system to predict how fast, for example, a rat would run down an alley to a food reward. To make this prediction, we would need to go through a number of steps. We would use the number of times the rat had already run down that alley and been reinforced to calculate the value of $_sH_R$. We would use the number of hours since the rat last ate to calculate the value of D. We would use the size of food reward that the rat had received on the last few trials to calculate the value of K. Then we would multiply those three values together to obtain the value of $_sE_R$. Finally, we would use $_sE_R$ to calculate the rat's speed on that trial. Each of these calculations requires using one of Hull's postulates, which would give us the necessary formula. To what extent it is possible to make such calculations in practice is difficult to say; we will get some idea of why it is difficult as we go along.

What Figure 5.1 shows, and what we have considered so far, is only the barest outline of Hull's system (1952). The final version of his theory had 17 postulates and 15 corollaries (theorems that follow immediately from a single postulate), which he hoped would cover the whole range of known behavioral phenomena. For example, he postulated the existence of unlearned stimulus-response connections, but did not elaborate the topic and rarely referred to such innate connections in his theorems. He discussed the effect of a delay between the response and the reinforcement in weakening the response tendency. He went into considerable detail about generalization and about the way generalized habit strengths combine (i.e., what happens when the same response is learned to two different but related stimuli). These details are beyond the scope of this book.

We have seen that Hull's goal was to derive the laws of behavior logically from a simple system of postulates. After considering the number of concepts and assumptions that Hull packed into his 17 postulates, we may begin to wonder if there is anything simple about the system. However, its relative simplicity is more evident if we remember that *A Behavior System* contains 133 theorems, some with several parts, all following from the 17 postulates. Moreover, these 133 represent the limitations of Hull's time and energy rather than the limitations of the theory—there could have been many more. There is no question that the system represents an accomplishment of major proportions.

STRENGTHS AND WEAKNESSES OF HULL'S SYSTEM

Hull saw the value of his theory not so much in the particular intervening variables it included as in its rigorous quantification. The postulates do not merely state that certain variables are related; they give equations by which one variable can be computed precisely from the other. For example, the postulate regarding habit formation contains the equation $_sH_R = 1 - 10^{-.0305N}$, where N is the total number of reinforced trials. Using this equation, we can state the exact level of habit strength for any given number of reinforcements. Similar equations are presented connecting the other second-stage intervening variables to the independent variables and also connecting excitatory potential to the dependent variables. The equation connecting the second-stage intervening variables to $_sE_R$, which involves simple multiplication, has already been given.

Hull dedicated much of his effort in the last years of his life to the problems of quantification. He wanted to develop a scale of measurement for excitatory potential that would be applicable to any response. Such a scale of measurement would make it possible to say, for example, that one rat's excitatory potential for pressing a lever was either greater or less than another rat's excitatory potential for running down an alley, even though lever-pressing is measured in presses per minute and running is measured in feet per second. He then wanted to find ways of combining different excitatory potentials that supported one another by the process of generalization or that competed with one another. Hull regarded this work on scaling (which is too complex to summarize here) as perhaps the leading achievement of his life.

The evaluation of Hull's work by others has, however, been rather different from his own evaluation. It is just on the matter of quantitative rigor that he is most vulnerable to criticism. To some extent, the reason is that his attempts at quantification were premature. The exact values in his equations, such as the $-.0305$ in the equation for habit strength, were typically based on the results of a single experiment. He made the suggestion, but never developed it, that the values in the equations might vary from individual to individual. Thus different people might have different equations for the development of habit strength, with the specific absolute value being greater than .0305 for fast learners and smaller for slow learners. Moreover, when Hull came to derive theorems from his postulates, he sometimes used different values in his equations from the ones given in the postulates. For all these reasons, it seems clear that these values were intended to be illustrative rather than literally correct. What Hull attempted to present in his books was the general outline of a rigorous theory together with some suggestions as to how the outline could be developed into a full-scale, quantitatively exact system. He was still a long way from actually having such a system when he died.

Even if we leave aside the matter of precise, quantitative values, the system does not live up to the ideals that Hull set for it. In a system such as Hull's, it should be possible, given the values of the independent variables, to compute the values of the intervening variables and from these the dependent variables. Even if the precise numbers needed to make the computations are not available, it should be possible to explain how the computations would be made. In many of Hull's cases, however, it is not possible to do so. Sometimes the reason it is not possible is simply that a given issue is not covered by the postulates. An example of this kind of problem is the value of incentive motivation (K). Since K is defined by the weight of food or other nutriment consumed, it is impossible to apply Hull's equations to a situation where some other reward is involved. This might have been an easy problem to solve, but Hull died before he had a chance to deal with it.

A second type of problem that occurs in Hull's theory is that the same question can logically be answered in two or more different and logically conflicting ways, so that both cannot be correct, yet both follow from the postulates. A particularly egregious example is the question of how to predict resistance to extinction. Suppose we want to know how many successive nonreinforced trials it would take to produce complete extinction. There turn out to be not just two but three different ways of answering that question, depending on which postulates we look at, each way leading to a different answer. It is therefore impossible to say what prediction Hull's theory makes about the question of trials to extinction of a response.

The fact that different approaches can give different quantitative answers is not necessarily a crucial problem, since we have seen that the particular numerical values Hull used were mainly illustrative. However, the lack of internal consistency which this illustration points up is a serious weakness in the system, probably more so than any other flaw. When a theory makes incorrect predictions, it can be modified, as Hull intended that his theory should be. When a theory does not deal with a given issue at all, we can accept this limitation in its scope and hope that someday it may be expanded to include the neglected topic. However, when a theory is internally inconsistent, so that it makes conflicting predictions about a given issue, its worth as a rigorous theory is seriously compromised. To some extent we can blame Hull's failure in this regard on the revisions in his theory. Racing against time in the last years of his life, Hull considered it more important to show what could be done with parts of his system than to make the system as a whole complete and consistent. Nevertheless, we must recognize that the theoretical system Hull actually created falls far short of the standards he himself set for theories.

HULL'S INFLUENCE ON OTHER THEORISTS

By the irony of history, it appears that Hull failed where he most wished to succeed and succeeded in the respect that interested him least. He wanted both to build a deductive theory, at once broad in scope and rigorous in detail, and to encourage others to carry on the same sort of theoretical work. We have seen how far he fell short of his first aspiration. Moreover, his failure may have discouraged others from attempting such a task. Many observers have noted a trend in learning theory away from the sort of all-encompassing theories that we have been examining so far, toward theories of smaller scope designed to explain only certain kinds of learning. This trend may well reflect in part Hull's failure.

For many years, psychologists have dreamed of doing for their field what Newton did for physics—developing a theory that would be at once vast in its scope, precise in its applications, and elegant in its simplicity, a theory that would pull together the loose ends of psychology into one master system. (Guthrie's theory, as we saw, was partly an effort in that direction.) In pushing so far toward this goal and yet falling so far short of it, Hull convinced many psychologists that the day of such a master theory in psychology was still far off.

Yet in his failure, Hull also achieved striking success. His terms, his interests, and his ways of formulating psychological questions became more widespread than those of any other theorist of his time. A large number of experiments were inspired by his work. His interpretations of drive, reinforcement, extinction, and generalization became standard starting points for discussion of these topics. He was attacked, defended, and elaborated on until to many people "learning theory" and "Hullian theory" became synonymous.

Moreover, Hull's interest in quantification in learning theory was clearly an idea whose time had come. Though we have not looked at how he went about it, we can note in general terms that it was a statistical theory, based on small random fluctuations in excitatory potential. To say that the fluctuations are random means that the individual fluctuations cannot be predicted, but that collectively the fluctuations follow regular laws, just as individual rolls of dice are not predictable, but the proportion of rolls that are sevens can be predicted within a small margin of error. Such statistical regularities are valuable not only to gamblers but also to insurance actuaries, to experimenters analyzing their data, and to psychologists studying individual differences. Hull recognized that these regularities are also useful in the construction of learning theories.

Statistical Learning Theories

However, he was not alone. Shortly before Hull's death, other theorists began to develop *statistical learning theories,* theories that were even more explicit in their statistical basis than was Hull's. Instead of talking about excitatory potential, they took the probability of a given response as their basic unit. Using this unit and a few postulates about the nature of the learning process, they were able to predict theorems about the shapes of learning and extinction curves and a number of other learning phenomena. Particularly noteworthy was the work of William K. Estes (b. 1919, currently at Harvard), a student of Skinner's who used postulates drawn largely from Guthrie to deduce theorems dealing with generalization, forgetting, spontaneous recovery, drive, and other phenomena.

How did the work of these theorists relate to Hull's? Obviously they were similar in a number of ways: deducing theorems from postulates, using statistical methods, and otherwise trying to make theory construction a precise, formal, quantitative operation. Moreover, (not surprisingly) they gave many of the same predictions. But there were also differences from Hull. For all his interest in statistical methods, Hull remained basically the engineer; he built a structure of theory and then added random statistical fluctuations at the end, as an engineer would add an extra margin of safety to his or her calculations in order to allow for unexpected fluctuations. The newer statistical theorists, however, built their whole theories on probabilities, which by their very nature have an inherent element of uncertainty. As it turned out, this made it possible for them to deduce certain things as theorems that Hull had put in as postulates. Since the ideal theory is one in which a very large number of (true) theorems can be deduced from a very small number of postulates, this permitted these theorists to out-Hull Hull.

These statistical theories were only some among a large number of formal, mathematical theories that were developed in the field of learning and in other areas of psychology. Many, as we noted earlier, were fairly narrow in their coverage, trying to deal precisely with one aspect of learning. These were often referred to as *models* of learning. They are models in much the same sense as a hardware model of an atom, with wooden balls for electrons, protons, and neutrons. No one claims that such a classroom model is a complete and accurate representation of an atom; we know that electrons are different from wooden balls and that their orbits are not much like pieces of wire. Nevertheless, there are certain respects in which the model and the real atom are alike. Given these similarities, the model enables us to predict certain things about the way the atom itself will behave. In many cases the model does not include any actual physical representation, but is merely a precise, usually mathematical description.

To the extent that a model enables us to predict some aspect of reality, it is useful. We need not argue whether or not the model is true, since at best it is never more than a partial description or representation. This is basically the same logic of theory construction that Hull used, but with extra emphasis on the fact that the model is a logical construction separate from the reality that it describes. A given model may describe one aspect of learning very well (e.g., the learning curve for number of correct responses on a particular lab task), another aspect less well (e.g., how quickly the individual responds on that same task), and still another quite poorly (e.g., performance on a different task). We would not say that the model is either true or false, just that it is accurate and therefore useful to varying degrees for predicting certain kinds of events.Clearly, there is no sharp distinction between a model and any other theory. The many models, statistical and otherwise, that have been applied to various aspects of learning are all in the same logical tradition as Hull's grand theory, but most of them are a good deal more modest in their aspirations than was Hull's.

Hull's Influence on Personality and Psychotherapy

In the later years of his life, Hull gathered around him a group of people in a number of academic disciplines, including clinical and social psychology, anthropology, sociology, and psychiatry. Though working independently, they all tried to apply

Hull's ideas to their own areas of study. Many lines of work emerged from this cross-fertilization of ideas; topics included the relationship of frustration to aggression, the reinterpretation of Freudian ideas in terms of learning principles, the psychological bases of social influence, and the explanation of worldwide cultural differences on the basis of different forms of child rearing. Of these many ideas, we will look at only one: an attempt to explain abnormal personality development and the ways that psychotherapy works to cure it. The analysis was developed by John Dollard (1900–1980), a clinical psychologist and social scientist, and Neal Miller (b. 1909), an experimental psychologist, working together at Yale (Dollard & Miller 1950).

Dollard and Miller begin the analysis by pointing out three characteristics of neurotic people: that they are miserable because of their conflicts, that they seem stupid about certain aspects of their lives, and that they have symptoms. The researchers then proceed to explain these three characteristics according to the neurotic's previous learning. The crucial element here is the learned drive of fear. This drive is the basis of the conflict, the source of the misery, the cause of the apparent stupidity, and the reason for the symptoms.

What is a learned drive? Dollard and Miller begin their discussion of the topic with an experimental demonstration involving rats. A rat is placed in a box with two compartments, one of which has white walls and a grid floor, the other black walls and a wooden floor. The rat explores both parts and shows little preference between them. Then it is placed in the white compartment and given strong electric shock through the grid floor. Most rats soon escape the shock by running into the black compartment. This sequence of shock in white and escape to black is repeated several times. Then the rat is placed in the white compartment without shock. It runs rapidly to the black compartment. Since there is no longer a pain drive to motivate this escape behavior, Dollard and Miller explain it on the ground that a learned drive of fear has been conditioned to the stimuli of the white compartment.

What is the nature of this learned drive? Like all drives, say Dollard and Miller, it involves strong stimulation. These strong stimuli are produced by the rat's own responses. When the rat was first shocked in the white compartment, it made a variety of responses to the shock, such as tensing the muscles, increasing the heart rate, and other involuntary indicators of emotion. These in turn produced strong stimulation, which was added to the drive produced by the pain of the shock. These strong stimuli produced by the emotional responses make up the drive of fear. These emotional responses became conditioned to the stimuli of the white compartment, owing to the fact that they occurred in the presence of those stimuli and were followed by drive reduction when the rat escaped the shock. Now when the stimuli of the white compartment are presented without shock, they produce the emotional responses that in turn produce stimuli of the fear drive.

The fact that fear is a drive can be demonstrated by using it as the basis of new learning. This demonstration was done by closing the door from the white to the black section and making it possible for the rat to open the door only by turning a wheel on the wall near the door. The animals learned to turn the wheel and then run into the black compartment, even though there was no shock in the white compartment. Thus fear was the drive, turning the wheel the learned response, and escape from fear (by escaping from the white compartment) the reinforcer. Then the situation was changed so that turning the wheel would not open the door but pressing a lever would. As a result, the wheel-turning response was extinguished and the lever-pressing response was acquired. Thus the learned drive of fear operated like a primary drive to motivate learning.

How does this kind of learning occur when we go from experimental rats to neurotic humans? Let us consider a child who is severely punished for any kind of self-assertive behavior. Whenever she tries to get her own way, she is subjected to pain, which produces emotional responses, which produce the learned drive of fear. These fear-producing responses become conditioned to the stimuli that are present at the time, including the cues that come from her own self-assertion. As a result, any self-assertive behavior comes to produce fear, while submissiveness reduces the fear. Moreover, the fear is not merely of overt self-assertive behavior, but even of those self-assertive thoughts and feelings that go with it. The child is then afraid of self-assertion in the same way that the rat is afraid of the white compartment, and the child's submissiveness (in thoughts as well as deeds) is an escape from fear-provoking cues, just as the rat's running to the black compartment is an escape from the fear-provoking white compartment.

However, the child's problem is worse than the rat's. As long as the rat is able to run to the black compartment, its fear is brief and does not disrupt its life. The child, however, is often placed in positions where self-assertive behavior might get her things that she wants. These positions occur even more often after she becomes an adult. The fact that she is afraid to be self-assertive is a great handicap in such situations. She is placed in a conflict between her desire for something and her fear of the self-assertive behavior that would get it for her. This conflict, in which she loses no matter what she does, is a source of misery. If she recognized the great difference between her present situation and that in which she was punished for self-assertion, she might be able to relieve the fear and resolve the conflict. However, this course requires that she recognize her problem and think about it. But she cannot do either, since she has become afraid not only of behaving self-assertively but even of saying (to others or to herself) that she would like to be self-assertive. It is this fear of saying or even thinking that she would like to be self-assertive that makes her behavior stupid. She cannot make the thinking responses that would help her to understand and to solve her problems. She can, however, obtain some relief in a variety of ways. She may, for example, become so dependent, perhaps through symptoms of apparent physical illness, that others will feel obliged to take care of her and provide her with some of the things she wants. This would not be a deliberately adopted policy but a response learned through its drive-reducing effects. The "illness" would be called a symptom. It is, however, only a partial solution to the problem posed by fear and conflict, and it interferes with finding a more effective solution. This individual has all the characteristics of the neurotic; she is miserable, in conflict, stupid about her troubles—and she has symptoms.

How can the neurosis be eliminated through psychotherapy? Since fear is the crucial cause, extinguishing fear is the crucial element of the cure. If the rat is given enough experience in the white compartment without shock, its tendency to make the fear-producing responses will eventually extinguish. Similarly, if the neurotic can be persuaded to make self-assertive responses (or do whatever else it is that she is afraid of) under conditions in which she will not be punished, her fear will extinguish. Since the cues for fear come from the individual's own responses, she must gradually be induced to make these responses, first in very weak and indirect form, later more directly and strongly. Thus in the early stages of therapy the neurotic may timidly say that she sometimes thinks that if she were permitted to she could make helpful suggestions to her boss, while in the later stages she may express a violent desire to tell the boss off with assorted insults. As the patient extinguishes her fear of making self-assertive statements, she becomes more able to think sensibly about her conflict. Since talking about an act and doing it are somewhat similar, she also becomes by stimulus generalization less afraid of overt self-assertive behavior. Thus Dollard and Miller, through a considerably different theoretical system, came to a practical conclusion somewhat like Guthrie's threshold method for the elimination of undesirable emotional habits.

Some people regard Dollard and Miller's interpretation as mainly a translation of Freudian ideas into simplified Hullian language. Others regard their work as a direct application of learning theory, inspired in some ways by Freud but very different from Freud's own thinking. Either way, it represents an interesting and potentially useful combining of two approaches from quite different sources. A third possibility is to see their work as a historical bridge between the older Freudian ideas and newer behavioristic approaches to personality and psychopathology. These newer approaches begin with the work of B. F. Skinner, to whom we next turn.

Chapter
6

Skinner's Form of Behaviorism

During the period of Hull's greatest influence, and beginning several years before Hull published his *Principles of Behavior,* B. F. Skinner had been studying learning in his own distinctive way. He did not consider himself a theorist and had little use for the theories of others. Both the data he gathered and the pungent opinions he expressed soon brought him to general attention, but his distinctive research methods and his lack of interest in theories kept him outside the mainstream of learning theory for a long time. Yet by the same sort of irony that made Hull a great success even as he was failing in his choicest ambitions, Skinner came to be the best-known learning theorist of the 1970s and 1980s. Like Hull in a slightly earlier period, he is widely praised, condemned, and imitated, but rarely ignored, and many of his terms have become part of the standard vocabulary of learning.

Skinner was born in 1904 and received a Ph.D. in psychology from Harvard in 1931. After teaching at the Universities of Minnesota and Indiana, he returned to Harvard for the rest of his career. His first book, *The Behavior of Organisms,* was published in 1938, three years after the first edition of Guthrie's *Psychology of Learning* and five years before Hull's *Principles of Behavior.* Thereafter his influence increased gradually, until somewhere around 1970 he replaced Hull as the most talked-about figure in the behaviorist tradition. Even after his official retirement, he remained an active writer, and his last lecture, at a meeting of the American Psychological Association, was given only a week before his death in 1990.

THE BASIC ELEMENTS OF SKINNER'S SYSTEM

Of the theorists we have considered so far, the one whom Skinner most resembles is Thorndike. The two are alike in being connectionist theorists of a sort who emphasize reinforcement as a basic factor in learning, who take a keen interest in problems of education, and who deemphasize theory. This lack of interest in high-level theorizing was only implicit in Thorndike's writings, but Skinner made it quite explicit in his system. However, the fact that Skinner does not elaborate theorems, postulates, and intervening variables in the same formal way as Hull does not mean that Skinner is not a theorist at all. It does mean that his contributions as a theorist and as an experimenter are more closely intertwined than is the case with most of the system builders we have considered.

Two Kinds of Learning

In contrast to the other theorists we have discussed so far, Skinner recognizes two different kinds of learning. They are different because each involves a separate kind of behavior. *Respondent* behavior is elicited by specific stimuli. Given the stimulus, the response occurs automatically. The learning of respondent behavior follows the pattern referred to earlier as classical conditioning. A new stimulus is paired with the one that already elicits the response, and after a number of such pairings the new stimulus comes to elicit the response. The presentation of the old (unconditioned) stimulus during training may be considered the reinforcer, since without it learning will not occur. Thus the learning of respondent behavior in Skinner's system is similar to the kind of learning that Watson assumed made up all learning.

Skinner maintains, however, that most behavior is of a different sort. This kind he refers to as *operant* behavior. Whereas the distinctive characteristic of respondent behavior is that it is in response to stimuli, the characteristic of operant behavior is that it operates on the environment to secure particular consequences. There is no specific stimulus that can be identified that will consistently elicit a given operant (i.e., a given unit of operant behavior). Skinner speaks of operant behavior as being emitted by the organism rather than elicited by stimuli. Most behavior is of this sort; walking, talking, working, and playing are all made up of operants.

Skinner does not mean to say that operant behavior is not influenced by stimuli. Much of his analysis of behavior is concerned with ways in which operant behavior is brought under the control of stimuli. However, such control is only partial and conditional. The operant behavior of reaching for food is not simply elicited by the sight of food; it also depends on hunger, social circumstances, and a variety of other stimulus conditions. In these respects it is in contrast to the respondent jerking back of one's hand from a hot stove, which is regularly elicited almost without regard to other conditions. Because of this distinction, Skinner does not consider it useful to think of operant behavior as made up of specific stimulus-response connections in the sense that respondent behavior is. Whereas Guthrie analyzes every bit of behavior in terms of the stimuli that produce it, and Hull includes the S in $_sH_R$, Skinner prefers to think of most behavior (the operant kind) as emitted by the organism, without bothering to consider the multitude of stimuli that have something to do with its occurrence. The difference on this point is mainly one of emphasis and convenience rather than of direct disagreement. All three theorists agree that behavior depends on the total pattern of stimuli, external and internal, that are present when it occurs, but Guthrie and Hull prefer to emphasize this point for all responses, whereas Skinner prefers to ignore it in those cases where no one particular stimulus is crucial to the occurrence of the response.

The learning of operant behavior is also known as conditioning, but it is different from the conditioning of reflexes. Operant conditioning is the same sort of learning that Thorndike described. Because for Skinner this is by far the more important kind of learning, this topic is one on which he and Thorndike are in close agreement. If an operant occurs and is followed by reinforcement, its probability of occurring again increases. Whereas for conditioned respondents the reinforcer is an unconditioned stimulus, for operants it is a reward (or, as Thorndike would say, a satisfier). Thus we may say that reward following an operant makes that response more likely to occur again. (Even though the stimulus for an operant is unknown, Skinner still often refers to the operant behavior as a response.) This is the pattern of operant learning, which is to say, of most of the learning discussed by Skinner.

Whereas a respondent is usually a single bit of behavior, easy to identify separately, it is sometimes less clear where one operant stops and another starts. If a series of operants must occur in a particular sequence in order to obtain reinforcement, they become organized in a *chain*. The whole chain then comes to have some of the characteristics of a single operant, since the whole chain is the response unit that gets reinforced. In order to get a drink of water, for example, a person may have to get up from a chair, walk into the kitchen, open a cupboard, take down a glass, turn on the faucet, fill the glass, raise it to the mouth, and drink. Clearly this chain is made up of many operant responses, yet in another sense it functions as a single operant. If at any point the chain is broken—if there is no glass or if the faucet is broken or if there is some other obstruction—the whole chain up to that point will tend to undergo extinction. A large part of human behavior consists of such operant chains, which function in some degree as units but can nevertheless be analyzed into their component parts.

Positive and Negative Reinforcers

Although Skinner is largely concerned with *positive reinforcers,* he also recognizes the existence of *negative reinforcers.* Negative reinforcers are aversive stimuli, ones that the individual commonly seeks to avoid. The *removal* of a negative reinforcer increases the probability of the preceding response, just as does the *presentation* of a positive reinforcer. Electric shock, for example, is a negative reinforcer because the termination of the shock is reinforcing. Thus a response can be reinforced either by presenting a positive reinforcer or by removing a negative one.

An important point about reinforcers, both positive and negative, is that they can be conditioned. If a stimulus occurs repeatedly with a positive reinforcer, it tends itself to acquire the capacity to reinforce behavior. It then is called a conditioned positive reinforcer. A sign reading "Restaurant" will serve as a conditioned positive reinforcer for a hungry person in a strange city, because such signs have been associated with food in the past. Similarly, a stimulus that occurs with a negative reinforcer tends to become a conditioned negative reinforcer, as in the familiar case of the burned child who learns to avoid the stove even when it is cold.

The topic of negative reinforcement is obviously related to punishment, but the exact relation is not obvious. Negative reinforcement results from the *removal* of a negative reinforcer, whereas punishment involves the *presentation* of a negative reinforcer. Like Thorndike in the latter part of his career, Skinner regards the effect of reinforcement as simple and direct, but the effects of punishment as indirect and less predictable. Though reinforcement, by definition, increases the reinforced behavior, punishment does not always reduce the punished behavior. The reason is that negative reinforcers, and hence also punishers, are typically also stimuli for respondent behavior. Punishment may therefore elicit both general emotional arousal and such specific respondents as crying, cowering, or biting. Because of these respondents, punishment can sometimes "backfire," as when punishing a child for crying produces more crying rather than less.

In general, Skinner regards punishment as a poor method of controlling behavior. One reason is precisely this possibility that it may backfire, producing the opposite effect from the one desired. Another is the fact that its effects in suppressing undesirable behavior are often temporary, making punishment sometimes appear dramatically successful when in the long run it is actually quite unsuccessful in changing behavior. Also, the emotional behavior it commonly produces is often undesirable, so that even though the punishment works in a narrow sense, it fails in its broader goal of improving behavior. Replacing misbehavior with crying or anger, for example, is seldom a good solution. Moreover, the emotional responses may become conditioned to stimuli other than the ones the punisher wishes, including the stimuli of the punisher. For example, a child punished for some misbehavior in school may learn to respond with anger to the stimulus of the teacher or with avoidance to the whole school situation. For all these reasons, punishment is both a rather unreliable technique for controlling behavior and one that is likely to have unfortunate side effects. Finally, punishment is unpleasant, and that alone is reason enough to avoid it if an effective and more pleasant alternative (such as reinforcement of desirable behavior) is available.

Nevertheless, Skinner would not claim that punishment is worthless as a device for changing behavior. When it is possible to arrange a situation so that punishment immediately follows the undesirable behavior, but does not occur at other times, it may be effective in suppressing undesirable behavior without producing harmful side effects. Under such conditions of very specific punishment, the individual learns emotional respondents only to stimuli closely associated with the punished behavior. Since the person is exposed to all the other stimuli in the situation at other times when behavior is not being punished, whatever respondents the individual learns to these other stimuli soon extinguish.

Punishment is most effective, according to Skinner, when combined with reinforcement of other responses that are preferable to the punished ones. It then does not greatly matter that the effects of punishment alone may be temporary, since punishment is not being used alone. Instead, it is being used along with reinforcement to provide an opportunity for new learning of more desirable behavior. Skinner's interpretation of just how and why particular forms of punishment work are surprisingly elaborate for someone who does not consider himself a theorist, and we will not explore them further.

In any case, such carefully arranged punishment situations are hard to maintain, and are a far cry from the haphazard and sometimes vengeful way that punishment is commonly used in everyday life. Moreover, because punishment works fast, there is a temptation to overuse it relative to its actual long-term value. Because of this temptation, even some users of Skinnerian techniques employ punishment in ways that Skinner would deplore. So, although Skinner recognizes that punishment, properly used, can sometimes be a valuable method for modifying behavior, in general he regards punishment as a technique to be avoided.

The Role of Stimuli

Although stimuli do not elicit operants in the sense that they elicit respondents, they may determine whether or not any given operant will occur. A stimulus acquires this influence through the process of discrimination. If an operant is reinforced in the presence of one stimulus but not reinforced when it occurs in the presence of a different stimulus, the tendency to respond when the second stimulus is present gradually becomes extinguished, and a discrimination is formed. The operant will then occur in the presence of the first stimulus but not of the second. Since the individual has learned to discriminate between the stimuli, they are referred to as discriminative stimuli. A positive discriminative stimulus is one that indicates that responding will be reinforced; a negative discriminative stimulus indicates that responding will not be reinforced. In some cases the main focus of interest is on the positive discriminative stimulus, as when the ringing of a phone indicates that someone is calling, and the negative stimulus is simply the absence of the ringing. In such cases the (positive) discriminative stimulus often is abbreviated S^D. In other cases the positive and negative stimuli are more symmetrical, as when the sign "Open" indicates that trying the restaurant door is likely to be reinforced and the sign "Closed" indicates that it is likely not to be reinforced. In such cases the positive and negative stimuli are usually labeled, respectively, as S+ and S−.

When one has learned a discrimination thoroughly, one may respond so rapidly to the onset of S^D that it looks almost as though the response were a respondent, elicited by S^D. It is not, however, since occurrence of the operant depends on factors other than the S^D. For example, a pigeon can be taught to peck a key when it is green (S+) but not when it is red (S−) by reinforcing with food the pecks of the green key but not those of the red key. However, the pigeon will show little tendency to peck the green key for food when completely satiated. The S^D is a major determinant of the operant pecking response, but it does not produce it in the automatic way in which a stimulus elicits a reflex. It sets the occasion for the occurrence of reinforcement. Under these conditions the operant is said to be under *stimulus control.*

Is Skinner a Connectionist?

Skinner's rejection of theorizing is largely an objection to intervening variables, which he regards as useless at best, and often actually harmful, since they focus our attention on imaginary constructs instead of on reality. As a result, he is sometimes said to study the "empty organism"—not empty in fact, of course, but empty so far as Skinner's interpretations are concerned. Therefore, though Skinner will talk about the tendency for a given operant to be emitted in the presence of a given discriminative stimulus, he will not talk about any habit or stimulus-response bond as being responsible for the tendency. Even in the cases of respondents, he will say only that the stimulus reliably elicits the response, not that there is a stimulus-response connection in the nervous system. Here he diverges not only from the archtheorist, Hull, but even from Thorndike.

Skinner certainly gives a good deal of emphasis to stimuli, both as elicitors of respondents and as discriminative stimuli for operants. At the same time, he points out that stimuli are only one set of variables that influence the emission of operants; such factors as food deprivation must also be considered. Although he sometimes speaks of the strength of a given operant, he completely rejects any reference to the strength of a stimulus-response bond. Moreover, he insists that the proper measure of the strength of an operant is the rate at which it occurs, not how often or how quickly it occurs to a given stimulus. Skinner is not, therefore, a connectionist in the same sense as the other theorists we have looked at so far. The only stimulus-response connections he will discuss are relationships in behavior, not bonds in the nervous system, and at least as far as operant behavior is concerned, they are relationships that depend heavily on other factors as well. In a narrow sense of the term, therefore, we might say that Skinner is not really a connectionist at all.

Nevertheless, in a broader sense Skinner is still a connectionist. In contrast to the cognitive theorists, whom we will consider in later chapters, but like the other connectionist theorists, he analyzes behavior in terms of responses and the stimuli that influence them. His concept of causation runs rather directly from independent to dependent variables, without discussing any system of beliefs or any pattern of mental activity that might occur between. Though the connections he studies between stimuli and responses are not interpreted as habits or bonds within the nervous system, they are connections nonetheless, and as direct connections as in any other theory. So, although he relates responses to stimuli somewhat differently from other connectionist theorists, it makes sense to include him as a connectionist. Indeed, for some years Skinner has been in a broad sense the best-known exemplar of the connectionist tradition.

THE EFFECTS OF REINFORCERS

Skinner's antitheoretical bias makes it difficult to discuss his system apart from his research and its applications (a fact of which Skinner would be proud). His research has been conducted almost entirely in one version or another of an apparatus that has become known as the *Skinner box* (so named by Hull, not by Skinner). This varies in size and form according to the organism being studied, but basically it is simply a box (or, from the subject's point of view, a room) containing a simple *manipulandum* (i.e., something the subject can manipulate) and a device for delivering reinforcers. The manipulandum may be a lever for rats to press, a key for pigeons to peck, a vending-machine plunger for humans to pull, or anything else appropriate for the kind of subject using it. The mechanism for providing reinforcers is typically some sort of feeder, delivering food pellets to rats, grain to pigeons, or candy bars to humans. Other sorts of reinforcers may be used, however, from drops of water for thirsty rats to peep shows for monkeys and humans. In some cases escape from electric shock to the feet is used as the reinforcer, in which case no separate reinforcement dispenser is required.

The basic principle on which the box operates is that responses to the manipulandum produce reinforcers. These responses are called *free operants,* since the subject is free to emit them at his or her own speed. The rate at which the free operant is emitted is the response measure. Whereas other experimenters may study speed of running, number of correct choices, or other aspects of operant behavior, Skinner and his followers study only the rate of emission of free operants. Whatever variable they manipulate, they study its effects in terms of this measure. However, as we have seen, there are many different free operants that can be studied. The important thing, says Skinner, is to find an appropriate operant for the kind of individual one wants to study—that is, an operant that the subject can emit conveniently and fairly rapidly. If this condition is met, the particular operant chosen makes little difference to the laws that will be found. Levers are used for rats and keys for pigeons rather than vice versa because these manipulanda suit the response capacities of these animals, but similar laws are found for rats and for pigeons when each learns an operant appropriate for its own capacities.

Schedules of Reinforcement

The rate at which the free operant is emitted (the dependent variable) can be related to a great variety of independent variables. In practice, however, Skinner and his followers have concentrated most on one independent variable, the *schedule of reinforcement*. This term refers to the particular pattern according to which reinforcers follow responses. The simplest schedule is *continuous reinforcement*, in which a reinforcer is given for every response to the manipulandum. This schedule generally is followed when the subject is first being trained to use the manipulandum. After the response is learned, the schedule usually is shifted to some form of *intermittent reinforcement*, in which only some of the responses are followed by reinforcement. Skinner has collaborated with Charles Ferster on a book, *Schedules of Reinforcement* (Ferster & Skinner 1957), describing a great many different schedules of intermittent reinforcement and their effects, but fortunately for the student they tend to represent variations on two basic patterns. If the frequency with which reinforcers are presented depends on the rate at which responses are emitted, this is called a ratio schedule; if it depends simply on the passage of time, it is called an interval schedule. In addition, each of these two kinds of schedules may be either fixed or variable. Combining these two bases of classification gives four main kinds of schedules.

In a *fixed-ratio* schedule, the subject is reinforced after every so many responses. Thus a reinforcer may be delivered after every fourth or every tenth or every twentieth response. A *variable-ratio* schedule differs from a fixed-ratio schedule in that the reinforcer, instead of being presented consistently after every so many responses, is presented after a different number of responses on different occasions. In this case the ratio is the average number of responses per reinforcer. Thus on a variable-ratio five schedule, reinforcers are delivered on the average after every five responses, but on one occassion two successive responses might be reinforced, while on another occasion the individual might have to make as many as ten responses after getting one reinforcer before getting another.

On a *fixed-interval* schedule, a fixed interval of time has to elapse after one reinforcer is delivered before another can be obtained. Once this interval has elapsed, the first response will be reinforced. Thus on a fixed-interval one-minute schedule, the subject cannot obtain reinforcers more often than one a minute regardless of how fast he or she responds. The subject can obtain one each minute equally well by responding rapidly all the time or by responding only once a minute. If the subject waits for a while after the minute has elapsed before making the response, the reinforcement will be correspondingly delayed. A *variable-interval* schedule makes it possible to obtain a reinforcer sometimes sooner and sometimes longer after the previous one. Thus on a variable-interval two-minute schedule, the average time after presentation of one reinforcer when another would become available would be two minutes, but on any particular occasion the interval might be considerably shorter or longer. Hence the only way to be sure of getting all available reinforcers as soon as possible would be to respond continuously.

What effects do these different schedules of reinforcement have on the rate and pattern of operant behavior? Figure 6.1 shows typical responding on five different schedules, as observed by many Skinnerian researchers studying various species, including humans.

What generalizations can be drawn about different kinds of schedules? First, ratio schedules typically give higher rates of responding than interval schedules. This difference is not surprising, since fast responding on a ratio schedule increases the number of reinforcements in a given period of time much more than does fast responding on an interval schedule. Second, on both kinds of fixed schedule there is a tendency for responding to be slowest immediately after reinforcement (more so than can be explained simply by the time required to consume the reinforcer). The reason is that responses immediately after reinforcement are never reinforced. Intuitively this effect is easier to appreciate in the fixed-interval schedule, since the individual has nothing to gain from responses during the interval. On

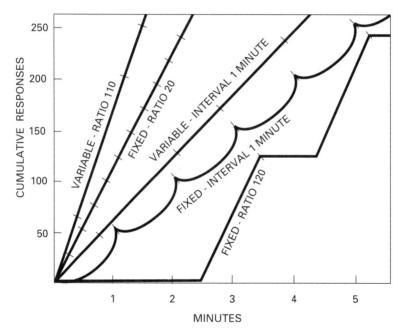

Figure 6.1 Performance on several schedules of reinforcement. Each curve represents the behavior of a single pigeon pecking a key on the designated schedule, plotted in the usual Skinnerian style. The vertical axis gives the number of responses emitted so far (cumulative responses), so steeper curves indicate faster responding and a horizontal line indicates a period of no responding. The delivery of each reinforcer is indicated by a short diagonal mark intersecting the cumulative response curve.

a fixed-interval schedule, the resulting pattern is a gradual increase in rate of responding from just after one reinforcement to just before the next. Because it looks on a graph like the edge of the familiar sea shell, this effect is known as *scalloping*. The fact that there is a gradual increase in rate during the interval rather than a sudden burst of responding just when the next reinforcer is due reflects the subject's inability to discriminate time perfectly.

On a fixed-ratio schedule we might expect the individual to respond just as rapidly after a reinforcement as at any other time, since a certain number of responses must be made before the next reinforcement regardless of when the subject makes them. This expectation, however, reflects a view of the organism as figuring out the most profitable strategy and acting accordingly. According to Skinner, we must simply look at the reinforcement contingencies. On a fixed-ratio schedule, the first responses after a reinforcement are never reinforced as quickly as the later ones; hence they occur at a slower rate. However, this makes a difference only when the ratio is high enough so that the subject cannot make all the necessary responses quickly and get almost immediate reinforcement. Consequently, low fixed-ratio schedules (i.e., those requiring only a few responses per reinforcer) show very little drop in responding after reinforcement, whereas high fixed ratios show a sometimes lengthy pause after reinforcement. This pause tends to be a total cessation of responding for some period of time, after which responses are emitted at a fairly constant rate until the next reinforcement. This pattern is therefore slightly different from the scalloping on a fixed-interval schedule, in which responding gradually increases during the interval, from a very low rate immediately after one reinforcement to a fairly high rate just before the next.

Finally, these variations in response rate during the interval between successive reinforcements are found only in fixed schedules, not in variable ones. Since all responses, early or late, have a chance of being reinforced on a variable schedule, responding is at a constant rate except for the brief period that may be required for actually consuming the reinforcer.

If a response that has been reinforced for some time then stops being reinforced, resistance to extinction will be greater if the reinforcement was intermittent than if it was continuous. Variable-ratio schedules are most effective for obtaining both rapid steady responding and high resistance to extinction. It is possible, in fact, to get animals to work for food reinforcement on ratios so high that they are actually operating at a biological loss: the energy expended in operating the manipulandum is greater than that obtained from the occasional food reward, so that if an animal stayed on the schedule for a long time it could literally work itself to death.

These schedules differ in their sensitivity to various disrupting factors. This fact has been of particular interest in connection with the effects of various drugs, and pharmaceutical companies have found it useful to test new drugs on animals responding to different schedules of reinforcement. One generalization that emerges from many studies is that interval schedules are more easily disrupted by a variety of drugs than are ratio schedules. Doses that will make responding on an interval schedule quite erratic will leave a ratio schedule largely unaffected.

Apparently the rat's counting mechanism is more stable or less vulnerable than its timing mechanism. Though Skinner is pleased that his experimental techniques have been found useful for studying drugs, it is characteristic of his approach that he makes no attempt to draw inferences about what these drugs are doing to the animal's body. There is a lawful relationship between what drug goes into the body and what behavior comes out; what goes on between the two is no concern of Skinner's.

It should also be noted that studies of different schedules of reinforcement are not concerned with how the response is originally learned. Ordinarily the subject is well trained to use the manipulandum before any form of intermittent reinforcement is introduced. Thereafter a given individual can adapt fairly readily to one schedule after another, changing behavior to suit each new schedule. Thus Skinner's formal research has been largely concerned with a short-run aspect of learning, the rapid shifts in performance level to match shifts in reinforcement conditions. (Some writers, in fact, consider such shifts too short-run to be called learning at all, and refer to them simply as changes in performance.) These studies are concerned not with an individual's learning how to respond, but rather with learning how rapidly to respond under a new set of reward conditions.

Shaping

We should not conclude from this emphasis, however, that Skinner has been uninterested in the process of learning how to perform complex tasks. Much of his less formal work has been concerned with this problem, and he has given striking demonstrations of training techniques. Though many experimental psychologists study animal learning, Skinner and his followers are almost unique in their concern with animal training. The technique by which they train animals to perform complex acts that are outside their normal range of behavior is known as *shaping*. The behavior is shaped through a series of successive approximations to the desired behavior, each made possible by selectively reinforcing certain responses and not others. Thus behavior gradually is brought closer and closer to the desired pattern.

Suppose you want to train a pigeon to bowl in a miniature alley with a wooden ball and toy pins (as Skinner has done). If left to its own devices, the pigeon might occasionally move the ball around, but would quite possibly never do so in a way that would get the ball down the alley and knock over any pins. If you waited to reinforce a full bowling response, therefore, you would have a quite impractically long wait, and even if the response finally did occur spontaneously, and you reinforced it, you would probably face another long wait before it occurred again. Yet this is not a particularly hard game for a pigeon to learn to play, given proper training.

To teach the pigeon to bowl, Skinner began, of course, by depriving it of food. Next, he trained it to eat from the food magazine. The operation of the food magazine made a distinctive sound, which, since it always signaled the availability of food, became a conditioned positive reinforcer. This conditioned reinforcer was a critical feature of the shaping process. If the food magazine had been silent, some of Skinner's attempts to provide immediate reinforcement would probably have failed, since it would have taken the pigeon some time to notice that the magazine was open. With the sound, however, Skinner could be sure that the opening of the food magazine would have an immediate reinforcing effect on the pigeon.

Given this means of reliably producing immediate reinforcement whenever he wished, Skinner proceeded to reinforce behavior that approximated the desired final performance: the pigeon's striking the ball in such a way that it would go down the alley and knock over some pins. First he reinforced merely being near and facing toward the ball. When that behavior had been reinforced often enough so that it was occurring much of the time, Skinner changed to giving reinforcers only when the pigeon pecked close to the ball. When that response had become common, he moved on to reinforcing only pecks that moved the ball. From there he narrowed the range of reinforced responses even further until the pigeon was sending the ball down the alley against the pins as reliably as a (novice) human bowler (Skinner 1958).

Though shaping is an application of the scientific principle of reinforcement, it involves a good deal of art. If the trainer proceeds too fast in narrowing down the range of responses that will be reinforced, the behavior already shaped will begin to extinguish. If the trainer proceeds too slowly, the training will take excessively long to complete. The trainer must therefore be constantly alert to the effect of his or her behavior on the learner's behavior and must be constantly ready to change it as needed in order to achieve the most effective shaping.

Given skillful application of the basic principle of shaping, striking results can be obtained. Skinner has not only trained single pigeons to bowl; he has also trained pairs of pigeons to cooperate (as well as compete) in a modified version of Ping-Pong. Rats have been trained to go through whole sequences of unratlike operations, such as pulling a string to obtain a marble, carrying the marble in their paws to a tube projecting above the floor, and dropping the marble into the tube. Pigs have learned to dance and play the piano (not well enough for the concert stage, but well enough for county fairs!). Some of Skinner's followers have found a considerable market for their talents in training animals for fairs and movies, as well as for more "serious" purposes.

Even though rapid and effective shaping requires a good deal of skill, the most striking significance of shaping is the impressive effects that can be obtained by applying the simple principle of reinforcement. Not all the demonstrations have been with animals. A technique for showing the automatic effects of reinforcement on human behavior is called *verbal conditioning*. In the first experiment of this sort (Greenspoon 1955), the subject was instructed simply to say words. The experimenter gave the subject no clue in the instructions as to what sorts of words were desired. However, whenever the subject said a noun in the plural form, the experimenter said "mmhm." There was an increase during the session in the frequency with which the subject said plural nouns. This increase occurred in spite of the fact that many subjects were quite unaware, so far as could be determined by questioning, either of the fact that they were saying more plural nouns or of any relation between the experimenter's behavior and their own. When the "mmhm" was discontinued, frequency of plural nouns declined (extinction).

In another, less formal experiment (Verplanck 1955) subjects were simply engaged in conversation without even being told that this was an experiment. The experimenter (who in this case might better be called the interviewer) expressed interest in and agreement with any of the subject's remarks that were presented as expressions of opinion (i.e., "I think. . . " or "It seems to me. . . "). Other kinds of remarks produced no reaction from the interviewer. Expressions of opinion became more and more frequent during the conversation. In both of these verbal-conditioning studies, verbal behavior was modified by reinforcing a given kind of verbal response and no other. Like any technique of operant training, this one depends on finding a reinforcer that will be effective for the particular kind of individual being studied, but once one is found the principle of reinforcement seems to apply as well here as elsewhere.

However, the "automatic" nature of these effects has been subjected to a good deal of question. In studies of animals, no problem arises: the experimenter need only note the systematic ways that behavior is influenced by reinforcement, and whether or not the effects are called automatic is pretty much irrelevant. With humans, however, the experimenter can ask subjects what they thought about the whole procedure and thus try to determine whether they reacted automatically and largely unconsciously to the reinforcement or whether they noticed what kinds of responses were being reinforced and then decided whether or not to work for reinforcers. From Skinner's point of view, the person's awareness is not a particularly important issue—the important question is whether the reinforcement influences the behavior, not whether the person can accurately describe what is going on or whether the subject feels that he or she is making a free choice. However, the issue of awareness in verbal conditioning has aroused considerable interest among other psychologists. Although the issue is far from settled, the weight of current evidence suggests that humans who are influenced by verbal reinforcement are usually at least partly aware of what is going on and have some sense of choosing how they will react to it (e.g., Spielberger & DeNike 1966). On the other hand, when a person is busy concentrating on one aspect of his or her own behavior, it may be possible to condition some other aspect of that behavior without the subject being aware of it (Rosenfeld & Baer 1969). The most likely conclusion is that reinforcement sometimes works automatically, without the learner being aware of what is going on, but that such events are the exception rather than the rule.

An interesting sidelight on the shaping of behavior is the way in which reinforcement can produce not only behavior that the experimenters intend but also behavior of which they have no advance idea. Suppose a timer is arranged to deliver a reinforcer every 30 seconds regardless of what the subject does. This is called a *fixed-time* schedule. (It differs from a fixed-interval schedule, in which the subject has to make a particular response after the interval is up in order to be reinforced.) Whatever the individual is doing when the reinforcement comes is more likely to occur again the next time. Purely on the basis of chance, the subject is more likely to be doing something at that moment that he or she commonly does than something that is done rarely. Given the fact that this behavior occurs commonly to start with, plus the fact that the behavior has now just been reinforced, it is all the more likely to be occurring when the next reinforcer is delivered. This reinforcement will strengthen the behavior more and make it even more likely to occur at the right time to receive the third reinforcement. Thus this particular behavior becomes more and more likely to occur because it is reinforced, even though the experimenter did not deliberately reinforce that response rather than others. Rather, the learning was the result of a vicious circle: because the response occurred frequently, it was reinforced, and because it was reinforced, it occurred more frequently. The experimenter did not know in advance which of the various responses that the individual made frequently would be learned in this way; that selection depended on chance. There might be a period during which several different responses were reinforced before any one gained enough of a lead to start the vicious circle going. Behavior might be too variable for any one response ever to get the necessary head start. However, when it occurs, this unplanned reinforcing effect appears to be an impressive demonstration of the automatic operation of reinforcement.

Skinner refers to this kind of unplanned learning through "accidental" reinforcement as *superstitious* behavior. The justification for this term is that the subject acts as though a certain behavior produced reinforcement, when in fact there is no necessary connection between the behavior and the reinforcement. The response is commonly followed by reinforcement only because both behavior and reinforcement occur frequently and hence often occur at the same time. The most successful experimental demonstrations of superstitious behavior have been with pigeons (though we will see a different interpretation of such demonstrations in Chapter 14). However, applications to human learning are not difficult to see. If a student carries a rabbit's foot into an examination for good luck, and does well, this experience will make the student more likely to carry it into the next examination. Repeated successes while carrying the rabbit's foot will make adherence to the foot as a source of luck stronger and stronger, even though it contributed nothing to success and the student would have done just as well without it. (We overlook the possibility that the confidence the talisman gave the student may have increased his or her effectiveness in taking the examination.) Many of our beliefs, not only in charms and magic, but also in medicine, mechanical skills, and administrative techniques, probably depend on such superstitious learning. A public speaker who thinks she is successful because she knocks three times on the podium before starting to speak is generally recognized as superstitious. But a speaker who thinks he is successful because he starts each lecture with a funny story may be equally superstitious by Skinner's definition. In humans, such superstitions are probably more often learned in the first place from other people than from chance occurrences. However, when people claim that their faith has been validated by experience, this experience probably often follows the learning pattern that Skinner has described and illustrated.

Chapter
7

Applications
and Implications
of Skinner's System

As you have probably already guessed, Skinner has shown much interest in the application of learning principles to complex practical situations. Many of these applications are at the level either of philosophical principles or of speculation about what might work. Two, however, have been extensively tested. In the treatment of behavior disorders, and in education, Skinner's ideas have not only demonstrated their validity outside the laboratory but have also had major practical effects on psychotherapy and at least some effects on schooling. Collectively, they are referred to as *applied behavior analysis.*

BEHAVIOR MODIFICATION

The term *behavior disorder* covers a wide range of problems, from those mildly irritating behaviors that we all notice in one another (and sometimes even in ourselves) through delinquency and neurosis to severe mental illness. Whether the problem is minor misbehavior on the part of a relatively normal child or a psychosis that has kept a patient hospitalized for many years, Skinner's approach to treatment is quite straightforward. Rather than focusing on early childhood, current psychodynamics, or possible organic abnormality, Skinner simply asks what this person is doing that we (including the person him- or herself) do not like and what we would like to have the person do instead. Once we have decided this, we can proceed to extinguish the undesirable behaviors and reinforce desirable ones. In other words, we can change the *contingencies of reinforcement,* the specific relationships according to which reinforcement is contingent on one or another behavior. This approach, basically similar to Guthrie's but with the additional element of reinforcement, forms the basis of various *behavior modification* techniques of psychotherapy.

The behavior modification approach may be illustrated by a case in which two nursery-school children were cured of excessive crying (Hart et al. 1964). The therapists (experimenters? educators?), like true Skinnerians, began by differentiating the crying into respondent (usually produced by physical pain and not influenced by the social situation) and operant (less directly influenced by specific stimulation, but occurring when an adult was nearby and involving frequent glances at the adult, apparently to see the adult's reaction). No attempt was made to modify the respondent crying, but all the nursery-school teachers were trained to recognize and to ignore the operant crying. However, when the children played constructively, the teachers often praised them and showed them affection. The attention from teachers that had previously reinforced the operant crying was thus removed, and a combination of extinction and retraining began. That the reduction in operant crying was really the result of this procedure is indicated by what happened when the teachers were instructed to resume paying attention to the children when they cried—there was rapid relearning of the crying. A second retraining was then begun, and the operant crying was virtually eliminated.

Similar techniques have been used in mental hospitals and in a variety of other settings to deal with such diverse behaviors as overeating and undereating, hoarding of towels (by a mental patient), inattention in school, adolescent aggression, and the extreme social withdrawal of autistic children and of many psychotics. However, the treatment is often considerably more complex than in the above example. It often includes the Skinnerian devices of shaping behavior by successive approximations, behavior that otherwise would probably almost never occur. This device may be supplemented by others that sound less Skinnerian, such as providing examples of correct behavior to be imitated or requiring individuals to keep performing undesirable behavior until they are thoroughly tired of it (as in Guthrie's method of fatigue). Some of these applications also raise the issue of whether, when, how, and how much to use punishment along with positive reinforcement. Already we see evidence that behavior modification, though it developed directly from Skinner's system, has still to some extent developed its own technology as it went along. We will see more of such trends in Chapter 12.

In many cases where the awarding of reinforcers for certain behaviors is central to the retraining, it has been organized and formalized in the form of *token economies*. In a token economy, the people in an institution (such as students, patients, or prisoners) can earn tokens by engaging in certain behaviors or by not engaging in others, and can then exchange these tokens (which become conditioned reinforcers) for primary reinforcers of their choice. For example, grade-school students might get a token for each workbook page completed, or mental patients one for each time they arrived at a meal on time. The children could later exchange a certain number of tokens for a toy of their choice, and the patients might exchange theirs for periods of grounds privileges. Actually having the tokens in hand (as conditioned reinforcers) would help to bridge the time gap between when the desirable acts were performed and when the toys or privileges were actually received. It is easy to belittle token economies by saying that what they show is that modern behavioral science has finally invented money. However, when a token economy changes disruptive behavior to constructive and cooperative behavior, and does so without the use of aversive stimulation, the fact that the basic idea is nothing new should not detract from the ingenuity of those who figured out when and how to apply it.

Though we commonly think of behavior modification as something that one person does to another, it is important to emphasize that it works in both directions. Whenever two people interact, they modify each other's behavior to some degree. When one of the people is more powerful than the other, that person's modification of the other is the more obvious of the two, but even in a setting as authoritarian as the army, soldiers modify the behavior of their officers by obeying some orders more quickly, completely, and enthusiastically than others.

Even when one of the interacting individuals is human and the other belongs to another species, the same two-way relationship applies. In some cases animals probably shape the behavior of their human companions more than vice versa. There is a joke about one rat saying to another: "I've really got this guy conditioned. Every time I press this lever, he gives me a pellet of food." Skinner repeated this joke as enthusiastically as anyone.

This two-way aspect of behavior modification makes it relevant to family therapy, where the problems of family interaction can be analyzed in terms of the ways family members do or don't reinforce each other. Training all family members in how to reinforce each other's behaviors for their mutual benefit can sometimes provide a way out of the frustrating, wheel-spinning interactions in a dysfunctional family. When it succeeds, it does so partly by giving each person specific steps to take and partly by replacing mutual recriminations with mutual benefits. Both changes are very much in the Skinnerian tradition.

Its stronger supporters regard behavior modification as the most significant innovation ever made in psychotherapy. In support of this view, they point out its many dramatic successes—beneficial changes in behavior which, though sometimes slow in absolute terms, are still often faster than traditional psychotherapies. Moreover, the same techniques can be used in a wide variety of settings to produce many different kinds of behavior change. Further details about the many uses of behavior modification (commonly abbreviated to behavior mod or B-mod) can be found in Schwartz (1982) and Kazdin (1994), and evidence of its effectiveness relative to other psychotherapies is described in Smith, Glass, & Miller (1980).

Critics of behavior mod have not hesitated to point out its difficulties. Interestingly, it has been attacked from two opposite directions. One criticism is that it produces only temporary and superficial changes. That the changes are often temporary is to be expected, since Skinner would not predict that changes in behavior would last unless the changes in the contingencies of reinforcement also lasted. In some cases, behavior modifiers are satisfied if, by arranging proper contingencies of reinforcement, they can get students to study harder or mental patients to behave in more "normal" ways in the hospital, without worrying about anything further. In other cases they hope to produce more lasting changes, but they expect success only if they can bring about lasting changes in the contingencies of reinforcement. If a schoolchild who has acquired good studying behavior as a result of a token economy in the classroom continues to show that changed behavior after the token economy is gone, it will be because other reinforcers have taken over, whether they are the fun of learning, the usefulness of the knowledge, or the satisfaction of pleasing the teacher. If none of these reinforcers is strong enough to keep the child studying, perhaps the problem is neither in the child nor in the token economy but in the curriculum!

However, the question remains: What is the most efficient way to change from a situation in which behavior is controlled by reinforcers delivered as part of a behavior modification program to one in which behavior is controlled by the "natural" reinforcers of everyday life? The general answer given by behavior modifiers is to make the transition gradually, reducing the frequency of the programmed reinforcers bit by bit, a process known as *fading*. In addition, behavior modifiers have various ways of enhancing the natural reinforcers—for example, by enlisting the help of relatives and friends to provide such reinforcers to an extra degree. These procedures are discussed in detail in Kazdin (1994).

The opposite criticism of behavior mod is that, far from being too weak and trivial, it is too dangerously powerful. The worry these critics have is that someone exposed to planned contingencies of reinforcement loses freedom and comes under the control of the person who controls the reinforcers. Skinner's reply to this challenge is that we are all controlled by many contingencies, some deliberate, some accidental. If the contingencies of positive reinforcement used by behavior modifiers are more effective than others, and at the same time more pleasant for the learner and more beneficial in their effects, why is that a criticism? Isn't it better, says Skinner, to be controlled pleasantly by a beneficent controller than to be subjected to all the conflicting, selfish, and often aversive attempts at control that so often occur? Not necessarily, say his critics: the worst enemy of freedom may be a gentle, beneficent dictator. To pursue the argument further would take us too far afield, but at least these latter critics do behavior mod the honor, however dubious, of being afraid of it.

EDUCATION

As the above discussion indicates, behavior modification is as much an educational as a psychotherapeutic technique. It is therefore not surprising that one of Skinner's applications has had important practical effects in the field of education. This is the study of programmed learning, first popularized through its use in teaching machines. Though Skinner was not the first to suggest this approach to teaching (Sidney L. Pressey of Ohio State University is generally credited with making the first teaching machine, in 1927), he gave the idea much of its early impetus. His object was to treat classroom learning like any other situation in which certain behavior—in this case, largely verbal behavior—is to be shaped. The student must progress gradually from familiar to unfamiliar material, must be given an opportunity to learn the necessary discriminations, and must be reinforced. The classroom situation has many disadvantages from this point of view. A rate of progress appropriate for one student is too fast or too slow for another. Opportunities for each individual to make the required responses are limited, and reinforcement is often greatly delayed. Individual tutoring could solve all these problems, but in most cases it is out of the question except perhaps for occasional supplementary work. What, then, can be done to give students in school the same advantages that pigeons in boxes have? Skinner's answer to this question was the teaching machine.

The basic component of the machine is the program. This is a series of combined teaching and test items that carries the student gradually through the material to be learned. An item may or may not convey new information, but in any case it calls for the student to fill in a blank in a statement and then to look at the correct answer. If it agrees with the student's answer, this agreement constitutes the reinforcement. If not, the student can study the correct answer so as to increase the chance of being reinforced next time. However, Skinner prefers to make the learning requirements so gradual that the learner rarely if ever does make mistakes. If this effort is successful, then on every item the student makes a correct response and is reinforced, which in Skinner's view is the best possible arrangement for learning. Individual differences then are reflected in the rate at which the student proceeds through the program. (For a discussion of the logic and the advantages of this approach to teaching, see Skinner 1962.)

At this point you may be wondering, "Where does the machine come in? This is just the old, familiar workbook method." To some extent this is a valid point. Much programmed instruction has been in workbook rather than machine form. The student fills in a blank, then turns to another page to check the answer. However, these programmed workbooks differ from the more familiar types of workbooks in that they do all teaching through the items in the program, rather than serving to supplement lectures and textbooks. The same series of items that calls forth the student's responses also provides the information necessary for making the responses. This arrangement, in turn, forces the author of the program to plan the sequence of items very carefully in terms of just what the student needs to learn and just how it can best be presented. Whether the program is in a workbook or in a machine is of secondary importance. Machines have some advantages in speeding up the reinforcement and reducing the likelihood of cheating by the student. It is probable, however, that much of Skinner's preference for machine presentation results from two factors: (1) the novelty effect of the machine, which very likely makes its use more reinforcing to the student; and (2) Skinner's personal liking for mechanized procedures. Although the machine itself has sometimes been a bone of contention between those who favor increased classroom efficiency and those who fear the loss of more personal values in education, this is a misplaced emphasis. The pertinent question is about the value of programmed methods of instruction in whatever form, not about teaching machines as such.

Even now it is hard to judge how valuable programmed teaching, by machine or otherwise, will prove in the whole context of education. Many factors besides efficiency as a specific teaching device are involved. Moreover, the increasing availability of computers provides for more varied forms of presentation than either workbook programs or the original form of teaching machine. Although Skinner favors *linear programs,* in which every learner goes through the same sequence of steps, which are easy enough so that mistakes are rare, computers have increased the use of *branching programs,* in which the learner's answers determine what material will be received next. In some computer teaching programs, the learner and the computer carry on quite a spirited dialogue, including both praise and sharp admonishments from the computer as it responds to a great variety of possible behaviors by the learner. The computer can decide how lavishly to praise or how strongly to reprove the learner, as well as what material to present next, not just on the basis of the learner's last response, but on the basis of the learner's whole record of performance. Though the computer usually communicates in writing on a cathode-ray tube, it can also be designed to speak. Both of these capabilities are illustrated in a program teaching children to read (Atkinson 1974).

As a result of the computer's great flexibility, computer-assisted instruction (CAI) has largely replaced programmed instruction as an active topic of research and an expanding area of education (e.g., Chambers & Sprecher 1983). The technology of programmed instruction has now gone far beyond Skinner's initial contribution, but it continues to demonstrate the value of Skinner's innovation.

OTHER APPLICATIONS

In addition to behavior mod and programmed instruction, both of which have given rise to much research and development, Skinner has presented a number of other logical applications that are still largely at the level of talk. One (appropriately enough) is the analysis of language. In his book *Verbal Behavior,* Skinner (1957*b*) analyzes language as a system of operants. He notes that each of us lives in a *verbal community,* a group of people who share a common language and who shape the language each of us uses by reinforcing correct usage and extinguishing incorrect usage. This shaping process is most noticeable with children, who must learn the language from scratch, but it continues to operate in adults as they learn new words and as they are either reinforced or not for the various spicy elements they include in their speech. Some utterances, such as requests and demands, are reinforced by another person's compliance; these utterances are called *mands.* Other utterances, which include most conversations, are reinforced in subtler ways by signs of understanding, such as smiling and answering appropriately. Utterances of that sort are called *tacts.* It is easiest to learn correct speech when the events that the speech refers to are external ones that everyone in the linguistic community can observe. When the events are unobservable, as in discussing one's own or someone else's feelings, it is much harder to decide whether a tact is correct or not. A child learns to describe his or her own feelings correctly only to the extent that others can infer those feelings from other evidence and reinforce the child's descriptions when they are accurate. No wonder our vocabularies for describing feelings lack the precision of science!

A second area of interest is the application of Skinnerian principles to complex social behaviors. Any social interaction is a situation in which two or more people are providing one another with stimuli and with reinforcers, and perhaps also failing to reinforce one another in some critical ways. The situations to which this type of analysis has been applied vary from a single conversation between two people to the continuing dynamics of dysfunctional families to the major institutions of society. Whether the interaction is formal or casual, friendly or hostile, dominant or egalitarian, it can be analyzed in these basic terms. For example, a factory worker who is paid on piecework (pay proportional to the amount produced) is being reinforced by her employer on a form of fixed-ratio schedule. For a quite different example, a mental patient diagnosed as depressive may be on a schedule where almost nothing he can do is reinforced, so that he complains of feeling helpless, hopeless, and worthless. Once you are familiar with Skinner's thinking, you can probably predict some of Skinner's comments on the mutually reinforcing or non-reinforcing contingencies in politics, business, religion, and the family.

Finally, Skinner has devised a utopian community called Walden Two (in honor of Thoreau, who might or might not feel honored), in which the principles of learning are used to create a more ideal form of social organization (Skinner 1948). In contrast to such negative utopias as those described in Huxley's *Brave New World* (1932) and Orwell's *1984* (1949), Skinner's novel *Walden Two* describes what he believes would be a desirable community, one in which principles of behavioral engineering would be used to create a more fulfilling environment for all the residents.

Many of the details of this imaginary community run sharply counter to what we are used to considering appropriate. The economy is socialized; government is by self-perpetuating committees instead of by elected representatives; children are reared primarily by child-rearing professionals, rather than by their parents. Particularly noteworthy to many readers is that a graded series of arbitrary frustrations is imposed on the children, such as having to wait for dinner even though it can be seen ready to serve, a device designed to build up gradually the children's toleration for frustration. This sounds a lot like Guthrie's method of thresholds, but may seem inconsistent with Skinner's own emphasis on designing teaching programs so that learners will not make mistakes. However, Skinner objects to learners' making mistakes not because mistakes are frustrating, but because they are missed opportunities for reinforcement of correct responses. Since some frustration is unavoidable in even the best regulated societies, he argued that children should learn to deal with it constructively.

It is not at all clear that these particular ways of doing things follow from any of Skinner's data as a researcher. How did he happen to select them for his utopian community? One possibility is that the particular suggestions were intended for their shock value in showing how different a behaviorally engineered community might be from what we would at first think desirable. In the second volume of his autobiography, Skinner leaves this possibility open by saying: "I let Frazier [the founder of the fictional community] say things that I myself was not yet ready to say to anyone" (1979, p. 298). He adds, however, "Eventually I became a devout Frazierian" (ibid.).

Another possibility, not necessarily contradicting the first, is that Skinner made Walden Two the kind of community that reflected his own felt needs at that point in his life. He remembered as the worst year of his life the one immediately after college when he was trying to become a novelist while his parents urged him to settle down to a more conventional career. Is that why he designed Walden Two as a community in which children are largely freed from family pressures, and in which it is easy to combine artistic creativity with "honest toil"? Later, when writing the book, he was faced with problems and disruptions in both family and professional life. Is that why Walden Two sometimes impresses readers as a fine community for an overburdened person to retreat to but not much of a place for the restless or the ambitious? Is such a community one that Skinner desired only at that point in his career? Elms (1981) thinks so, and further speculates that writing the book may have been the therapy Skinner needed, since he made no effort to put his ideas into practice.

Nevertheless, several attempts have been made to establish real-life communities modeled on his book. For the most part, these attempts have had no better success than the many other secular utopian communities that have been tried over the years. One, however, known as Twin Oaks, has lasted for over 25 years and has achieved at least a modest degree of success (including one special modern criterion of success: appearing on television). Though its membership of less than 100 appears small beside the 1000 in Skinner's fictional community, it still represents a fairly stable, functioning community. The first five years of Twin Oaks were described by one of its founders (Kinkade 1973), and a more recent period has been portrayed by Komar (1983). The problems that the community has struggled with seem much like those that any commune would face, irrespective of any special behavioral principles. Judging by Komar's book, Twin Oaks has been most successful in dealing with the emotional and social needs of its members, and least successful in solving the problems of government organization and economic incentives.

Regarding this real community's relation to Skinner's utopian novel, Kinkade (1973) wrote: "The debt we owe Dr. Skinner is enormous, but there is nothing sacred about the institutions we derived from his book. All of our systems are subject to change, and most of them have changed even over the few years that we have been a community" (p. 57). This comment Skinner presumably would approve. Later, however, Kinkade wrote (as quoted in Komar 1983): "Behaviorism at Twin Oaks was important to us in 1969 and 1970, still got lip service for a year longer, and then was overrun and sacked by a more primitive and vigorous idea which is now called the 'human potential movement'" (p. 92). The description concludes: "I think the accepted theory now is that behaviorism was one of several early religions that Twin Oaks went through, and now that the group has matured, behaviorism is thought of as a discarded ideology" (p. 113). The Walden Two idea, like other ideas that Skinner started, has clearly gone far from its origins in directions that its creator would not necessarily approve.

SKINNER'S RELATION TO OTHER PSYCHOLOGISTS

For many years, Skinner and his followers formed a small in-group within the psychology of learning. Whereas the followers of other theorists argued with each other and tried to best each other in experimental tests of their respective theories, the Skinnerians remained aloof and went their own way. They published their own journal, held separate meetings at psychological conventions, and eventually established a separate Division of the Experimental Analysis of Behavior within the American Psychological Association. (Many non-Skinnerians may feel that what they are doing is also "experimental analysis of behavior," but the expression has become a label for Skinner's approach.) As Skinner's research techniques and his ideas have become increasingly prominent, much of this separatism has disappeared, but some remains. What are the differences between Skinner and other psychologists of learning that account for it, and what factors eventually made him, in spite of it, such an important spokesperson for the field?

It is hard at first to see what differences could account for the historical schism between Skinner and other learning theorists. We have already noted his similarity to Thorndike. Though he differs from both Watson and Guthrie in placing heavy emphasis on reinforcement, he resembles both of them in his practical emphasis. In analyzing a response, Guthrie's first question was "What stimuli evoke it?" while Skinner's is "What reinforcer sustains it?" Both of these, however, focus on a specific, manipulable detail of the situation. Guthrie went further in relating specific situations to a general statement of what learning is, while Skinner has gone further in actually experimenting with the situations he analyzes. Their differences are substantial, but their similarities are nonetheless noteworthy.

As for Watson, he and Skinner have in common a missionary zeal about what psychology should be and what it should contribute to human affairs. Both react vigorously against what they regard as vague, overtheoretical interpretations of human nature and in favor of strictly scientific study of behavior. Both present systems that their supporters regard as highly useful and their foes regard as highly oversimplified. (Both judgments may, of course, be valid, for oversimplifications can be useful for many purposes.) Both theorists appear as prophets, seeking to purge the errors from psychology as it is and to proclaim the glories of psychology as it should be. Both have a vision of what humankind can become if guided by proper application of the principles of learning.

On the issue of reinforcement, Skinner is closer to Hull than either is to Watson or Guthrie. Moreover Skinner's views of social influence and of behavior disorders are rather similar to those already described for Dollard and Miller. Nevertheless, Skinner's difference from Hull is sharp, since Hull was a theorist par excellence, while Skinner scorned theory building. Even so, the difference is not as fundamental as it might at first appear. There are two aspects to Hull's theorizing: postulating intervening variables, and deducing theorems from postulates. Certainly Skinner does not do either of these in anything like the formal way that Hull did, but neither do many other learning theorists, and Skinner does do things that bear a certain resemblance to both of these activities of Hull's.

Regarding intervening variables, Skinner has no such concept as excitatory potential, but he does speak of the strength of a response, even though the strength may be measured in various ways depending on the situation. (Skinner usually preferred measuring it by the rate at which an operant is emitted, but in some cases substituted speed or probability.) Is the "strength of a response," then, so different from "excitatory potential"? Also, though he scorns completely unobservable entities, Skinner does not mind talking about ones that are merely hard to observe, like the many different emotional respondents that can interfere with making a punished response.

As for deducing theorems from postulates, Skinner often does something one step removed from that: expressing one law of behavior in terms of another. For example, why do subjects on a fixed-interval schedule produce more responses relatively late in the interval rather than earlier, as was shown in Figure 6.1? Skinner replies that they have formed a discrimination between these two parts of the interval, since responding in the early part is never reinforced while responding in the later part sometimes is reinforced. In other words, he starts with the law that subjects can learn to discriminate between two specific stimuli, S+ and S−, and then applies that law to a new and somewhat different case. In this new case, the discrimination is not between two observable stimuli but rather between whatever stimuli there may be to distinguish the first part of an interval from the last part. Skinner cannot say just what stimuli the subject is using to distinguish early in the interval from late, but he knows there must be some such stimuli, so for him this is a straightforward case of discrimination learning. To Skinner, this line of reasoning is simply a matter of showing that a scientific law applies in a new situation, but it does not seem so terribly far removed from Hull's more formal deductions.

Given that Skinner's differences from the other theorists we have considered are not much greater than their differences from one another, why has there been such a schism between him and them? Part of the impetus for the separation has come from Skinner's conviction that he has a whole new approach, one that makes nearly all previous theorizing and a large part of previous research obsolete. Whether or not it is correct, his expression of this opinion in his publications has naturally tended to keep him and his followers aloof from other psychologists of learning. The rest of the impetus has come from objections by other psychologists to the research methods Skinner uses. Though he puts great emphasis on the scientific character of his work, many others have felt that his methods are untrustworthy as sources of scientific data.

The main objection to Skinner's research methods is that his experiments have typically been conducted on one or a very few subjects. Skinner believes that only by looking at the behavior of a single individual can one find the lawfulness in behavior. Many psychologists, however, take the contrary view: that stable, general laws can be obtained only by averaging the behavior of many individuals. Only thus, they say, can individual differences and accidental fluctuations be ruled out so that the widely applicable, general laws remain. The arguments on both sides of this question are too complex to consider here. Whatever the rights and wrongs of the argument, for a number of years journal editors and convention program committees often rejected Skinnerian research on these bases, thus forcing Skinnerians to find their own publication outlets and further isolating them from other researchers in learning.

Given this division, how is it possible that Skinner came to be such a dominant figure in the psychology of learning? To some extent this dominance was due to the very methodological factors that so long isolated him. The Skinner box has proved to be a most valuable research tool for studying learned behavior, and Skinnerians have had enough success in demonstrating lawfulness with single individuals to impress other researchers. This success in dealing with individual cases has made Skinnerians strikingly successful in their applications of psychology, which we have already discussed, and thus given them extra credibility with practical-minded observers. Finally, Skinner has been a tireless popularizer of ideas about psychology that many non-Skinnerians share. He has preached the gospel of objective research on learning and its practical applications, presented in a relatively simple, no-nonsense way, more vigorously and persistently than anyone else since Watson. As a result, more outsiders have heard of him and more insiders have had reason to be proud of him. As the psychology of learning has moved into more complex channels of research and theory (some of which we will see in later chapters), Skinner has stood as the most conspicuous spokesperson for those simple, traditional ideas that Thorndike, Watson, Guthrie, Hull, and Skinner himself, whatever their differences, have all shared.

In this role as spokesperson for a point of view about human behavior, Skinner has again been the focus both of enthusiastic support and of angry criticism. Supporters see his views as marking the way to a new era of scientifically based human improvement; critics see them as the mechanization and enslavement of the human spirit. He threw additional fuel on these fires of controversy in *Beyond Freedom and Dignity* (Skinner 1971). Answering those critics who claim that his system deprives people of freedom and of dignity, he argues that freedom and dignity are merely the terms we apply to behavior when we cannot detect the reinforcers that control it. All behavior, he insists, is under the control of contingencies of reinforcement, planned or unplanned. The fact that in some cases we have trouble determining what the contingencies are does not make the behavior any more desirable. We should give up pursuing these shadowy goals of freedom and dignity and instead work on building a society in which well-planned contingencies of reinforcement give rise to desirable behavior.

This book made clear that, while his position within psychology had changed, his confrontational presentation of controversial ideas had not. In his still later books, some people thought he was finally mellowing, since these books consisted less of challenges to everyone he disagreed with and more of such gentle thoughts as how to prepare for a visit with one's grandchildren and such whimsical thoughts as how to swat a fly most effectively. However, his final address to the American Psychological Association, a week before he died, refuted any thoughts of his mellowing. Frail but firm, he dismissed a viewpoint in psychology that he disapproved in terms that elicited an audible gasp from the audience. Whether debating other behaviorists, other kinds of psychologists, or the biases of the public at large, Skinner began and ended his career with more conviction than intellectual tolerance.

In spite of the sometimes sharp differences between Skinner and the other theorists we have considered, he is now the outstanding exponent of the connectionist tradition. Thorndike, Watson, Guthrie, and Hull all died long before Skinner, and Miller's interests have changed. These changes left Skinner for a number of years as the spokesperson for those approaches to psychology which he and these other theorists, for all their differences, had held in common. A look at Skinner is both a look backward at this tradition and a look forward to the direction in which Skinner thought that psychology should be headed. Others, of course, disagree about this direction. Indeed, the approach that Skinner dismissed contemptuously in his farewell address will occupy us for four of the next five chapters.

Chapter
8

European Cognitive Theory

All of the theories we have considered so far were of the sort that can be called *connectionist*, that is, those that regard learning as a matter of forming connections between stimuli and responses. To be sure, these theories varied in how explicitly they emphasized such connections. Thorndike was most explicit, with frequent references to S-R bonds, while Watson, Guthrie, and Hull were not far behind in their emphasis on S-R connections. At the opposite extreme, Skinner accepted S-R connections only for respondent behavior, and specifically ruled them out for operant behavior. Nevertheless, his focus on specific operants and the conditions under which they are emitted still placed him fairly close to the others in this respect. For all of them, what is important is what we do and when we do it, not what we think or know or understand.

To many readers, this may seem a strange imbalance in these theories. Can we really do a good job of predicting behavior if we don't take account of what people know and believe and understand? Aren't both school learning and practical learning about getting along in the world a lot more than just learning to make certain responses under certain conditions? Moreover, if we don't pay attention to knowledge and beliefs and understanding, aren't we overlooking a good deal of what makes us human?

The connectionist theorists were not troubled by such questions. If they considered them at all, it was to explain words like "knowledge" and "beliefs" as just everyday shorthand for certain responses, such as responses of talking subvocally to oneself. However, not all psychologists agreed with them. We turn now to some of these others, who are known as *cognitive* psychologists, from the Latin word for "know." The majority of early twentieth century cognitive psychologists were European, so we will look first at them.

GESTALT THEORY

One year before Watson published his first challenge to American psychology, Max Wertheimer (1880–1943) published a challenge to the established psychology of Germany. The orthodoxies against which these two revolts were directed were, as noted in Chapter 3, much alike. Both the American and the German versions were largely concerned with the structure of the mind. They tried to analyze conscious thought into its fundamental units, such as sensations, images, and ideas. Particularly in America, there was some trend toward studying behavior for its own sake, but psychology was still regarded as primarily the study of conscious experience. Experimentation was directed toward a more complete analysis of the contents of consciousness.

The forms that these two revolts took, however, were strikingly different. Watson's objection, on the one hand, was that psychology should be concerned not with consciousness, but with behavior. He wanted to abolish the discussion of images and ideas in favor of a discussion of stimuli and responses. He still agreed with the earlier position, however, in being interested in analysis. He still wanted to work with fundamental units, though they were now to be units of behavior instead of units of consciousness.

Wertheimer, on the other hand, objected to the concern with analysis. It seemed to him that breaking consciousness into its parts destroyed what was most meaningful about it. He had none of Watson's objection to the study of consciousness; indeed consciousness was his main concern. What he wanted to do was to study consciousness as it appears, rather than break it down into parts. The traditional psychology regarded anything we look at as a mosaic of tiny patches of color. Only as all these tiny patches are put together do they make up the scene we observe. Wertheimer challenged this view. We actually see the scene, he insisted, as a meaningful whole. Only by a very artificial process of analysis can we break down this whole into patches of different colors and shades. The same applies to thinking. The traditional psychology regarded all our thoughts as made up of images connected by a process of association. This analysis, too, Wertheimer rejected. Our thoughts are whole meaningful perceptions, not associated collections of images.

Wertheimer's first publication in this revolt against analysis was concerned with the phenomenon of apparent movement. It is well known that when a light in one place is turned off and a light in another place is immediately turned on, we experience the phenomenon as a single light moving from one place to another. This illusion is the basis of the apparent movement in lighted advertising signs. Prior to Wertheimer, the phenomenon had been regarded as a minor curiosity of no theoretical importance. To Wertheimer, however, it was striking evidence of the futility of analyzing a whole into its parts. The components were two separate lights going on and off, but the resulting whole was an impression of movement. The observer does not see the two lights flashing and infer that something is moving. Rather, the impression of movement is immediate and direct; only by careful study can we determine that there are two lights and no physical movement. This phenomenon of apparent movement so impressed Wertheimer that he named it the *phi phenomenon* and began a series of studies on it.

What is a Gestalt?

The phi phenomenon was only the starting point of an intellectual movement within German psychology. This movement was primarily concerned with perception, but came to include learning and other topics as well, treated according to the same principles as were used to study perception. Its emphasis was on whole systems in which the parts are dynamically interrelated in such a way that the whole cannot be inferred from the parts taken separately. Wertheimer applied the German word *Gestalt,* which may be roughly translated as "form" or "pattern" or "configuration," to these dynamic wholes. Such gestalts (treating *gestalt* now as an English rather than a German word) are of many sorts, and they occur in physics as well as in psychology. We have already considered the phi phenomenon as one example. A melody is another, since it depends on the relation between the notes rather than the notes themselves. "Die Lorelei" (to take an appropriately German example) is still the same tune when transposed into another key so that every note is different. A whirlpool is a third example, since it is a whirlpool not because of the particular drops of water it contains but because of the way the motion of the water is patterned. Because of this concern with gestalts, the movement that Wertheimer started came to be known as *gestalt psychology.*

The emphasis of the gestalt psychologists on unified wholes does not mean that they never recognized separateness. Indeed, a gestalt may be referred to as a distinctly separate whole. Of particular interest is the way that gestalts come to stand out as distinct entities separate from the background against which they appear. This interest was expressed in the concepts of figure and ground. The *figure* in any perception is the gestalt, the entity that stands out, the "thing" we perceive. The *ground* is the largely undifferentiated background against which the figure appears. A melody, for example, is a figure against a ground that includes many other sounds. What appears as figure at one moment may not at another. If the listener stops paying attention to the melody in order to hear what a friend is saying, the friend's speech becomes figure and the melody becomes part of the ground. Such changes in figure-ground relationships play a part not only in perception but in learning and thinking as well.

It is of course possible to analyze a gestalt figure into component parts. The fact that three black dots on a white page appear as a triangle does not keep them from still being three dots. However, the important thing to a gestalt psychologist is that what we see immediately is a triangle. Afterward we can analyze the triangle into three dots and study what it is that makes these three dots appear as a triangle when another three, differently placed, do not. We cannot say, however, that the triangle is nothing but three dots. The triangularity, which depends on the pattern of the dots rather than on the dots themselves, is the most essential aspect of what we see. The gestalt figure is more than just the sum of three dots. This relationship is the basis of an expression often applied to gestalt psychology: "The whole is more than the sum of its parts."

It is evident that Wertheimer and Watson, though rebels against similar traditions at the same time, were moving in opposite directions. Each may be considered both a pioneer and an extreme prototype of a certain approach to psychology.

Watson's was the mechanistic approach, concerned with the components of behavior and the connections between them. Wertheimer's was the dynamic approach, concerned with unified patterns in consciousness. Without judging their importance relative to that of other theorists, we can say that in terms of conspicuous intellectual movements, Watson was the outstanding pioneer of connectionist theory and Wertheimer the outstanding pioneer of cognitive theory.

From the first, however, Wertheimer shared the spotlight with various colleagues, particularly Wolfgang Köhler (1887–1967), who eventually surpassed Wertheimer as a publicist for the new movement. The group that gathered around them became known as the Berlin school, though both men eventually moved to the United States. Perception remained their primary interest, but learning was by no means neglected. Throughout, the emphasis was on organized wholes, separated from other wholes but united within themselves by their dynamic patterning.

The interpretations of learning presented by Wertheimer, Köhler, and other gestalt psychologists tend to be presented in the terminology of perception. Instead of asking, "What has the individual learned to do?" the gestalt psychologist is likely to ask, "How has the individual learned to perceive the situation?" Gestalt interpretations thus make an interesting contrast with the connectionist interpretations we examined earlier. Gestalt theorists do speak of memory traces, which are the effects that experiences leave in the nervous system, but these are different from the stimulus-response bonds discussed by connectionist theorists. The memory traces of the gestalt psychologists are not isolated elements, but organized wholes—in other words, gestalts. Consequently, learning is primarily a matter, not of adding new traces and subtracting old ones, but of changing one gestalt into another. This change may occur through new experience, but it may also occur through thinking or through the mere passage of time. The way in which these restructurings occur is the concern of gestalt learning theory.

Gestalts in Problem Solving and Learning

The most important contribution of gestalt theory to our understanding of learning is in the study of *insight*. Often learning occurs suddenly with a feeling that now one really understands something that was previously a baffling puzzle. This feeling is not limited to mystery stories—it is common in learning math, in interpreting other people's behavior, and in looking for solutions to everyday practical problems. Such learning is likely to be especially resistant to forgetting and especially easy to transfer to new situations. We speak of such learning as involving insight. In such cases the gestalt language of perceptual reorganization is particularly applicable. The learner who has insight sees the whole situation in a new way, a way that includes understanding of logical relationships or perception of the connections between means and ends.

Such insight is by no means restricted to humans. During World War I Köhler, interned in the Canary Islands, did extensive studies of insightful problem solving in apes. These are described in his book *The Mentality of Apes* (1925). He presented chimpanzees with problems in which bananas were displayed out of reach and could be obtained only by using techniques new in the apes' experience. For example, a banana might be hung from the top of the animal's cage, with boxes elsewhere in the cage that could be piled under the banana so the ape could climb up and get it. Or a banana might be outside the cage, far enough away so that it could be obtained only by pulling it in with a stick. Such arrangements had the advantage, from the gestalt point of view, of making all the necessary elements of the solution visible to the animal, which is not the case in a puzzle box or maze. Köhler found that these problems not only were often solved suddenly, but frequently were solved immediately after a period of time during which the ape was not actively trying to reach the banana. Sometimes it appeared that the animal, having failed to obtain the banana by familiar methods, sat and thought about the problem and then suddenly saw the solution. Such incidents are well suited to a description in terms of perceptual restructuring. Köhler could say that an ape suddenly saw the boxes, for example, not as playthings to be tossed around but as supports to be climbed on. It saw the relationship between the boxes and the bananas. During the time that it was not actively doing anything about the problem, the ape was undergoing a process of restructuring which, when complete, made an immediate solution possible.

It should not be supposed, however, that only such dramatic examples of sudden and complete insight can be explained in gestalt terms. Gradual learning by trial and error can be interpreted as a series of small, partial insights. Köhler's problems, on the one hand, were so arranged that the ape could see all the necessary elements of the solution at once. All that was necessary was for these parts to become organized into an appropriate gestalt. A rat in a maze, on the other hand, cannot see any relation between a particular turn and the food at the end until this relation has been discovered by experience. The rat's restructuring must therefore be gradual and piecemeal, since the situation permits no other kind. Nevertheless, the discovery that a certain pattern of turns is the way to food is no less a cognitive restructuring than the discovery that boxes piled on one another are the way to food. The suddenness of the restructuring depends on the problem and the way it is presented to the subject, but the principle is the same.

Insight in Education

Wertheimer's most noted contribution to the development of gestalt psychology, once the enterprise that he started was under way, was in applications to education. He was concerned with insightful learning in schoolchildren. Whereas Köhler studied insight in apes for theoretical reasons, Wertheimer had a very practical interest in the topic in schoolchildren. It seemed to him that teachers put far too much emphasis on rote memorizing at the expense of understanding. He therefore directed his studies toward finding ways in which learning could take place with greater insight on the part of the learner.

In his book *Productive Thinking,* Wertheimer (1945) makes a distinction between two types of attempted solutions to problems. Solutions of type A are those in which there is originality and insight; solutions of type B are those in which old rules are inappropriately applied, and hence are not really solutions at all. This distinction does not imply that B solutions depend on previous experience and A solutions do not. Both depend on previous experience; the difference lies in the original organization that characterizes A solutions.

Wertheimer found geometry an especially useful area in which to study different approaches to problems. One of his problems, which he presented to adults as well as children, required the subject to find the area of a parallelogram. Wertheimer would begin by showing the subject how to find the area of a rectangle, not simply the formula of length times height, but the reason the formula works. He did so by dividing the rectangle up into small squares (Figure 8.1, part A) and showing that the area was the number of squares in a row times the number of rows. He then presented the subjects with a parallelogram cut out of paper (Figure 8.1, part B) and the instruction to find its area. Some people replied that this was a new problem and that they could not be expected to solve it without being told how. Some blindly repeated the now incorrect formula of multiplying one side times the other: a B type of "solution." Other people attempted to find an

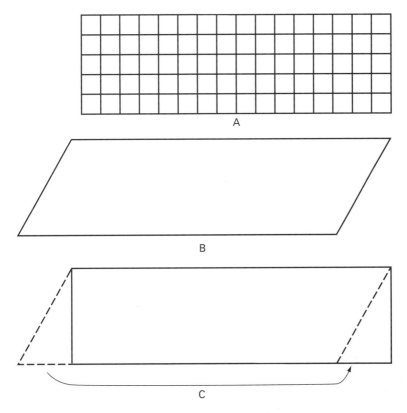

Figure 8.1 Wertheimer's parallelogram problem. Part A shows Wertheimer's way of explaining why the area of a rectangle equals the product of length times width—in this case, 16 by 5. Part B shows the parallelogram for which he asked subjects to find the area. Part C shows how one person solved the problem by cutting off one end and moving it to the other end, thus converting the parallelogram into a rectangle.

original solution, but were unable to see the essential relationships. A few, however, came up with genuine A solutions. One child, noting that the two projecting ends were what made the problem difficult, asked for scissors, cut off one end, and fitted it against the other end, thus converting the parallelogram into a rectangle (Figure 8.1, part C). Another subject achieved the same goal by bending the parallelogram into a ring, so that the two ends fitted together, and then cutting the ring vertically to convert it into a rectangle. These two individuals showed a genuine understanding of the situation that made possible correct, original solutions.

The rule for solving the original problem, with the rectangle, could also be stated as "base times height." If a student applied that version of the rule to the new problem, it would have given the correct answer. However, as a blind application of an old rule, it would still have demonstrated no understanding. Thus it would have been much like a B solution, even though it would have happened to be correct. What the A solutions involved, however, was finding an original way of converting the new problem into a familiar one, one that they knew how to solve. The final solution depended very much on previous experience, but it was previous experience organized in a novel way. The important thing about these solutions, what made them true A solutions, was the insight by which the new problem situation was restructured. From the solvers' point of view, they converted the parallelogram into a better gestalt, a rectangle.

Thus, even when a solution is correct, it is important to distinguish whether or not real understanding is involved. Understanding is not the same as logic. Both the inductive and the deductive methods of logic may be applied blindly. The inductive method, in which a person reasons from particular instances to a general conclusion, is really just trial and error. Another person might have tried various possible formulas for the area of a parallelogram, found that base times altitude gave the same answer as the book in several cases, and concluded that this was the correct formula, but without having any idea why. Though adequate for practical purposes, this would be a solution without understanding.

Wertheimer is amused by cases where blind induction leads to absurdly wrong conclusions. He once arranged a series of four examples so that in each of them the area of a parallelogram happened to equal the sum of the base and the other side. A student noticed this relationship and proudly pointed out that the area could more easily be found by adding the two sides than by the more difficult multiplication of base times altitude. Some teachers might have been impressed by that student's alertness, but to Wertheimer such blind induction demonstrated lack of real understanding of the geometric relationships. When Wertheimer then gave another problem in which the addition method did not work, the student said sadly, "I am sorry; it would have been so nice." "Would it?" replied Wertheimer.

The deductive method, in which a person reasons logically from one principle to another, can also be applied blindly. A student may fumble around algebraically until he or she finds a valid proof that a certain equation is correct, but the student may still not understand the equation in the sense that Wertheimer means. Understanding implies not merely logical correctness but a perception of the problem as an integrated whole, of the ways in which the means lead to the end. In going through an algebraic proof, for example, the student should ask at each step not only "How does this follow logically from the previous step?" but also "How does this lead toward the solution I am looking for?" In Wertheimer's opinion, education should make such understanding, or perception of whole gestalts, its primary goal.

The value of creative problem solving is not restricted to such "purely intellectual" situations as the above. Wertheimer illustrates its value in social situations with an anecdote about two boys playing badminton. The older boy was so much better at the game than the younger that he won nearly every point, and the frustrated younger boy finally refused to play any longer. Since this spoiled the fun for the older boy, it posed a problem for him. How could he get the younger boy to go on playing with him? He might have exhorted him to be a good sport (probably in vain), or he might have offered a handicap (a better approach, but still not an answer to the fundamental problem posed by the one-sided competition). Seeing the competition as the crux of the problem, the older boy was able to propose a constructive solution. The competitive game of winning points was replaced by a cooperative game of seeing how long the two together could keep the bird going back and forth, and both were then able to enjoy playing. Again, understanding of the situation led to an insightful solution.

This simple example of Wertheimer's, in addition to being an illustration of insightful problem solving, is also an early example of negotiation and conflict resolution, a topic that has recently received a lot of attention. In areas as diverse as family counseling, labor-management relations, and peacekeeping in situations of international tension, there has been interest in how to turn a competitive situation into a cooperative one (see, e.g., Bazerman & Neale, 1992). The people involved in such situations often interpret them as purely competitive, as cases where one party's gain has to be balanced by the other party's loss. Often, however, some arrangement is possible in which both parties gain more than they lose. In a particular factory, for example, management might care most about holding the line on wages, while labor cared most about getting more freedom in the work situation. If management agreed to a large change in the work situation, while the union agreed to accept only a very small raise, both parties would be better off than before—what has come to be called a win-win situation. Not only did Wertheimer provide the above early example of a win-win solution, he also suggested the importance of understanding the situation and finding insightful solutions for human conflicts.

This book of Wertheimer's, set beside Guthrie's *Psychology of Learning*, points up the contrast between cognitive and connectionist views of learning in their extreme forms. Both books show a keen interest in the applied psychology of learning, especially as applied to children. Guthrie's emphasis, on the one hand, is on training the child to make the right responses to the right stimuli. His question is always "What does the child do?" Wertheimer, on the other hand, is concerned with educating the child to have insights into the material. His question is "What does the child understand?" This emphasis on understanding, on the perception of relationships within an organized whole, is the great contribution of gestalt psychology to the interpretation of learning.

PIAGET AND COGNITIVE DEVELOPMENT

Cognitive theories became popular in Europe well before they did in the United States. We have seen how gestalt theory, starting with the topic of perception, went on to become a theory of learning and thinking as well. Another European theory came to a cognitive interpretation of learning and thinking by way of the study of human development. It began a little later than gestalt theory, and in the French-speaking part of Switzerland rather than in Germany. Its best known exponent was Jean Piaget (1896–1980).

Since Piaget was French-speaking, his name is pronounced somewhat like "John Peeah*zhay*." He spent about the last half century of his life in Geneva studying processes of thinking in children. His early scientific interest was in biology, and at the age of 15 he had already achieved renown for his publications about mollusks. However, his interest in logic and the sources of knowledge led him into cognitive psychology. He studied with Alfred Binet, the developer of intelligence tests, but found that he was more interested in how intelligence develops than in how to measure it, and began doing studies on the way his own children's understanding of various topics changed over time.

He first became widely known among psychologists through his book *The Language and Thought of the Child*, which was published in French in 1923 and translated into English in 1926. This has been followed by so many other books, articles, and lectures, continuing up to his death, that even a sampling of the titles would be excessively long. Since his writings are not only voluminous but also theoretically rather complex, we can get a better overview of his system from such secondary sources as Flavell (1963) and Phillips (1981). Over the years his status in the English-speaking world has risen from that of a strange but intriguing outsider to that of an outstanding theorist who (like Hull in his heyday) could be followed, modified, or opposed, but not ignored.

Basic Concepts of Piaget's System

One way of identifying a theorist is by the key intervening variable(s) that he postulates. Piaget used as his favorite intervening variable the *schema*. Schemas are a little more general than most of the cognitions we have considered so far. They are ways of perceiving, understanding, and thinking about the world. One might speak of them as frameworks or organizing structures for mental activity. They are broad types of expectancies, dealing with general ways in which events occur. The formation and change of schemas are the essence both of cognitive development and of learning.

A child, of course, has schemas relevant to a great many topics, and the number becomes even greater as the child approaches adulthood. Piaget was particularly interested in those schemas pertaining to the physical world. In what ways does a given child understand relationships of size and weight and causality? How does the child reason about physical changes, about constants and variables, about the sources of actions and the nature of living and nonliving things? Though the exploration of these schemas was Piaget's greatest contribution, he was not unaware of children's social worlds as well. How does a child understand social relationships? How does the child reason about moral issues? What justification can be provided for the rules of games or the rules of decent behavior? Piaget studied these schemas, too, and influenced the research of others interested in those aspects of development.

Schemas can change, and such change is important in cognitive development. The process by which they change is known as *accommodation*. When a child (or any person, for that matter) has an experience that is inconsistent with a schema, there will be some tendency for the schema to change so as to accommodate this new input. For example, it is common for children around the age of 6 to operate on the schema that objects that are light to lift will float and those that are heavy to lift will sink. When asked to make predictions, they indicate that a large (and therefore heavy) block of wood will sink, while a small piece of metal will float. However, as they repeatedly see disconfirmations of these predictions, the schema becomes increasingly difficult to maintain. Gradually they fumble their way toward a new, more adequate schema. For a while they may manage with a group of more specific schemas such as that wood floats, while metal and stone sink. Eventually they achieve a new schema that is as general and almost as simple as the old, but more accurate: that objects of low density float, while those of high density sink.

The process of accommodation by which children improve their schemas is similar to that by which scientists improve their more technical ones. Indeed, the question of how to differentiate consistently between objects that float and those that sink was once as much of a problem for scholars as it is now for children. All of us sometimes find our views of the world disconfirmed, try to explain why, and (perhaps) learn from the experience. Accommodation applies equally well to an infant discovering that an object that has gone out of sight has not ceased to exist and to Einstein replacing Newton's description of the world with the theory of relativity. Accommodation is thus, for Piaget, the most important and most interesting form of learning, responsible for our understanding of the world in all its manifestations.

This emphasis on the process of accommodation might suggest that schemas are unstable, constantly being changed by new inputs. Actually, however, the opposite is true; schemas tend to be quite stable. A child is no more likely to give up an old schema in response to one or two disconfirming inputs than is a scientist to give up a pet theory because only one or two experiments failed to work out as expected. For both child and scientist, the reaction is more likely to be: "Something odd happened that time. I wonder how I can explain it." To explain it, of course, both child and scientist need to use their existing schemas. Even more common than accommodation, therefore, is the opposite process, by which schemas influence the interpretation of experiences. This process is known as *assimilation*.

Everything we experience, from the simplest physical stimulus to the most complex new scientific or philosophical idea, is interpreted in the light of what we already know and believe. One way of expressing this relationship is to say that the stimulus (however simple or complex) is assimilated into the existing schemas. The meaning of the stimulus is determined by the schemas that the person uses to recognize and interpret it. This "modification" of the stimulus into a part of the individual's total cognitive world is what Piaget means by assimilation.

When a schema is stable and can easily assimilate whatever relevant new experiences come along, a state of equilibrium exists, in which new experiences that might otherwise disrupt it are counteracted by the forces of assimilation. As more new experiences come along that cannot easily be assimilated, disequilibrium results. If eventually accommodation occurs, so that a new schema can assimilate these troublesome experiences, a new equilibrium results. This process of striving toward equilibrium of schemas and experiences—by assimilation where practical, more gradually by accommodation where necessary—is similar to the ideas of the gestalt psychologists about gestalts and how they change through insightful learning. Piaget's schemas are more durable than their gestalts, but both involve an organization within the nervous system, resulting from the interaction of experience with existing structures, and always striving toward its best possible form. Though Piaget's background is not that of a gestalt psychologist, his thinking is congenial to theirs.

Stages in Cognitive Development

If we look only at the process of accommodation, we can imagine a person's schemas constantly changing throughout life. Though in a sense this is true, it would not give a very accurate picture of Piaget's writings. Much of what he has written deals not with changes in schemas but with their characteristics at any given period in life. Since schemas change slowly, it is possible to describe the way a person interprets the world at any given time during life without worrying about the changes that are slowly going on in those interpretations. One of the most conspicuous features of Piaget's theory is his list of developmental stages. At each stage, children's schemas have certain characteristic features that are different from those of earlier or later stages. Knowing at what stage a given child is now, we can predict with a fair degree of accuracy how the child will answer various questions about the way things happen and why.

Many psychologists have described development as a series of stages, and several comments are appropriate to all of them, including Piaget's. For one thing, the number of stages and the boundaries between them are somewhat arbitrary. What one scholar would call two stages, another might call two parts of a single stage. Moreover, a given person at a given time might be judged by one observer to be in an earlier stage, but starting to make the transition to the next stage, and by another observer to be in the later stage, but still showing many remnants of the earlier.

Further, some children will enter a given stage earlier than will other children, and some children will pass through the stage more rapidly than others. The order of stages is assumed to be the same for all children, but the timing is somewhat variable and the ages specified for any given stage are therefore only approximate. In addition, there is typically some ambiguity as to why everyone passes through the same order of stages and to what extent, if at all, the sequence could be changed. Psychologists who describe systems of stages nearly always assume that the order, at least, is fixed, regardless of the environment. It may be possible to speed up progress through the stages, or slow it down, or even stop it completely, but it is not possible to reach a "higher" stage before passing through the lower ones. Though this assumption of stage theories often is challenged, Piaget could defend it in his case by pointing to the way in which schemas build on one another. Since one cannot solve a problem without first having mastered the necessary components, Piaget would claim that one cannot enter a later stage until one's schemas have reached the necessary level of complexity and abstraction, represented by the previous stage.

With these general warnings, let us look at Piaget's system of stages. The matter of distinguishing between main headings and their parts or subheadings, mentioned above, is a bit of a problem. Probably the clearest version of his classification is in four stages: sensory-motor, preoperational, concrete operations, and formal operations. Each stage represents an increase over the previous one in the child's ability to think abstractly, predict the world correctly, explain reasons for things accurately, and generally deal intellectually with the world.

The first stage is known as the *sensory-motor.* It extends roughly from birth to age 2. As the name implies, the schemas that develop during this stage are those involving children's perception of the world and the coordinations by which they deal with the world. It is during this period that children form their most basic conceptions about the nature of the material world. They learn that an object that has disappeared can reappear. They learn that it is the same object even though it looks very different when seen from different angles or in different illuminations. They relate the appearance, sound, and touch of the object to one another. They discover ways in which their own actions affect objects, and acquire a primitive sense of causality. Thus their world becomes increasingly an orderly arrangement of more or less permanent objects, related causally to each other and to their own behavior.

The second stage is the *preoperational,* extending from about ages 2 to 7. In this stage children begin to show the effects of having learned language. They are able to represent objects and events symbolically: not just to act toward them, but to think about them. However, Piaget does not regard this change as due entirely to language. Children have internal representations of objects before they have words to express them. These internal representations give children greater flexibility for dealing adaptively with the world, and attaching words to them gives them much greater power of communication. However, their intellectual abilities are still very limited compared with those of an adult. Their thinking is still decidedly concrete by adult standards. They tends to focus on one aspect of a situation to the exclusion of others, a process that Piaget calls *centering.* Their reasoning can be a logician's nightmare, and they find it difficult to understand how anyone else can see things from a point of view other than their own. They are thus, as the name of the stage implies, still early in the process of acquiring a logical, adult intellectual structure.

The third stage is that of *concrete operations,* extending from about ages 7 to 11. Again, this stage represents an increase in flexibility, in this case over the preoperational. The sorts of operations to which the name of the stage refers include classifying, combining, and comparing. Children in the stage of concrete operations can deal with the relationships among hierarchies of terms, such as robin, bird, and creature. They are aware, as preoperational children are not, of the reversibility of operations: what is added can be subtracted, and a substance that has been changed in shape can be restored to its original shape. A girl in this stage will not fall into the fallacy that a preoperational girl may, of saying: "Yes, I have a sister. No, my sister doesn't have any sister!" Just as the advances of the preoperational stage can be related to the beginning of language, so the advances of the stage of concrete operations can be seen as related to the beginning of school. Again, however, Piaget points out that this is not the whole story. One child may have learned arithmetic operations by rote but fail to apply them when appropriate, while another child may deal effectively with problems without ever having studied arithmetic. (Wertheimer would certainly agree.) Learning of symbolic manipulations may be helpful to children in going from the preoperational to the concrete-operations stage, but experience with a wide variety of concrete situations is more important.

The fourth and final stage is that of *formal operations*, starting around age 11 and involving improvements in abstract thinking continuing to about age 16. In this stage the capacity for symbolic manipulation reaches its peak. Though children in the previous stage have been able to perform a number of logical operations, they have done so within the context of a concrete situation. Now the persons (intellectually no longer children) can view the issues abstractly. They can judge the validity of syllogisms in terms of their formal structure, independent of content. They can explore different ways of formulating a problem and see what their logical consequences are. They are at least ready to think in terms of a realm of abstract propositions that fit in varying degrees the real world they observe. (In short, we might suggest, they are ready to study Hull's theory!) They may not demonstrate all these tendencies in every possible situation—how many of us ever do?—but they have reached the stage at which they are capable of doing so. The intellectual apparatus of formal reasoning that provides the basis for so much human achievement is at least potentially at their disposal.

As children pass from one stage to another, as well as through substages we have not considered, their schemas are changing through accommodation to new experiences. At each stage they try to assimilate new experiences to their existing schemas, but often find discrepancies. (The same observations at a younger age would not have been discrepant, since their schemas were not well enough developed for them even to recognize an inconsistency.) Though a single such discrepancy is merely puzzling, a series of them will gradually produce accommodation and change the relevant schema toward the next stage. Formal schooling helps the process along, but confrontation with discrepant information is critical, and even that produces its effect only slowly.

Of the many schemas that change during development, there is one group that Piaget has studied in particular detail. They are the most studied changes that take place as the child moves from the preoperational stage into and through the stage of concrete operations. They are grouped together under the heading of conservation, to which we now turn.

Conservation

Most people, on hearing the term *conservation,* probably think of virgin redwood forests or some other natural resource in danger of depletion. Piaget's use of the word, however, is more like that in the physical expression "conservation of matter." It refers to the fact that some quantitative property of matter remains the same in spite of changes in other properties. For example, a lump of clay keeps the same weight no matter how its shape is changed, and a given number of buttons is still the same number whether the buttons are bunched close together or spread out widely over a tabletop. These constant properties may seem ridiculously obvious to us, but they are not at all obvious to most children in the preoperational stage. Just as an infant must learn that an object remains the same object as it moves, so a somewhat older child must learn that a substance conserves its weight through changes of shape and a group of objects conserves its number through changes of spacing. The mastery of these various forms of conservation takes place typically at somewhat different ages, extending from the beginning to the end of the stage of concrete operations.

A favorite demonstration among Piagetians is to show a preoperational child two pitchers of different-colored liquids, the same size and shape, and equally full. When the child has agreed that there is the same amount in both pitchers, the experimenter pours the contents of one of them into a tall, narrow beaker and asks the child which liquid there is now more of. Some children will say there is now more of the one that was poured ("since it's higher"), others will say there is more of the one that is still in the pitcher ("because it's fatter"), but they generally agree that there are no longer equal amounts of the two liquids. The children have failed to show conservation of volume. This failure may be attributed in part to their unawareness of the reversibility of operations. It is obvious to most adults that the liquid could be poured back into the pitcher and would then take up the same space as before; its volume never changed. To the child, however, the change was more fundamental; he was not aware of its reversibility. This characteristic of his thinking interferes with his achieving conservation.

Failure to conserve number or weight follows from the same characteristics of the preoperational child. A child lines up eight buttons next to eight pennies and agrees that there are the same number of pennies as buttons. Then the pennies are spread out to make a longer line, and in reply to the experimenter's questioning the child now indicates that there are more pennies. Again, this failure of conservation represents a nonrecognition that the change in spacing is reversible. Similarly, when a child has seen two balls of clay balance on a scale and has then watched the experimenter mold one of them into a different shape, he is likely to decide that now the changed piece is either heavier or lighter, not realizing that the clay can be restored to its original shape.

Failure to show conservation seems so strange to most adults that one is tempted to think that the problem is merely a trivial misunderstanding about words. Maybe the child really knows that the number, or volume, or weight remains the same, but just gets the words for them mixed up with words for length or height, and so appears not to be showing conservation. This is a tempting inter-pretation, and there is evidence to suggest that confusion about words does play some part in children's failure to show conservation. However, most people who have worked with children on these problems, asking children the same question in different ways, have concluded that there is much more to it than that. If the child is confused about the words, it is largely *because* he is confused (from an adult point of view) about the whole matter of quantities—what they are and how they behave. However strongly he may defend his "wrong" interpretations, he is still, as Piaget claims, in the process of developing and refining the schemas by which he interprets the world.

Though modern cognitive theory got its start in Europe and continued to receive greater support in Europe than in America, it was by no means ignored in the United States. Translations of the gestaltists and of Piaget found an interested, if somewhat skeptical, audience west of the Atlantic. In addition, a few Americans soon joined the cause with their own versions of cognitive theory, as we will see in the next chapter.

Chapter
9

American Cognitive
Theory

During the greater part of the history of American learning theory, connectionist theories were dominant, and the sorts of cognitive theories discussed in the previous chapter had relatively little influence. Only in the last third of the twentieth century have cognitive approaches become prominent. In retrospect, it seems surprising that it took so long. There were, however, a few pioneers in this approach whose work goes back as far as many of the connectionist psychologists we have considered. Of these pioneers, the most conspicuous was E. C. Tolman.

TOLMAN'S PURPOSIVE BEHAVIORISM

Edward Chace Tolman (1886–1959) spent most of his professional life on the faculty of the University of California at Berkeley. His major work, *Purposive Behavior in Animals and Men,* was published in 1932. Though his system later underwent a number of modifications, its essential spirit remained the same. Writing in the heyday of behaviorism, Tolman was impressed with behaviorism's objectivity, its concern with the precise measurement of behavior, and its faith in the improvability of man. At the same time he felt that behaviorism showed too little appreciation of the cognitive aspects of behavior. We do not simply respond to stimuli, he argued; we act on beliefs, express attitudes, and strive toward goals. What we need, therefore, is a theory that recognizes these aspects of behavior without sacrificing objectivity. To fill this need, Tolman undertook to create what he called a *purposive behaviorism.*

    What is a purposive behaviorism like? Much of its meaning can be inferred from the name. First, since it is a form of behaviorism, it is concerned with objective behavior, not with conscious experience, and with how behavior is affected by external stimuli. Second, it is concerned with learning, with the way that behavior changes with changing experience of the external world. It is thus a traditionally American learning theory in contrast to the more perceptual gestalt theories and the more developmental theory of Piaget. Third, it is concerned with the purposes that impel and guide behavior. Whereas most connectionist theorists treat behavior as a matter of responses to immediately present stimuli, Tolman emphasized the relation of behavior to goals. Most of our behavior is not so much a response to stimuli as a striving toward some goal. Stimuli of course guide us toward the goal and determine at every step what means we will use to reach it, but the search for the goal is what gives unity and meaning to our behavior. We may shift from one approach to another as circumstances require, while still continuing to direct our efforts toward the same goal. As a result it would be necessary for anyone who wanted to predict our behavior to know the goal we were seeking as well as the particular stimuli we were encountering along the way. Tolman called his system a purposive behaviorism because it studies behavior as it is organized around purposes.

The behavior that Tolman wanted to study is *molar* behavior. This term refers, not to the kind of behavior, but to the way in which it is analyzed. Molar behavior is analyzed in fairly large commonsense units, such as driving to work or cooking a meal. In practice, this is the way all theories of learning analyze behavior. However, some theories include an interest in *molecular* behavior, which is behavior analyzed in terms of single movements of particular muscles. Walking a city block, for example, is a molar act made up of an enormous number of molecular movements—expansions and contractions of the various muscles of the legs and other parts of the body. Guthrie is an example of a theorist who puts a good deal of emphasis on molecular analysis. Tolman, however, states explicitly that he is concerned only with molar behavior. The ways in which molecular movements work together to produce molar acts are of no concern to his system.

Cognitions as Intervening Variables

A given goal may be approached by a great variety of different acts, not only as sequences of responses but also as alternative possible ways of gaining the objective. Tolman's problem was to develop a theory for dealing with this complex variability of molar behavior as it operates in search of goals. To do this, he considered it necessary to take account of the individual's cognitions—one's perceptions of and beliefs about the world. How could Tolman take them into account without sacrificing the objectivity of behaviorism? His answer was to make use of *intervening variables*. To appreciate the importance of this answer we must see it in historical context. The existing behaviorist theory (more than a decade before Hull's *Principles of Behavior*) regarded anything more complex than a stimulus-response bond intervening between the stimulus and the response as itself a response, just as physical and potentially just as measurable as any other response. If the word *cognition* had any meaning at all for such behaviorists, it was as a shorthand name for tiny movements of the speech muscles; any other meaning they rejected as a figment of some mentalistic theorist's imagination. Tolman, however, considered it possible to use the term *cognition* objectively without treating it as a physical, directly measurable movement. He therefore designated cognitions as intervening variables. In doing so he both made the concept of cognition more respectable in behaviorist circles and introduced the concept of intervening variables into psychology.

As an intervening variable, a cognition is not a thing. It is an abstraction defined by the theorist. While it is possible that physiologists may some day find some particular activity in the brain that corresponds to a cognition, this possibility is no concern of Tolman's. The meaning of the word *cognition* is determined by the definition that the theorist gives it. For Tolman, this definition is in terms both of stimuli and of responses, since it intervenes between them. Hence, we can infer that a person has a given cognition either from the way that person behaves in certain situations or from the experiences the person has had that would have produced those cognitions. This linking of intervening variables both to stimuli and to responses is of course very similar to what Hull did, even though Tolman's particular intervening variables are markedly different from Hull's.

Experience with certain stimuli results in the formation of certain cognitions. For example, when one of Pavlov's dogs repeatedly heard the sound of a metronome just before seeing and smelling food, the dog learned a cognition that the sound of the metronome was a signal for food. Likewise, when a cook sets the oven hotter than usual and bakes an especially good cake, he is likely to form the cognition that using a hotter oven will result in a better cake. Of course that conclusion may be mistaken, as something else may have been responsible for the success. If so, then further experiences with hot ovens and average or below average cakes will change the mistaken cognition.

In addition, certain needs produce *demands* for certain goal objects. (Deprivation of food, for example, produces a demand for food.) These demands are also intervening variables. Cognitions and demands work together to produce responses.

Predictions from Tolman's Theory

How is Tolman's theory different from a connectionist one? Both attempt to predict behavior from stimuli and other antecedent conditions. Does the fact that Tolman uses cognitions as intervening variables make any real difference? Consider an individual who makes a certain response to certain stimuli and obtains a reward. What learning does this experience tend to produce? For Guthrie, Hull, or Skinner, it produces a tendency for those stimuli to be followed by that response, provided other conditions such as drive are appropriate. For Tolman, it produces a cognition that making the response will lead to the reward. If one now has a demand for the reward, one will make the response. How are these two interpretations really different?

The answer to this question is that not all cognitions take the form "If I do this, I will get that." We form many other kinds of cognitions about the way the environment is structured, about things that go together, about what paths lead to what places. These various sorts of cognitions can then be used when needed to help the individual achieve life goals. Cognitions from several different learning experiences may be put together so that the individual can respond adaptively to new situations. Attention to such combination makes it possible for Tolman's theory to deal with more original and flexible behavior than is covered by the connectionist interpretations of learning that we have discussed so far.

One example of this greater flexibility is in cognitions about what leads to what. Once an individual has learned how to get from one place to another, this knowledge can be used to obtain rewards quite different from the one obtained while learning. A rat that has learned its way around a maze while satisfying its demand for exploration can use this knowledge later to obtain food. This changeover is illustrated in an experiment by Buxton (1940). Rats were given several experiences of spending a night in a large maze. There was never any food in the maze, and the rats were taken out of the maze at different places on different occasions. This variation was designed to ensure that no part of the maze or path through the maze would be rewarded more than any other. After this experience, the rats were fed in the goal box of the maze while they were hungry and were then put in the start box of the maze. About half the rats ran to the goal box without a single error on this first trial, a record far above that of a control group without the previous experience in the maze. Since the rats had never been reinforced with food (or, presumably, with anything else) for following this particular path, it is difficult for stimulus-response theories to deal with this experiment. For Tolman, however, it is simple enough; the rats had formed a cognition (or perhaps a group of cognitions) about how the maze was arranged. They did not make use of this knowledge until they were given a reason to do so. In other words, the learning about the layout of the maze remained latent until food was experienced in the goal box. Hence this study is said to demonstrate *latent learning*. Several different kinds of latent learning have been studied; this experiment illustrates one of them. Whenever learning goes on without its being evident in performance at the time, latent learning is taking place.

Another way in which Tolman's theory achieved greater flexibility than connectionist theories was through its emphasis on learning the location of reward. Once an individual has learned where a given kind of reward is located, that location can often be reached by means other than those originally used. If a shopper finds an intriguing store while exploring the city on foot, the person can return later by car or bus. Similarly, a rat that has learned the location of food may, if the experimental arrangements permit, take a detour to get there faster. This is illustrated by another experiment (Tolman, Ritchie, & Kalish 1946). Rats ran a roundabout route across a tabletop, through an enclosed alley, and then along a series of elevated pathways to obtain food (Figure 9.1, part A). After they had learned to use this route, the alley was blocked, but 18 new pathways were made available, leading in various directions from the tabletop (Figure 9.1, part B). The rats did not, as one might expect from the principle of generalization, choose the paths closest to the one they had previously used. Instead, they tended to choose the one that pointed approximately toward the location of the goal. Many, to be sure, chose other paths, but the goal-pointing path was the only one chosen by a large proportion of the rats. In other words, the rats tended to choose the path that appeared to be a shortcut to the goal rather than those close to the original path. They had not merely learned a route to food; they had also learned the location of the food in space.

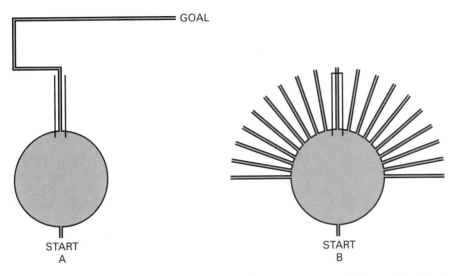

Figure 9.1   Learning the direction to a goal. This is a top view of Tolman, Ritchie, & Kalish's (1946) apparatus. In part A, rats followed the roundabout route from the round tabletop to the goal, where they found food. In part B, the original route was blocked and 18 new paths were made available. The rats tended to choose the path pointing toward the goal.

The two above experiments are typical of many that were done by Tolman and his students or were done by others but quoted by Tolman in support of his position. Because of their importance to the controversy between cognitive and connectionist interpretations of learning, these studies often were criticized for various details of their procedures and often were repeated by both friends and foes of Tolman's ideas. In some cases it turned out that animals show the insightful behavior predicted by Tolman only under quite special conditions. However, whether or not rats behave according to Tolman's theory in any given situation, there is no doubt that this kind of flexible, insightful behavior does occur in some species (particularly humans) under some conditions. The very fact that Tolman considered these experiments necessary shows how strong a hold connectionist interpretations of learning had on American psychology.

Tolman used a number of terms to refer to the cognitions that are learned in various situations. Perhaps his most popular term is *cognitive map*. It is easy to see how the two experiments discussed above can be interpreted by saying that the rats had cognitive maps of the areas they had explored. Those in the maze had a cognitive map of the various alleys, indicating which were blind and which led on to other choice points. Those in the roundabout path had a map that included not only the path but also the surrounding space with its possible shortcuts. If someone asks how it is possible to have maps in the brain when the brain is made up of nerve fibers that conduct impulses from one place to another, Tolman is not concerned. Cognitive maps are intervening variables, and if they explain learning Tolman does not care how they relate to physiology.

For all their differences, Tolman's ideas are in some ways close to those of the cognitive theorists we considered in the previous chapter. Indeed, at various points in his theorizing Tolman borrowed ideas not only from the gestalt psychologists but also from Freud, from the reinforcement theorists, and even from Guthrie. His breadth is also reflected in the variety of variables that he took into account in explaining behavior. In addition to all the aspects of the situation, he listed four main kinds of individual-difference variables. Only one of these, we may note, involves learning. The four are heredity; age; training; and endocrine, drug, or vitamin conditions. Using the initial letters of these four, Tolman labeled them the HATE variables. (One wonders how Tolman, a devout Quaker, came to arrive at this particular set of initials.) The HATE variables help to illustrate the breadth of Tolman's concern with different aspects of behavior. Discussions of such diverse factors as age and vitamin conditions are rare in learning theory. They are valuable as a reminder that learning, for all its great importance, is far from being the only determinant of behavior.

Of Rats and Humans

Tolman was atypical among cognitive theorists in having given more attention to the behavior of animals than of humans. (This was also Köhler's emphasis at one stage of his career, but he did extensive work in human perception as well.) To some extent, the preference reflects the same factors that have influenced behaviorists in general toward animal work: the greater simplicity of animals and the greater opportunity to control their environments. It probably also reflects Tolman's special concern to show that a cognitive system could still be objective, that it need not depend at all on anything the individual says. Tolman himself, in the tongue-in-cheek manner so characteristic of his writing, presented a third possible explanation. He suggested that psychologists typically begin with an interest in solving the great problems of human life, then become frightened by the awesome implications of such a task and flee to safer aspects of the study of behavior, such as learning in the rat. Certainly Tolman was right in saying that many psychologists are aware of a conflict between their desire to attack the great questions of life directly and their desire to concentrate on other questions that are less exciting but that they have more chance of being able to solve. Tolman's own career reflects this conflict clearly.

On the one hand, Tolman was a man of strong social conscience. (He was one of the faculty members who left the University of California rather than sign the controversial loyalty oath in 1950.) In 1942 he published a small book called *Drives Toward War*, in which he analyzed the psychological causes of war and presented some suggestions for removing them. His analysis of the biological drives, social techniques, and psychological dynamisms leading to behavior—warlike or otherwise—combined experimental, clinical, and historical sources. On the basis of this analysis he suggested several fairly radical changes in our political, economic, and educational systems, changes that he thought would reduce the impetus toward war. Among these was a plan for a world state, along with some psychological suggestions for making this admittedly visionary idea a bit more practical.

On the other hand, Tolman had as his principal ambition the development of a schematic rat world, a system from which he could predict completely the behavior of rats in a laboratory environment. This is reflected in his whimsical dedication of *Purposive Behavior* to *Mus norvegicus albinus* (actually the white mouse, but he meant the white rat). He wanted to include enough different variables and to have flexible enough constructs to achieve this goal completely. When we consider the tremendously complex human social situations that people usually want psychologists to deal with, this seems like a very modest ambition. Tolman did not, however, achieve his goal.

Evaluation of Tolman

If we consider how Tolman incorporated the best aspects of behaviorism within a cognitive theory, what a broad range of variables he took into account, and how early he anticipated future developments in the logic of theory building (e.g., the use of intervening variables), we could easily conclude that Tolman is the greatest learning theorist we have considered. In its conception, his theory may be the best there is. The conception, however, was never really carried into execution. Tolman discussed the kinds of laws psychology needs, but he did not develop these laws. He did experiments intended to show that cognitive formulations are better than connectionist ones, but he did not do experiments to make these cognitive formulations precise enough to be really useful for prediction. He pointed the way toward an extension of cognitive theory to include the best aspects of connectionist theory, but he did not carry the program through. He gave us a cognitive framework (or perhaps we should say a gestalt) for interpreting learning, but he did not provide us either with detailed laws of learning like Skinner's, or with a detailed theory like Hull's, or with a principle of learning as general as Guthrie's. Thus his system is more a road sign or a preliminary attempt than it is an accomplished fact.

This shortcoming is not really a failure on Tolman's part, however, for his attitude toward his own theorizing was always tentative and whimsical. He regarded theory construction not as a serious business of building great intellectual edifices for the future but as a half playful trying out of different approaches. As a result he was constantly revising his theory, making suggestions and then abandoning them before he had time to explore their implications. His writings are a mixture of earnestness and whimsy, of high-flown theorizing constantly being pulled up short by a chuckle. His desire to construct a schematic rat world was thus partly an aspiration but also partly a joke. He wanted not so much to build a truly adequate theory as to explore the whole activity of theory building, both playing with it himself and puncturing the excessive claims of others. As a result, he was widely respected and widely liked, but not widely followed. In fact, of all the major learning theorists considered in this book, he may well have been regarded most affectionately by his students but at the same time have had the fewest students follow in his footsteps. This apparent contradiction was analyzed 15 years after his death in a symposium (see Campbell & Krantz 1974) suggesting that to be a "tribal leader," that is, to found a school of loyal followers, one must have a strong and somewhat intolerant conviction of the rightness and importance of one's ideas.

Tolman lacked that conviction. Possibly his intellectual style was influenced by his being the younger brother of a distinguished scientist in a better-developed science: physics. In any case, compared with other major theorists, he had little faith in the lasting rightness of his theories, but much interest both in exploring ideas and in encouraging students to develop in their own directions.

Tolman himself put it best. His final theoretical statement appeared in the same book as Guthrie's (and he and Guthrie died in the same year). He ended his chapter with this concluding statement, which became in a sense the concluding statement of his professional life.

> The system may well not stand up to any final canons of scientific procedure. But I do not much care. I have liked to think about psychology in ways that have proved congenial to me. Since all the sciences, and especially psychology, are immersed in such tremendous realms of the uncertain and the unknown, the best that any individual scientist, especially any psychologist, can do seems to be to follow his own gleam and his own bent, however inadequate they may be. In fact, I suppose that actually this is what we all do. In the end, the only sure criterion is to have fun. And I have had fun. (Tolman 1959, p. 152)

The same casual approach to theorizing that prevented Tolman from founding a school also made it easier for him to present many tentative suggestions about the interpretation of learning. We have noted his openness to other people's ideas, to aspects of learning that many other theorists neglected, and to different formulations of different kinds of learning. As a result, it has been hard for later cognitive theorists to come up with anything that Tolman had not already suggested. Much of the work of later cognitive theorists, therefore, has been either to make ideas quite similar to Tolman's somewhat tighter and more formal, or to continue his efforts to get cognitive approaches more accepted. In both respects they have been quite successful, as we shall see.

TOLMAN'S CONTINUING INFLUENCE

Tolman's immediate effect on the psychology of learning was on the connectionist theories of his time, particularly on Hull. Without Tolman, it would have been easier for the connectionist theorists to go on assuming that of course stimulus-response interpretations of behavior and learning are the correct, scientific ones. Cognitive interpretations would have been easier to dismiss as either the sloppy way that everyday people talked about scientific matters they didn't understand, or the way European psychologists wrote because they were still more influenced by philosophy than by science. Tolman, by his sophistication about intervening variables and his insistence that a cognitive system can still be behavioristic in a broad sense, made American psychologists take cognitive theory seriously.

Taking cognitive theory seriously meant primarily arguing against it, which connectionist theorists did vigorously. However, since they could not simply dismiss Tolman as silly or irrelevant, they needed to do experiments to show that he was wrong. A number of their experiments did indeed show that Tolman's findings were not as general as he supposed, thereby weakening Tolman's argument that even the behavior of rats cannot be adequately explained without cognitive intervening variables. However, others of their experiments confirmed Tolman's findings.

At the same time, connectionist theorists were of course also doing experiments that were not concerned with Tolman, but merely with the development of their own theories. Some of these experiments turned out also to raise questions about strict stimulus-response interpretations, questions that these theorists needed to deal with. Perhaps these findings would have moved the dominant connectionist theories in cognitive directions in any case, but Tolman's influence made such changes seem less radical, and thereby encouraged them. Thus both Tolman's influence and factors internal to connectionist theories led to changes in connectionist theories that moved them in cognitive directions.

Some of these changes were extensions of connectionist theory. Hull deduced from his postulates various theorems that described insightful behavior in rats, the kind of intelligent, flexible navigation in space that Tolman emphasized. Others of these changes were actual modifications in directions that brought them closer to Tolman. Nevertheless, despite such changes during the 1940s and 1950s, the mainstream of American learning theory remained connectionist and regarded its concessions to cognitive theory as minor adjustments.

Tolman also gave encouragement to cognitive approaches, and a number of psychologists did research and wrote with a cognitive bias. An example is the work of Krechevsky, a student and later a colleague of Tolman's at the University of California. Krechevsky, studying discrimination learning in rats, challenged the traditional connectionist interpretation that discrimination learning involves attaching responses to specific stimuli. He suggested that rats instead form hypotheses about how to predict where food will be. They then test these hypotheses until they find one that consistently predicts the location of food correctly. This cognitive view of rats as rational, problem-solving creatures is obviously one that Tolman approved.

How could one tell whether rats are forming and testing hypotheses? Suppose a rat is presented with a complex discrimination problem in a T-maze, a simple maze offering a single choice between the two arms of the T. Food is always in one arm of the maze or the other but not both. On some trials the left arm has a little hurdle over which the rat must jump, while on other trials the right arm has the hurdle. There are thus four possible simple rules as to where the food will be on a given trial: on the left, on the right, in the arm with the hurdle, or in the arm without the hurdle, in addition to various possible more complex rules. Each such possible rule represents a hypothesis that a rat might have. When a rat has a particular hypothesis, said Krechevsky, it will go consistently to whichever arm the hypothesis predicts will have food on that trial (e.g., to the left arm regardless of whether it has the hurdle). If after a while this hypothesis turns out not to lead consistently to food, the rat will try a different hypothesis (e.g., to the arm with the hurdle regardless of which side it is on). When the rat tries the correct hypothesis, that hypothesis will be confirmed, so the rat will continue to follow it.

In the experiment just described, with "choose the hurdle" as the correct solution, Krechevsky (1932) demonstrated that rats did indeed choose one side consistently for some time (with the result that they got rewarded only half the time) before discovering the correct (hurdle) solution and thereby getting rewarded every time. Though this finding is consistent with Krechevsky's own hypothesis (that rats have hypotheses), it does not demonstrate conclusively that they do. Perhaps the rats just prefer turning right (or left) and therefore keep doing so until the habit strength for going to the hurdle gets strong enough to overcome that preference. The rat's consistent choice of one side would thus not be due to anything as cognitive as a hypothesis, but merely to a bias toward making one response rather than the other. Connectionists like Hull considered that explanation more plausible than Krechevsky's.

How could one choose between these two explanations? If Krechevsky was right that the rats chose one side consistently because they were testing the hypothesis that food was always on that side, then the rats should not learn anything about whether going to the hurdle was reinforced until they gave up their hypothesis about the side and instead started testing the hypothesis that the food was on whichever side had the hurdle. Hull maintained, however, that habit strength for going to the hurdle was building up even when the rat was going consistently to one side. Since Hull claimed that habit strengths built up continuously, his position was called the *continuity position*, while Krechevsky's position was called the *noncontinuity position*.

Various methods were used to find out whether rats actually did learn anything about one cue (such as hurdles) while they were consistently responding to a different cue (such as position on the left or right). A long controversy ensued, called the *continuity controversy*. Different methods of studying the question to some extent gave different results (Woodworth & Schlosberg, 1954). Though the continuity position probably came out a little ahead in research on rats (Osgood, 1953), the noncontinuity position obtained strong support from studies of human problem solving (Levine, 1970). So, although the cognitive approach to discrimination learning was not greatly strengthened by this line of research, it did gain some additional publicity and respectability.

As they gathered data like this and argued about what the data meant, cognitive psychologists liked to joke that being a little cognitive is like being a little pregnant. In other words, even if much of behavior can be explained adequately in purely connectionist ways, as long as even a little of it can only be explained by cognitions, something must be wrong with connectionist theory. Such arguments kept the controversy lively, but cognitive psychologists were still much in the minority. The field was dominated by Hull and later by Skinner, not by those in Tolman's tradition. Nevertheless, a major change in a cognitive direction had begun, and was soon to revolutionize the field.

THE COGNITIVE REVOLUTION

The change came after Tolman's death. The cognitive approach, so long an embattled minority position, began to occupy more of the American stage. To some extent, this happened because of developments in fields other than learning. One such field was perception. This area of psychology was well suited to a cognitive approach, since its dependent variables were largely people's descriptions and interpretations of what they saw or heard. Such dependent variables lend themselves more readily to cognitive intervening variables—what the observers think they are seeing—than do dependent variables like running and eating and working. In an earlier period, interest in perception gave rise to gestalt psychology, and more recently it gave rise to *information processing*, the study of how we convert information from stimuli into interpretations of what we are perceiving and what it means.

Another field that contributed to the increase in cognitive interpretations was one outside psychology: linguistics, the study of language. Within linguistics, interest was shifting from the comparison of different languages and the history of their development to the analysis of how individuals acquire and use language. This more recent interest of linguists is of course also of interest to psychologists, as is indicated by Skinner's (1957*b*) book, *Verbal Behavior.* Indeed, one of the landmarks in the new approach to linguistics was a scathingly negative review of *Verbal Behavior* by the linguist Noam Chomsky (1959). One aspect of this approach to linguistics that particularly interested psychologists was how we understand the language we read or hear. How do we decide whether the word *bat* in a given sentence refers to an animal or to a device for hitting a ball? Why are some complex sentences still easy to understand, while others are almost incomprehensible? As with perception, these questions are concerned rather directly with the way we understand and interpret the world, and thus fit a cognitive approach better than they do a connectionist one.

The result of these and other influences was a major change in the theoretical bias of American psychology. The cognitive approach, so long a relatively minor influence, became dominant, while the connectionist approach, so long the mainstream view in the field, was largely displaced. This transformation became known as the *cognitive revolution.*

Sources of the Revolution

When did the cognitive revolution happen? That is a hard question to answer precisely. Even though the change was rapid in contrast to the long previous period of connectionist dominance, it still took place over a number of years. One significant date was 1960, when a book was published with the Tolmanian-sounding title: *Plans and the Structure of Behavior* (Miller, Galanter, & Pribram, 1960). This book argued in considerable detail that behavior is best analyzed, not in terms of responses or even of operants, but of plans for carrying out certain activities to achieve certain goals. If we call these plans "cognitions about what behaviors will achieve certain purposes," the similarity to Tolman is clear.

Another significant date was 1962, when Robert Gagné (b. 1916) published an article on the application of learning principles to military training (Gagné, 1962). When he first worked on such applications, the sorts of things he tried were drawn from behaviorism: providing immediate reinforcement, making the crucial stimuli as distinctive from each other as possible, and the like—approaches that Skinner would have approved. However, these approaches turned out not to be as useful as most learning theorists would have expected. Some were simply not applicable to a given learning task, and those that were, all too often made relatively little difference in rate of learning.

What did help in training was an analysis of tasks into their component parts. The psychologist needs to ask the following kinds of questions: "What items of knowledge and skill must a person have in order to do this job?" "How do these items of knowledge and skill depend on one another in such a way that certain ones should be learned before others?" "Into what more basic components can these items be analyzed, and how are they in turn organized?" The answers to these questions tell the psychologist what needs to be taught, in what order, and to some extent how. Thus Gagné, starting from a traditional behaviorist position, soon found himself trying to analyze the cognitive structure of learners. We will return to his analysis in Chapter 12.

A third significant date was 1967, in which Ulrich Neisser (b. 1928) published the book *Cognitive Psychology* (Neisser, 1967). In this book Neisser discussed a number of topics, particularly ones related to perception but also including thinking and language, from a cognitive point of view. What was most important about the book was that it brought together the various threads that had been developing, noted their common focus on cognitions, and defined both an area of and an approach to psychology. Many people would therefore date the cognitive revolution from 1967.

That date may still be too early, however, for a revolution that made the cognitive approach dominant over the connectionist. By that date the Skinnerian approach, though a major influence, had not yet replaced the Hullian approach as the chief expression of behaviorism. Many psychologists, if told in 1967 that a revolution had just swept the cognitive approach ahead of both the Hullian and the Skinnerian, would have reacted with puzzled amusement—"Says who?" To a considerable extent their puzzlement and amusement would have been justified, since Neisser's book indicated merely that the cognitive approach had become a more serious challenge to the connectionist approach than ever before, not that it had become *the* dominant approach.

However, their reaction also reflects the fact that it took longer for the cognitive approach to become dominant in the study of learning than in such other branches of psychology as perception and thinking. Probably this difference resulted from so much of the research on learning being with animal subjects. When human subjects tell you what they see or what they are thinking, cognitive interpretations are more natural than when all you can observe is what an animal does. Learning thus became one of the last branches of psychology to show the full influence of the cognitive revolution.

Causes of the Revolution

What caused the cognitive revolution? Considering how extreme the traditional connectionist behaviorist theories were in their rejection of anything cognitive, we might better ask why it took so long to come. The "person in the street" has traditionally used both connectionist terms ("I just did it automatically, by habit") and cognitive ones ("I knew that had to be the way to fix it because I understood how it works"), but with the cognitive being more frequent. Tolman and other cognitive theorists gave the cognitive type of interpretation some respectability, yet a quarter of a century after Tolman's *Purposive Behavior in Animals and Men*, connectionist interpretations were still firmly in control. Why?

The main explanation seems to be that psychologists wanted very much for their young field to be scientific. It was not enough that they use the scientific method; they must also have theories that fit comfortably in the natural-scientific view of the world. Their argument went something like this. "Biology tells us that learning depends on the nervous system, which consists of neurons that sometimes send impulses and sometimes do not. A psychological explanation of learning must be consistent with this biological explanation, and what could fit better than stimulus-response connections that are sometimes active and sometimes not? If we talk instead about beliefs and ideas and such similar vague, mentalistic entities, we will lose our connection with the world of science and become instead part of philosophy." Since psychology had only recently separated from philosophy, returning to philosophy seemed like a serious threat to its newfound status. Thus connectionist theories continued to hold sway beyond the point at which one might reasonably have expected cognitive interpretations to be more widely accepted.

Why, then, did the cognitive revolution finally come, and come when it did? We have already seen various developments in perception and in linguistics that helped to create a fertile environment for it. However, the single biggest factor in encouraging the cognitive revolution was probably the rise of computers. As a piece of engineering, a computer is a connectionist device, with elements that do or do not pass current. However, many of the things that computers have been programed to do seem quite cognitive. It is to these "electronic brains" that we now turn.

Chapter
10

Cognitions, Computers, and Production Systems

S ince their origin during World War II, computers have become ever more widespread, powerful, and important to society. What would now be considered a child's starter computer has more processing capacity than the roomful of vacuum tubes that constituted the world's first true computer. From weather research to business record-keeping to military planning, it has become hard to imagine society functioning without them. At the same time, they take the blame for everything from mistakes in billing to students' failures to get their assignments finished on time to the alleged dehumanization of society. For better or for worse, in the past half century they have become a crucial factor in society.

What have they meant to psychology? For one thing, of course, they have made old types of research easier to do and made new types of research possible for the first time. For another, they have provided a way to trace the implications of a theory, making more complex predictions from a set of postulates than was previously possible. Third, they have provided a metaphor for human thought, a way of talking about how we think, that has influenced theory-building in cognitive psychology. Comparing how humans and computers process information and solve problems has become important enough in psychology so that we may say, only partly in jest, that psychologists study three kinds of organisms: humans, animals, and computers.

WHAT COMPUTERS CAN DO

The phenomenal rise in the use of computers in the past third of a century has had several effects on psychology. Computers are used to analyze data, to generate stimuli for experimental subjects, to present instructional programs, and to perform various other tasks. For theorists, a particularly interesting application has been the attempt to draw an analogy between the operation of computers and the operation of the human intellect. Computers carry on various processes that bear marked resemblances to human learning, remembering, and thinking. Can the way that computers carry on these processes tell us anything about how humans do so?

Robots

In these days of computerized games it may be appropriate to begin with a relatively simple connectionist "toy," not even using a computer. A small machine can be built, far less complicated than a computer, that will behave like a real organism in that it moves around, seeks certain goals, avoids others, and demonstrates simple forms of learning. Walter (1953) produced such a machine several decades ago and named it (imitating biological taxonomy) *Machina docilis* (the teachable machine). This little machine would ride around on its wheels, approaching lights of moderate intensity and moving away from very bright lights. It could be conditioned to approach a whistle that was paired with the turning on of a "reinforcing" light, and this conditioning was subject to both extinction and forgetting. It would avoid obstacles, show "fear" of a stimulus that had been paired with a kick, and behave ambivalently toward other members of its "species." In the days before computers became widespread, when the behavior of machines was widely regarded as something completely different from the behavior of living organisms, such a machine constituted quite a striking demonstration. Even after looking at its wiring diagram, one tended to feel that there was something magical about a "mere machine" behaving in so lifelike a fashion. Now, when computers have taken over many business operations and computerized robots are a stock-in-trade of movies and television, some of the magic has gone out of such a demonstration, but it has still not completely lost its power to beguile us.

As computers have become smaller, it has become increasingly practical to use them in the design of robots, so that more recent robots have far more "intellectual power" than *M. docilis*. One example, created in the late 1960s, was named Shakey. Whereas *M. docilis* was designed to resemble an animal, Shakey was designed to resemble a human manual laborer. Its principal job was moving and stacking boxes. Though this might be considered "mindless labor" for a human, it requires quite sophisticated behavior from a machine. Shakey had to perceive the environment well enough to locate boxes, avoid obstacles, and know in which of eight rooms it was located at any given time. Shakey had to be able to pick up a box, carry it into another room, and put it on another box stably enough so that the stack would not fall over. Given such a moving job to do, it had to figure out just what sequence of moves would accomplish the task. Moreover, it could remember such a plan and use it again later in another context.

Twenty years later, Shakey had a successor, Flakey, that seemed to demonstrate relatively little improvement on Shakey (Brooks, 1991). Knowing what complex operations computers can perform, we might think such simple manual labor would be trivial for a computerized robot. Why didn't Shakey do something more impressive?

On the one hand, computers are best at calculating and at making logical decisions, activities that many humans find difficult. On the other hand, computers have difficulty doing things that are simple for most humans, such as recognizing patterns in a visual display and making well-coordinated movements in a variable environment. In other words, when the input and the output are simple, computers can do impressive jobs of processing the information in between, but both getting the information and controlling the output are difficult. Shakey's abilities thus represent more of an achievement than we might at first think.

One example of such limitations of computerized robots is their form of locomotion. Like *M. docilis,* Shakey rode on wheels. Given the number of stair steps in most human environments, walking on legs would have made these robots more adaptable. However, walking is a complex operation that, however natural for humans, is a major problem for robots, even with the power of computers. The robots of fantasy, striding skillfully on insectlike legs, are being developed, but in the meantime robots do much better on wheels. Whereas people joke about "reinventing the wheel," robots have only partly succeeded in reinventing legs.

Computer Problem Solving

For the most part, computer analogs have been of more complex, cognitive processes. They typically involve problem solving, game playing, language comprehension, and the like—not so much models of learning per se as of those behaviors that in humans are the results of learning. A number of them are discussed in Feigenbaum and Feldman (1963) and in Schank and Colby (1973). One impressive model is the Logic Theorist developed by Newell, Shaw, and Simon (1958). This is a computer program whose function is, given the postulates of geometry, to prove certain theorems. The manner in which it goes about doing so is quite comparable to what a good high school geometry student does. It works forward from theorems already proved to try to find ways of turning one of them into the theorem to be proved. It works backward from the to-be-proved theorem to other statements which, if true, would permit the proof, and then treats these statements as subgoals to be proved. Clearly, it deals with cognitive structures rather than with stimulus-response connections. Though Logic Theorist's concern with postulates and theorems would appeal to Hull, Tolman would feel more at home with its mode of operation than most of the other theorists we have discussed, and Wertheimer might be proud of its creative problem solving.

Soon after Newell, Shaw, and Simon developed Logic Theorist, it was expanded to deal with a wider variety of problems. The result was known, appropriately, as General Problem Solver, or GPS (Ernest & Newell 1969). A problem may be regarded as any discrepancy between an actual state of affairs and a corresponding desired state of affairs, and the job of a problem solver is to reduce that discrepancy. In real life, problems vary from "I am in Chicago and want to be in New York, but a snowstorm has closed O'Hare Airport; How can I get to New York?" to "I need an A in organic chemistry to get into medical school, but at this rate I'll be lucky to get even a B; How can I raise my grade?" Though a computer program to solve such problems for us would indeed be useful, illustrations of how GPS works are generally more artificial problems. They are, however, still challenging enough to keep most people occupied (and sometimes frustrated) for at least a few minutes. Here are two examples of problems that GPS can solve:

PROBLEM 1

Present state: There are three missionaries and three cannibals on one side of a river.

Desired state: To have all six of them on the other side.

Difficulties: The only way across is by a boat that can carry only two people at a time and must always have at least one person to row it (i.e., it cannot cross the river empty). If more cannibals than missionaries are ever left together on one side while the boat is crossing, the cannibals will eat the missionaries. (Getting missionaries across in cannibals' stomachs is not considered a solution!)

Question: What sequence of crossings with the boat will accomplish the transfer?[*]

PROBLEM 2

Present state:
$$
\begin{array}{r}
\text{D O N A L D} \\
+ \text{G E R A L D} \\
\hline
\text{R O B E R T}
\end{array}
$$

Desired state: An example of correct addition in which one particular numeral corresponds to each of the letters above.

Difficulty: The codebook to tell what numeral each of the above letters represents is lost, and we know only that D = 5.

Question: What code will convert the letters into numerals to give a correct example of addition? (Simon & Newell 1971)[†]

A computer program that can solve problems as different from one another as logic proofs and the puzzles above is clearly quite an accomplishment, and GPS is one of several that can. Nevertheless, some people feel that problems of this sort are rather trivial. Humans have been able to analyze completely the various possible approaches to these problems and to say which will work efficiently, inefficiently, or not at all, so perhaps it is not such a wonder that computers can be programmed to find a solution. However, computers have also been programmed to work on problems that no one has been able to analyze so exhaustively. Chess playing is probably the most famous example, one in which computers have done remarkably well. Though the prediction that someday the world's chess champion would be a computer program has not yet been fulfilled, in 1996 a program called Deep Blue won a game from world champion Garry Kasparov, the first time a program had done so under standard tournament conditions. Though Kasparov rallied to win the match with three wins and two draws out of six games, the event brought the possibility of a computer as world champion a step closer.

---

[*]The boat crossed five times, each time carrying one missionary and one cannibal. The first and fourth times a missionary brings the boat back; the second and third times a cannibal. (There are numerous versions of this problem, varying in difficulty.)

[†]The solution is as follows:
$$
\begin{array}{r}
526485 \\
197485 \\
\hline
723970
\end{array}
$$

Even though a computer can search the implications of many possible moves very quickly, it cannot win by that power alone. Fast as it is, it still cannot come anywhere near to following every possible sequence of moves through to eventual victory or defeat; there are just too many possible combinations of moves in the course of a game. The program must therefore recognize, as a human player does, which situations are promising and which are threatening and then try to create or avoid those situations. In other words, it "understands" that it is typically desirable to trade a knight for a rook or to threaten the opponent's king, but undesirable to lose one's queen or to have one's own king put in check. Each sequence of possible moves is then analyzed according to whether it leads to desirable or undesirable consequences within the next few moves.

Though human players and computer programs are alike in that they examine and evaluate various possible moves, it does not follow that they do so in just the same way. Computers, because of their great speed, can examine more total moves. They are less efficient, however, in deciding which possible moves to explore most deeply. As a result, they tend to play rather uninspired chess (as do most human players), with little ability to formulate long-range strategy. The best human players can usually beat the best chess programs partly because of such long-range strategy and partly because of having gradually learned the significance of a great many specific chess positions—which are favorable, which are risky, which call for a particular move or series of moves. Programs might obtain such detailed knowledge about chess positions either by having it included in the original program or by being programmed to learn by experience (an approach discussed, though not specifically for chess, in Chapter 11). So far, neither approach has been altogether successful, so the greatest advantage of these programs is still their speed in exploring possible moves. These similarities and differences between human players and computer programs, and their implications for understanding both people and computers, are explored in Frey (1983).

Though these examples suggest (correctly) that computers are more effective thinkers than one would have imagined 50 years ago that any machine could be, they are a long way from being able to do all that humans can do. One of their conspicuous failures is translating from one language into another. Fairly early in the development of computers, it looked as though they should be ideally suited for translation. To translate Russian into English, for example, you should need only to provide the computer with a Russian-English dictionary and to program it with appropriate grammatical rules. These hopes have not, however, been realized. The main reason for the failure is that the meaning of a sentence cannot be determined by vocabulary and grammar alone. Does "We don't have enough different woods" refer to a shortage of forest preserves, cabinet-making materials, or golf clubs? It depends on the context. Does "That kills me!" mean that the speaker is dying? Fortunately not in most cases. Because of such ambiguities, a passage translated into a foreign language and then translated back again by another person may be unrecognizable, as when "He shot off his mouth without thinking" comes back as "He absentmindedly fired a bullet into his jaw!" Given such difficulties, it is understandable that computerized translation has not yet achieved great success.

Efforts to make computers better problem solvers are continuing. Recently Newell and a new set of collaborators developed a program called SOAR (for "State, Operator, and Result") that goes well beyond GPS (Waldrop 1988*a*, *b*). It provides better ways of resolving indecision about what step to take at any given point, and it can store the solution to a problem efficiently for future use. SOAR is currently being tried out in a number of contexts and modified in various ways. (Presumably Hull would have approved.) How well it can solve the various difficulties we have considered remains to be seen.

COMPUTERS AND LEARNING THEORY

What do computer programs tell us about the actual processes of learning and thinking in living organisms? Nothing directly; as just noted, the fact that a computer can be programmed to learn or think by certain processes does not demonstrate that either humans or rats learn or think by the same processes. What these programs can show are the implications of certain assumptions about how organisms learn. A theorist can write a computer program to follow the laws of learning that he or she thinks organisms follow, then run the program to see what happens. If what happens is similar to the outcome of human or animal learning, this finding makes it more plausible that humans or animals do in fact follow those hypothesized processes when they learn. If what happens is quite different from the outcome of "real" learning, the theorist's assumptions are probably false. Thus the computers provide a more precise way of doing what Hull wanted to do; if he had made use of computers he might have avoided some of the contradictions in his system. The role of the computer program is much like that of mathematical analysis—not to change the logic of theory construction, but to carry out that logic more precisely and more thoroughly.

Though most psychologists working with computers have not been concerned primarily with the arguments between connectionist and cognitive theorists, their work is quite relevant to that controversy. As a piece of engineering, a computer is a connectionist "organism"; its chips, which do or do not pass currents, are comparable to neurons in the nervous system that do or do not fire. At a molecular level, therefore, a connectionist analysis of a computer would be accurate. At the molar level, however, what we mainly note is the computer's ability to store and retrieve information, reason logically, break problems into sub-problems, and otherwise behave in very cognitive ways. A computer is thus a basically connectionist "organism" that gets programmed to operate in cognitive ways. If a "mere machine," built by humans from basically connectionist parts, can operate so effectively in such cognitive ways, cognitions can scarcely be as unscientifically mentalistic as earlier psychologists feared. Perhaps, indeed, there may be a resolution of the connectionist-cognitive argument in the definition of a human being as "the only movable, general-purpose computer that can be produced by unskilled labor!"

In the case of computers, the programming is done by humans. How do humans themselves get programmed? Their programming takes place through a lifetime of experience, some of it arranged deliberately by parents and teachers, some of it happening without anyone having planned it, and some resulting from each person's efforts to improve him- or herself. However, the "programming" of a person differs from the programming of a computer in that with humans the new learning cannot completely override all the earlier learning. In some cases this is unfortunate, as when someone in an emergency momentarily forgets his more recent learning and makes a mistake that he had been "programmed" not to make. However, this same feature of human learning means that we are never under the complete control of any one "programmer." This same difference from computers that makes humans in some ways less effective thus also contributes to our individuality and autonomy.

At first our "programs" are simple, but they soon get combined into more complex ones. A computer program often includes a command to call some simpler program to do a particular job needed by the larger program. Similarly, a person working on a large task can draw on previously learned ability to do smaller tasks that contribute to the larger one. For example, a carpenter's "program" for building a bookcase will be full of specifications to saw a board or pound a nail. The details of these actions do not need to be spelled out, since the carpenter is already thoroughly familiar with how to do them and can take the details for granted. When the appropriate point in his "program" for the bookcase arrives, the carpenter simply has to note that the board should be sawed, and his previously learned "subprogram" of skills will take care of it, after which the main program continues on its way.

The analysis in terms of programs and subprograms could be extended to more than two levels, with programs made up of subprograms and in turn combined into larger programs. The result would be a hierarchy of knowledge or skills at different levels, each depending on those lower in the hierarchy. We will see more about such hierarchies in Chapter 12.

ANDERSON'S ACT THEORY

One way in which computers have influenced learning theory is by providing a general analogy for use in theorizing. Just as earlier theorists interpreted humans as animals and both humans and animals as simple stimulus-response mechanisms, more recent theorists have analyzed people, and sometimes animals, as "wet computers," doing by means of neurons what computers do by means of chips. Since some of the things that computers do sound rather cognitive, such as storing information in their memories and making decisions on the basis of that information, these computer-based models are much closer to traditional cognitive than to traditional connectionist theories. They also take seriously the challenge to cognitive theories to show how cognitions give rise to actual behavior. As a result, some of them are called *production systems*, theories that attempt to show how cognitions actually produce action.

One such theory is appropriately called ACT, developed by John R. Anderson (b. 1947) of Carnegie-Mellon University (Anderson 1982, 1983, 1987, 1993). The theory has gone through various revisions, of which the most recent is called ACT-R, but we will simply use the general term ACT, which stands for Adaptive Control of Thought.

Declarative and Procedural Knowledge

Central to ACT theory is a distinction between two kinds of knowledge, designated as declarative and procedural. *Declarative knowledge* is what we usually call knowledge: propositions that are true. We may think of it as descriptions of the world, or as answers to questions, or as "knowing that." *Procedural knowledge* is the ability to carry out procedures appropriately. We may think of it as skill, or as "knowing how."

Procedural knowledge consists of rules of the form "If A is the case, then do B." Simple examples are "If you see a red traffic light, then stop at the edge of the intersection" and "If you want to know the time, then look at your watch." Slightly more complex examples would be "If you are hungry, and if you are far from home, and if you have money, then look for a restaurant" and "If you are adding a series of numbers, and if the sum of the right-hand column is at least 20 but less than 30, then record the last digit of that sum and carry a 2 to the next column."

It is not easy to provide procedural rules that will work for all cases where the "if" part of the rule applies, since the best rule to follow often depends on so many different factors. One way of dealing with this problem is to make rules more and more complex and specific by adding more and more "if" clauses to them. In principle, the process could be carried further and further until there were a large number of specific rules covering every possible situation.

However, this might not be a very efficient production system. It often works better to have both a simple general rule and a few exceptions. For example, so many English words form their plural by adding *s* that the most effective production system is to have the general rule "If you want to make a singular noun plural, then add an *s* at the end," plus a number of specific rules such as "If you want to form the plural of *man*, write *men*." The production system for plurals works by using a specific rule if there is one, and otherwise the general rule.

What reason is there to think that there really is an important distinction between declarative and procedural knowledge? Anderson gives several reasons, of which the most dramatic comes from *amnesics*, people who suffer from disorders of memory due to brain damage. One type, *anterograde amnesics*, generally have reasonably good memory for things they knew before the brain damage, but none for experiences since then. They can be introduced to the same person daily for months without remembering that person's name or even that they have ever met.

When this condition was first noted, it appeared that anterograde amnesics were simply incapable of any new learning. This turned out, however, to be an overstatement of their deficit. They did learn to find their way around the hospital, even though they had no recollection of having been there before. Moreover, they showed roughly normal learning of certain motor tasks. For example, it is quite difficult for normal people to trace a complex shape while guiding themselves by watching their own performance in a mirror. Because the mirror reverses the image, they constantly move the pencil in the wrong direction. However, with practice they gradually get better and better at the task. The same is true of these amnesics. Though each time they do the task they deny ever having done it before, they become more and more skillful with practice. In Anderson's terms, they have the capacity to learn procedural knowledge (skill) but not declarative knowledge (information).

As with so many distinctions, that between declarative and procedural memory is not always easy to make. Is it that declarative can be expressed in words but procedural cannot? Usually, but not always, since humans can have declarative knowledge of what something looks like without being able to describe it clearly in words, and animals can have declarative knowledge about their environments. Is procedural anything that amnesics can learn and declarative anything they cannot? No, amnesics are too diverse a group to use them for a technical definition. Anderson says that the distinction can only be made completely in the context of the theory, and the way he does so shows how much computers have influenced ACT theory. Declarative knowledge, he says, provides the data that are input, while procedural provides the operations that the person, like a computer, performs on those data.

When a person acquires a new ability, the process usually begins with acquiring declarative knowledge. This knowledge is acquired by observation, but Anderson has little to say about the details of how it is learned. Presumably it includes not only what we observe directly but also what we are told and what we read. However acquired, declarative knowledge represents the basis from which procedural knowledge develops.

Before we look in more detail at procedural knowledge and at how it develops out of declarative knowledge, we should note how different this idea is from traditional behavioristic notions. Behaviorists start with items of behavior (responses or operants or acts) and ask how they are learned. These are procedures; collectively they make up what Anderson calls procedural knowledge. What he calls declarative knowledge, including knowledge and beliefs and memories of experiences, is quite secondary in behaviorism. Some behaviorists ignore it and the rest treat it as derived from behavior. Even Tolman puts behavior first and sees cognitions (i.e., such declarative knowledge as where certain things are located) as being learned largely from behavior. Anderson, however, sees declarative knowledge as acquired first and then used to develop procedures for dealing with the world. He thus carries the cognitive approach to learning further even than Tolman. Teachers who tell their students it is important to acquire knowledge so that it will be available when needed to solve problems should be delighted with Anderson's approach.

If we ask ourselves how declarative knowledge can be used to develop specific procedures, we might come up with various ideas about how to reason from what is true (declarative) to what will work for a given goal (procedural). Indeed, we might look at all the ways in which the fields of engineering, medicine, and other forms of applied science go from basic knowledge to useful applications. In earlier versions of ACT, Anderson was open to such a variety of answers for explaining how to get from declarative to procedural. In the latest version, however, he maintains that it can happen in only one way, by taking a particular example of what has worked in the past, stored in declarative memory, and applying it to the present case. To understand how this works, we will now look at procedural memory and then work backward to the declarative memory from which it comes.

Problem Solving

Consider a person seeking a certain goal. How can this person achieve it? In all but the simplest cases, he or she must first select some subgoal that is likely to move the person closer to the final goal and that he or she can probably achieve directly. As noted earlier in this chapter, subgoals are often identified by working backward from the final goal, as when we say, "If I could find the meaning of this one key word (subgoal), then I could translate the whole sentence (final goal)." Subgoals may also be identified by working forward from where you are in directions that you hope will move you toward the final goal. In a geometric proof, for example, you might say: "I already know that angle ABC = angle XYZ; Now what follows from that about anything else in the figure?" (As you may have noticed, what is called a "final goal" for one purpose may itself be a subgoal toward some larger purpose.) Reaching the final goal may require going through a whole series of subgoals, but at any one time you are working toward a particular subgoal that seems to be both easier to reach now than the final goal and likely to help in reaching the final goal.

Next, one must find an act (a procedure, in Anderson's terms) that is likely to achieve that subgoal. As noted above, all procedural knowledge is organized in if-then instructions: "If a certain set of conditions is met, then take a certain action." To try to reach the subgoal, the person goes through all the procedures he or she can think of that have the right "if" structure. In order to qualify, a procedure must refer in its "if" both to the subgoal and to the particular conditions that currently apply. For example, if you want to light a fire in your fireplace, but can't find a match, you would first search your procedural knowledge for procedures that begin with "If your goal is to start a fire and you don't have a match . . . " The first one you came to might continue: "and you have a cigarette lighter, then strike the lighter." However, if you didn't have a lighter either, you would have to reject this procedure because its "if" clause didn't fit the actual conditions. Perhaps the next procedure you came to would continue: "and you have a gas stove that lights automatically, then turn on the gas and hold a piece of paper in the flame." You do have that kind of a stove, so this is a possible procedure for getting to the goal.

However, you would not necessarily proceed at once. Perhaps you would find other procedures that also fit the goal and the conditions. For example, another might be: "If your goal is to light a fire and you don't have a match but you do have an electric soldering iron, plug it in, wait until it is hot, and then hold it against the paper in the fireplace." Now you have two possible procedures and need to decide which one to try. According to Anderson, you would choose the one for which your experience with that procedure indicated that the chance of success, minus the cost, was greatest. In the present example, you might decide that the soldering iron had the greater chance of success, since the stove is so far from the fireplace that the paper might burn out before you got to the fireplace, but that the soldering iron would also have greater cost, since it would take more time to set it up and get it hot. Taking these and other factors into account, you would decide which to try.

In going through such a search, eventually one of two things happens. In some cases the best among the alternatives appears good enough, and you try it. In other cases, none of the available procedures seems likely to succeed, or any that does seem likely to succeed carries such a cost (such as risk of burning the house down) that you are unwilling to try it. You will therefore need to proceed in some other way.

At this point it is important to note that the procedures being compared are ones that the person has used in similar cases in the past, not merely ideas about what seems in principle as though it might work. The person therefore has actually practiced the necessary skill. So, although you need to decide whether to try it, you do not need to find out how to do it.

However, there is no guarantee that every procedure whose "if" fits the requirements will even show up in the search. Every procedure has a certain strength. Whenever the procedure is used, it is strengthened. Whenever a period of time passes without its being used, it is weakened by forgetting. (Anderson, like Hull, gives equations for the details of these two processes.) Therefore, only those procedures that currently have a certain strength will even get considered for possible use.

If no procedure that you come up with seems likely to achieve the goal at a reasonable cost, what next? You must then turn to your declarative memory. Whereas you previously searched your procedural memory for an actual procedure that you had used in the past, you now search your declarative memory for an experience in which you observed or heard about a successful solution to a similar problem. If you find one or more, you choose the one closest to the present problem and generate an actual procedure from it. If it works, you then have a new procedure available for solving such problems in the future. If it fails, you can try doing the same with another example from your declarative memory until you run out of examples that are close enough to be worth trying.

Being able to use declarative memory gives one a great advantage. You can potentially draw on a great deal of information from many sources. Moreover, the examples do not need to be very close to the problem at hand; they merely need to be analogous in some way. In the present case, an example need not necessarily have anything to do with fire; it might instead be concerned with what to do when you need something you lack. This line of search might lead you to find someone from whom you could borrow a match, or to go to a store from which you could buy matches.

Converting an example into a procedure, however, is not always straightforward. Having heard of, or even seen, a fire started by rubbing two sticks does not mean that the person can even go through the right motions, let alone do so successfully. So, although declarative knowledge places great resources for potential problem solving at the person's disposal, it is by no means a complete substitute for the skills of procedural knowledge, which typically require practice. Thus, some of the connectionist approach gets into even this quite cognitive theory.

When the procedure has become part of procedural knowledge, the declarative knowledge is no longer needed in order to carry out the procedure. The normal process of forgetting therefore takes over. If the declarative information is still being used for something else, such as answering questions, it will be retained, otherwise it will be gradually, though not completely, lost. Then one has the case of the person who is very skillful at doing a job but very poor at explaining how it is done, or why it works. Another similar example is a phone number that you dial often on a touch-tone phone but never write or tell to anyone else. Eventually you press the correct sequence of buttons without thinking of the numbers, and if asked to say the number may need to watch your own fingers on the buttons in order to be able to remember. At the beginning of learning you had declarative knowledge but not procedural; in the middle you had both; now you have only procedural.

The whole process of getting from declarative knowledge to smooth, integrated procedural productions is called *knowledge compilation.* The use of this term reflects Anderson's interest in computers as an analog to human thought. Just as a compiler converts instructions to a computer into the machine language with which the computer actually works, so knowledge compilation converts knowledge about the world into the skills of actual productions.

As we consider the various things that happen in problem solving, Anderson seems at times to be analyzing decisions that a person makes by careful conscious thought, such as reasoning by analogy or deciding when a potential solution is good enough; at other times he seems to be analyzing processes that happen automatically, such as remembering and forgetting, without making any distinction between the two. However, neither Anderson nor Tolman would see a problem in treating the two interchangeably. For both of these theorists, what we believe, remember, or decide is a matter of intervening variables. If they are useful in explaining and predicting behavior, they are good. To this Anderson would add that the real test of the theory is how well a computer program based on the theory resembles what people actually do. To worry about what the person is consciously aware of thinking about is to act as though the person's *real* thoughts were somehow different from the processes described by the theory. So far as Tolman and Anderson are concerned, it makes sense to ask whether the behavior the theory predicts is the same as the behavior that people actually show, but it does not make sense to ask whether the processes the theory describes are what people are aware of doing as they solve problems.

Learning

Although procedures originate from declarative memory, they can then become stronger or weaker according to their success in achieving a goal. However, ACT has an unusual feature in this regard. The system makes no distinction between a procedure's leading to success and its producing no indication of either success or failure. On the one hand, whenever a rule is used and nothing happens to indicate that it was wrong, the rule is strengthened—that is, the "if" part of the rule increases its tendency to produce the "then do such and such" part of the rule.

On the other hand, if something happens to indicate that it was a mistake to use the rule in that situation, the rule is weakened; its "if" is less likely to produce the "then do such and such" in the future. The ACT system thus has a mechanism of extinction, but no explicit reference to reinforcement. This places Anderson in contrast with Thorndike, Hull, and Skinner, all of whom regarded reinforcement as of central importance. In this rejection of simple reinforcement theory Anderson is more like Guthrie. However, Guthrie saw extinction as an active process of learning to do something else, whereas Anderson sees extinction as directly weakening the procedure that didn't work. Anderson's view is also in some ways like those of Tolman and Piaget, both of whom would say that the way to change a cognition is to provide disconfirming evidence. Anderson, however, would probably object to that paraphrase of his view, since "disconfirming evidence" sounds like a reference to declarative knowledge, and the above rule applies to procedural knowledge.

We have noted that some production rules are specific and others general. Specific rules become combined into general ones by a process that Anderson considers the same as generalization. He gives two rules as an example: (1) If you want to show that a coat belongs to you, then say "my coat"; (2) if you want to show that a ball belongs to you, then say "my ball." Just from these two rules, the system can generalize a third, much broader rule: If you want to show that any object belongs to you, then say "my [name of object]." In some cases such a new rule will be too general, so discrimination learning will be required before a fully correct rule is developed.

A rule may even be generalized from a single case, but then the risk of overgeneralization is even greater. A learner might reason, for example, that "in German the plural of *Gestalt* is *Gestalten,* so in German plurals are formed by adding *en.*" Since this rule is actually correct for only a minority of German nouns, further discrimination learning would be needed. Since generalization from a single case is a familiar learning phenomenon, this assumption of Anderson's may be good psychology even if it represents poor logic on the part of the learner.

Computers in ACT Theory

Computers figure in Anderson's thinking, and in that of other theorists with similar interests, in at least three ways. One is as a source of ideas. The analogy between the computer and the human brain has provided many hypotheses about how the brain may work, as well as a vocabulary for discussing human cognition. We can see the vocabulary changes in popular as well as technical language, in the way that such words as *input* and *interface* and *network* move back and forth between computer and noncomputer contexts.

The second way is as a means of testing ideas. If a computer is programmed to do what a theorist thinks the human brain does, and the result is what humans actually do, this supports the view that humans reach that result by the same sorts of processes as the computer did. The view is not necessarily true, but the success of the analogy strengthens that hypothesis.

This second use of computers goes beyond merely testing the theory; it also serves in some degree to shape the theory. We noted earlier that the latest version of ACT recognizes only one way of getting from declarative to procedural knowledge—by finding examples of successful problem-solving in the person's declarative knowledge. If Anderson were concerned with broad explanations of how problem-solving and learning work, he would probably have continued to recognize other ways of getting from declarative to procedural, involving the sorts of reasoning that Wertheimer considered (see Chapter 8). However, it would be extremely difficult to make exact predictions about the conditions under which such insightful solutions will or won't occur. In order to make predictions precise enough to put on a computer, Anderson needed to ignore that way of getting from declarative to procedural knowledge, and focus instead on a simpler, more reliable way. The result is a more testable and therefore a more scientific theory, but one that overlooks an important part of what sometimes occurs.

The third way computers figure in theories is in applying them to education. To the extent that theories like ACT give an accurate picture of how people learn and think, we should be able to take advantage of that picture in designing teaching devices. Moreover, these devices might best be in the form of computer programs, programs that present material to the learner in just the way that will make learning most efficient. Anderson and his collaborators have developed such teaching programs for geometry and (appropriately) for computer programming.

How does such a teaching program operate? Consider a student trying to prove a theorem in geometry. When the student takes a step that is both valid and a sensible step toward the final proof, the program makes no response. This lack of response would be inconsistent with Skinner's belief in reinforcement, but is quite consistent with Anderson's view, as given above. If the student takes a step that is either invalid or useless, the program "knows" enough about the structure of the proof to "infer" what the student is mistakenly thinking. It therefore explains to the student where he or she is mistaken. If instead of making a mistake, the student seems unable to think of anything to do, the program tells the student what to do next. (Though such strong prompting might seem to defeat the purpose of active, self-directed learning, Anderson maintains that this is likely to be the best procedure for getting a confused or baffled student back on track.) The computer thus helps the student through the proof very much as a good human tutor would (Anderson, Boyle, & Reiser 1985).

Anderson clearly shares Skinner's interest in the technology of education. Moreover, his approach to computerized tutoring resembles Skinner's programmed instruction in its "close control of the learning process, the immediate feedback during problem solving, the focus on minimizing errors, and the gradual approximation of experts' behavior by accumulation of components of the skill" (Glaser, 1990, p. 32). However, Anderson emphasizes the assumed cognitive processes of the student in a way that Skinner would consider somewhere between pointless and absurd.

Theories like ACT represent the convergence of ideas from several sources. They combine ideas from the long-established fields of psychology and linguistics with those from such newer fields as computer science, cognitive science, and artificial intelligence. Many psychologists in recent years have felt that such theories were just what was needed—a substitute for outmoded behavioristic theories, an improvement on the older cognitive ones, and at last a truly scientific answer to age-old questions about how the mind works. Not everyone has agreed, of course. Skinner, for example, liked to sneer that one can make any topic sound trendy by putting "cognitive" in front of it, as in "cognitive development" or "cognitive social psychology." However, not all the objections have come from theorists attached to older positions. New lines of criticism have also appeared, as we will see in the next chapter.

Chapter
11

The New Connectionism

*T*he analyses of problem solving in the previous chapter involved sequences of actions based on rules. Whatever form these rules took and whether they were used by a person or a computer, they were rational, goal-directed, purposeful. They were highly cognitive, the kinds of operations that would be expected to appeal both to Tolman and to Piaget. They, as much as anything in learning theory, gave the cognitive approach its great impetus.

This was the way computers worked, and theorists came to expect that this was also the way humans worked. For a long time the majority of theorists had regarded cognitive approaches as a bit disreputable, threatening to destroy the scientific respectability of connectionist interpretations. Now here was the computer, a basically connectionist "organism" that could nevertheless be programmed to "think" and act in quite cognitive ways. It is understandable that theorists who were sympathetic to the cognitive approach would feel that its time had come and would use this computer model as an analog to human thinking, helping to usher in what came to be considered the cognitive revolution.

PROBLEMS WITH COMPUTER MODELS

Then, in the 1980s, doubts began to appear. Many sources were responsible for them. One was the discovery that human experts do not solve problems simply by following rules. In fact, it is largely the novices who slavishly follow rules, while experts proceed more intuitively, using their great base of experience to select or eliminate courses of action without having to analyze them in any detail. What they do looks more like making learned responses to stimuli than like inferring actions from principles, though perhaps not a great deal like either.

A second source of doubt came from a consideration of the nervous system. Neurons operate a great deal less quickly than computer chips, and it seemed increasingly unlikely that humans could think as effectively as they do (perhaps we should say "even as effectively as they do") if they operated in the same step-by-step way as computers. However, the neurons in the brain are organized in complex ways, with each connecting with many others, so that it would be possible for the brain to increase its efficiency considerably by having different sets of neurons working on a problem at the same time in various complex ways. Moreover, as psychologists and physiologists studied those animal nervous systems that were simple enough to analyze in detail, they found evidence that they operated more like a network than like the single central processing unit of a computer. Maybe the difference between a computer's hardware and a person's or animal's "wetware" really does make a difference!

A third factor pushing theorists toward a different point of view came from within computer science itself. Computer scientists are constantly trying to devise more and more powerful machines. The amount of computing power that can be concentrated in a given amount of space has been increased dramatically by several engineering changes during the half century or so since the first computer was built. The first computers, made with vacuum tubes, are referred to as the first generation, those with transistors as the second generation, those with transistorized chips as the third, and those with miniaturized chips as the fourth. The next breakthrough, to the fifth generation, involves *parallel processing*, in which different components of the system are working on different parts of a problem at the same time. This, of course, is what we have just suggested that the human brain does. Thus, whereas for some time an attempt has been made to analyze people as if they were computers, now we might say that an effort is being made to design computers to be more like people.

NETWORK MODELS

The combination of these three lines of argument suggested that the nervous system should be analyzed as a network of neurons, multiply interconnected, in which impulses could pass through numerous complex loops, all working together to deal with a situation. Though such ideas were not altogether new, they received a major impetus from the lines of reasoning given above.

Along with this view went another, related one. The earlier computer-oriented views had focused primarily on how a system—human, animal, or computer—operates to solve problems. They had for the most part not concerned themselves with how the system comes to operate that way—that is, with the process of learning. The new approach, however, regarded the process of learning as of central importance. We can see the difference in the way each approach would set up an *expert system*—a computer program designed to do a job as a human expert would (for example, to diagnose illnesses like a medical specialist, or to play chess like a grand master). The older approach would involve discovering the rules a specialist uses for making decisions, and then programming the computer to follow those same rules. The expertness is thus built into the program at the start. The newer approach is to have the program learn from experience, keeping those procedures that work and dropping out those that don't. The system might be very inexpert at the beginning, but since it has perfect memory for its experiences, it would learn fairly rapidly what worked and what didn't. Though it would develop rules of thumb from experience, it would learn by examples rather than be programmed with rules. So, although in some ways it might operate quite cognitively, it would still be a lot like something Thorndike might have imagined.

This relatively new view has not yet focused on a single theory, but is instead a way of constructing specific models of one or another particular learning process. A general term for what this approach assumes goes on in the nervous system is *parallel distributed processing*. The kinds of interpretations it uses are often referred to as *network models*, and the approach is generally called *connectionism*.

Though this modern-day connectionism is obviously related to connectionism in the traditional sense of that word, it is nonetheless considerably different. Whereas the older connectionism referred to connections between stimuli and responses, which were assumed to be fairly simple and direct, the new connectionism refers to the whole interconnectedness of the network. The learning processes that are assumed to take place within a network are often more complicated than even Hull supposed, as well as often more cognitive than any of the older connectionist theorists would have considered. This new connectionism thus combines an emphasis on specific connections and on learning by reinforcement that would have appealed to Thorndike or Hull, with an emphasis on the organized operation of whole systems that would have appealed to a gestalt psychologist.

Two Approaches

Theorists within this general framework have followed two considerably different approaches. Some have focused on the real nervous systems of simple organisms. They analyze in detail how the individual neurons in, for example, a sea snail work together to produce conditioning. The advantage of their approach is that they are dealing with a real organism with real neurons. However, the disadvantage is that they are studying organisms that show only simple forms of learning. If many people feel that even rats are too simple to tell us anything interesting about higher mental processes, how much more so must they feel that way about the study of learning in sea snails!

The other approach has been to try to study more complex networks. However, to study humans directly has proved impractical. Although we can study people's behavior, ask them questions, and make inferences about their cognitive intervening variables, we are limited in our opportunity to study their nervous systems. Though a lot has been learned about human brain processes from studying people with brain damage and people undergoing brain surgery, and from recording electrical and chemical activity in the brain, researchers cannot do the kinds of thorough studies on people that they can do with lower animals. Partly they are limited by the sheer complexity of the human brain. There are more neurons in one human brain than there are people in the world, and the total number of synapses among all those neurons is hard to imagine; it has been estimated at 1,000,000,000,000,000. Another important limit is the ethical and practical impossibility of doing experimental surgery on humans for purely research purposes. The alternative is to construct physical models to imitate human thinking, and study them.

The new connectionist approach assumes that the crucial feature of neural networks is not the biochemistry of the neurons and synapses but rather the patterns in which neurons are interconnected by way of synapses so that they form networks. One can specify the characteristics of such a network, construct a device to act according to those assumptions, and see whether the device shows the expected "learning" (that is, whether its output changes in the predicted way). The logic here is the same as that of constructing and testing any theory or model. The difference is that the model is not just on paper; rather, it is a functioning physical model that goes through the specified operations and then either does or does not show the changes in behavior that are predicted. Like a robot, it provides a technological test of the theoretical model's adequacy.

If the device or working model shows the kind of learning that humans show, one is encouraged to think that the human brain does operate according to the same formal principles as the model, in spite of the many differences between them. However, one never knows for sure. As we noted when looking at Hull's theory, there is always the possibility that the brain and the computer model produce the same results by different processes. What is distinctive about the connectionist approach is not the logic but the particular assumptions of the model.

The principle on which these models operate would seem more familiar to Thorndike or Hull than to the more traditional computer modelers. To begin with, like traditional stimulus-response theories, they are concerned with how we learn to make the appropriate response to a given stimulus. Moreover, the operation by which this learning takes place is in effect reinforcement, since some mechanism is built in to indicate which responses were correct. The tendency of impulses to cross each "synapse" in the network can be set at any initial value, and these values then change as a result of the "reinforcement" mechanism.

An Example: NETtalk

An example of such a system is one called NETtalk. Developed by Terrence J. Sejnowski (b. 1947) of Johns Hopkins University and his collaborators (Sejnowski & Rosenberg 1987; Heppenheimer 1988), it is a system that learns to read aloud. The stimuli are written passages, made up of the 26 letters of the alphabet plus spaces and punctuation. The responses are sounds that resemble speech. A linguist decides what sequence of sounds is the best pronunciation of a written passage. This pronunciation is the "correct" response, which it is the machine's task to try to learn.

At the beginning of a learning session, all the connections in NETtalk are set at random values, unrelated to the correct pronunciations. At first, therefore, the sounds NETtalk makes are gibberish, not only unrelated to the written passage but also quite unlike any understandable speech. After each such effort, some of

NETtalk's connections are strengthened and others weakened in an effort to bring its speech closer to a correct oral reading of the written passage. After many "readings" of the passage, the program begins to sound more like real speech, even though it is still incomprehensible. The first step in that direction is the machine's learning that spaces represent periods of silence that divide the passage into words. Once that is learned, NETtalk's speech sounds more like speech in a foreign language, rather than just like gibberish.

Then the output begins to sound more and more like the actual written passage. First NETtalk distinguishes which letters correspond to vowel sounds and which to consonant sounds. Then it learns more and more about the sounds of particular letters. Eventually, after a number of hours, the computer reads the passage quite understandably. It accomplishes this success not by following preprogrammed rules, like most computer programs, but by creating its own rules through trial, error, correction, and changing strengths of connections between letters and sounds.

When NETtalk has achieved this success, has it simply connected each of the 26 letters of the English written alphabet with one or more phonemes (speech sounds)? No. We all know that English spelling is far too irregular for that to work. Has NETtalk learned the so-called rules of English spelling, such as to pronounce *c* like *k* when it comes before certain vowels and like *s* when it comes before others? To a considerable extent it has, but such traditional rules are both complex and incomplete. Moreover, NETtalk's responses, whether or not they correspond to any describable rules, keep changing to some extent as they encounter new written passages. Has NETtalk simply learned to do whatever works? Yes, but it was actually far from simple, and the result may fit many familiar rules to varying degrees and perhaps even show other regularities that no one yet has thought of stating as rules.

How Does NETtalk Do It?

Needless to say, building a machine that will show such learning is not easy. There were a number of unsuccessful attempts to build such machines in the late 1950s and the 1960s—so unsuccessful, indeed, that the whole approach was abandoned for over a decade. In the 1980s, however, the approach was tried again and has achieved some success, as NETtalk demonstrates.

One thing that has made success possible is that the stimulus units (for NETtalk, each corresponds to a letter) are not connected directly to the response units (for NETtalk, various characteristics of spoken sounds). Instead, the stimulus elements are connected to a set of "hidden units," which in turn are connected to the response units. Each hidden unit is connected to all the stimuli and the responses. Every one of these units in the machine—input, output, or hidden— acts like a neuron in the brain, either firing or not firing when it is stimulated. The hidden units act like intervening variables that give the network extra power, in somewhat the same way that Tolman's and Hull's intervening variables helped their systems.

When NETtalk reads a particular letter, that letter may or may not fire the connection to each of the hidden units with which it is connected. Each hidden unit, as a result, receives stimulation over some of its various connections from different letters, but not over others. The combined stimulation from all of those connections that fire may or may not be enough to get that hidden unit to fire. If the hidden unit does fire, it sends stimulation to a number of response units, representing characteristics of speech sounds. The pattern of firing in the 26 output units determines what speech sound NETtalk makes at that moment.

Each of the connections from an input unit to a hidden unit, and each of those from a hidden unit to an output unit, has a certain *weight*, which is the strength with which it affects the target unit. If the connection from an input unit to a hidden unit has a high weight, then when the input unit fires, it will send strong stimulation to that hidden unit. If, instead, the weight of that connection is low, there will be only weak stimulation to the hidden unit when the input unit fires. Whether or not a given hidden unit fires depends on the combined stimulation that it receives from all input units combined. The same principle applies to stimulation from hidden units to output units.

Each time NETtalk makes a sound and then finds out what the correct sound would have been, the weights of the various connections change. It is these changes that constitute the learning process. However, it is not simply that all connections leading to a correct response are strengthened. Rather, throughout the system, the weights of some connections increase and others decrease, according to the learning rules built into the system. Learning is thus a property, not of single connections, but of the whole system.

Another factor that helps NETtalk is that it does not simply read letter by letter. Rather, the actual stimulus is a given letter in the context of the three previous letters in the written passage and of the three following letters. This characteristic of the system makes it possible for NETtalk to deal with such complexities as the difference, mentioned above, in the pronunciation of *c* before *e* and before *o*. It also helps with such peculiarities of English spelling as the different sounds of *ough* in "through," "though," "plough," "ought," and "tough."

A Smaller Example

NETtalk's learning to talk sounds impressive, but trying to picture how its 80 hidden units and its huge network of connections with changing weights do the job is impossible. However, one can get some sense of how that kind of network operates by considering an extremely simple one, shown in Figure 11.1. This little network has two input units, two hidden units, and one output unit, represented in the diagram by boxes. On any given trial, each of these units may either fire or not. Whether an input unit fires or not depends on external stimulation. (In NETtalk, this meant that an input element fired when its particular letter was presented, and otherwise not.) Connections between units are indicated by arrows from the input to the hidden units and from the hidden to the output units.

The number beside each connection is the weight that it has at this particular point in the learning process. A positive (excitatory) weight means that when the input unit is activated, the connection tends to activate the hidden unit. A negative (inhibitory) weight means, in contrast, that when the input unit is activated,

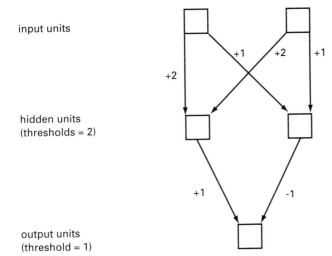

input units

hidden units
(thresholds = 2)

output units
(threshold = 1)

Figure 11.1   A very simple network model. When either of the two input units is fired by external stimulation, it sends a signal with a strength of 2 to the hidden unit on the left and a signal with a strength of 1 to the hidden unit on the right. If the resulting stimulation to a hidden unit is at least 2, that hidden unit fires, otherwise it does not. As a result, the hidden unit on the left will fire whenever either of the input units fires, but the hidden unit on the right will fire only when both input units fire. When the hidden unit on the left fires, it sends a positive (excitatory) signal to the output unit. When the hidden unit on the right fires, it sends a negative (inhibitory) signal to the output unit. Since the output unit requires a net signal of at least 1 to fire, it will fire when only the left hidden unit fires, but not when both hidden units fire. The final result of these two stages is that the output unit will fire if either of the input units alone fires, but not if both of them do. The units, connections, and thresholds are fixed characteristics of the model, but the weights are always subject to change.

the connection tends to prevent the hidden unit from being activated. The size of a weight indicates the strength of that excitatory or inhibitory tendency. In addition, each unit has a *threshold,* which is the minimum amount of net stimulation (positive stimulation minus negative) needed to make that unit fire. Whether the output unit is activated or not depends on the activation of the two input units, but just how it depends on the input units is determined by the weights of the six intervening connections and by the thresholds of the two hidden units and of the output unit.

With the weights shown in the figure, this tiny network has an interesting property. If either one of the input units fires, so will the output unit. However, if both input units fire, the output unit will not. Convincing yourself that this is true by studying the diagram may provide more of a feel for network models. Keep in mind, though, that this network is simpler than almost any that new connectionist modelers actually work with. To bridge the gap from this to somewhat more complex models, interested readers can consult Bechtel and Abrahamsen (1991).

Even for this simple model, we will not try to show the detailed process by which it learned to show this particular behavior. The specific steps through which it went to reach its present state depended on the particular random weights for each connection at which it started. We will consider the process only in general terms.

On each trial, whether the output unit was activated or not is compared with whether it should have been. If the outcome is correct, no learning takes place on that trial. However, if the outcome is incorrect (the output unit either should have been activated but wasn't, or should not have been but was), then the weights of the connections from the hidden units to the output unit are adjusted in the direction that would tend to correct the error. If the output unit was activated when it should not have been, the weights of any connection leading to it that was activated are made less positive or more negative, so that the output unit will be less likely to be activated next time. If, instead, the output unit was not activated when it should have been, the weights of connections leading to it that were activated will be made more positive or less negative, so that the output unit will be more likely to be activated next time.

Moreover, the weights will change similarly for the connections between the input units and the hidden units. If the error by the output unit was due to wrong activation by a hidden unit, the weights of the connections between that hidden unit and the input units will change in the appropriate directions to make that hidden unit fire if it should have or not fire if it shouldn't have. It is the combination of all these adjustments throughout the system that produces the learning.

Some readers may be disturbed at how abstract all these units and weights sound. Hull's intervening variables were abstract enough, you may think, but at least they corresponded to something we could relate to, such as feeling thirsty (for drive) or tending to run from one place to another (for habit strength). What are the units and connections and weights in a network model? Are they neurons in the brain? Are they items of knowledge? Are they ways of thinking? They are indeed more abstract than any of these suggestions, because they are the building blocks from which anything we learn can be constructed—or so at least the new connectionist theorists hope. They are the native endowment that gets programmed by experience, whether in NETtalk or any other network model, or in a child. Whether the learning takes place in the same basic way in network models and in children remains highly controversial, but at least models like NETtalk raise that possibility in a challenging way.

APPLICATIONS AND EVALUATION

These new connectionist models clearly show a resemblance to the older stimulus-response connectionist theories. However, this does not mean that these newer theories are very much like the older ones. Rather than habits connecting a given stimulus directly to a given response, the newer connectionist models specify entire interconnected networks, involving not only input and output units but also the hidden units in between. Moreover, there are not just a number of different pathways being reinforced; rather, reinforcement changes the weights of a number of parallel connections and thus changes the whole pattern of flow within the interconnected network. In this respect, the new connectionist models look like what the classical gestalt theorists would have appreciated. Thus we might say that two characteristics of Hull's theory, learning by reinforcement and the use of intervening variables (the hidden units), result in a total system that Wertheimer and Köhler would have found quite congenial.

One of the most popular applications of the new connectionist models has been to perception. Even though computers can solve many problems faster and more accurately than humans, they are notoriously poor at dealing with complex patterns. Most people are inferior to computers at playing chess or evaluating mathematical functions, but they are way ahead of computers in their ability to recognize individual faces. They are also much better than computers at recognizing a particular object even when it is surrounded and partly hidden by other objects. This fact makes it difficult to design computerized "smart missiles" that are as effective as human bombardiers at, for example, homing in on tanks but not on other large battlefield objects.

To traditional computer experts, the poor performance of computers at recognizing patterns is an embarrassment. To the new connectionist theorists, however, it is a sign that their approach is needed. The sorts of patterns that develop spontaneously in distributed networks seem just right for analyzing perceptual patterns. Whether the problem is how to recognize an object whichever way it is turned, or how to find a hidden picture within a larger picture, or how to distinguish one face from another, connectionists have worked enthusiastically at applying their methods to it.

What makes the connectionists' machines more effective for these purposes than are ordinary computer programs is that they work on the patterning of elements. As many of us know from painful experience, computers are exceedingly literal. Misspell a word or misplace a comma and the computer is baffled. This means that in order to match a picture to the computer's template for a certain person's face, there must be exact point-by-point correspondence between the two. Differences so small that a person would barely notice them will prevent the computer from detecting that the two are the same. Computers have ways around this problem, but they are still rather literal-minded ways, such as counting the number of features (long nose, closely spaced eyes, and so on) that the two faces have in common. The connectionists' networks, however, can react to the overall similarities in pattern between two faces, just as a human would, even though there is no point-by-point correspondence. Again we see why, of all the classical learning theorists, the ones who might sympathize most with this new approach are the gestaltists.

The connectionist network models illustrate in fairly extreme degree the use of modeling as an approach to the study of learning. Models such as NETtalk are not theories of learning; rather, they are models illustrating one particular way that a certain kind of learning could possibly occur. The general theory is that learning occurs through changes in the strength of connections in a network with many distributed connections. A specific model is just one example, illustrating how such learning could occur, not necessarily how it does occur in any particular organism or any particular situation. The model itself is a set of rules about how to change the weights of connections depending on the nature of the input (the stimuli) and on the success of the output (which corresponds to reinforcement). If following those rules leads to changes that resemble actual learning in real organisms, this suggests two things: that the model is an accurate representation of how learning occurs in some situation, and that the whole approach is a useful one.

At present these models are still in the early stages of development. Their supporters see at least two values in them. One is practical. A machine designed to learn through connectionist networks has the potential to become the ultimate expert system. Whereas an expert system constructed by people can never be better than the knowledge that is built into it, a self-teaching system has the potential to go beyond existing knowledge, learn by experience, and become more expert than any person or any system that could have been produced in some other way. The implications for computerized problem solving are enormous.

The other potential value of this approach is in finding out how learning occurs in humans and other organisms. Obviously these models do not tell us how learning occurs at the biochemical level—the connectionist machines are not made of living cells. However, they do show us how the neurons in a real brain could work together to produce learning. Of all the ways that real nervous systems might work, these models represent the most plausible guess as to how they actually do work, say their supporters.

Critics are more skeptical. The models are still only in a preliminary stage of development. None of them has yet done as good a job as the best of the competing models, which are computer programs designed to reason logically about information given to them by their creators. Quite possibly, for a variety of reasons, the connectionist models never will. At present they represent an interesting new approach, a set of high hopes, and the possibility of combining the best of connectionist and cognitive approaches more effectively than ever before. To what extent the hopes will be realized remains to be seen.

Chapter *12*

Some Current Cognitive Interpretations

*I*n the previous chapters, we have seen how much the cognitive revolution and modern cognitive theory owe to the computer. However, that is by no means the only source of current cognitive theories. Others have come from quite different sources. It is to some of these that we now turn.

As we saw in Chapter 9, the cognitive revolution came from a variety of sources. In Chapter 10, we focused on one particularly important source, the rise of computers, and saw how that source has been exemplified recently in ACT theory. In this chapter we look at a miscellany of recent cognitive developments that developed from other sources. Some represent behavioristic approaches that have become increasingly cognitive as they struggled with the complexities of human behavior. Others emerged directly from earlier cognitive theories. These approaches vary a good deal both in the topics with which they deal and in their balance between interest in abstract theory and interest in applications. What they have in common is confidence that cognitive models are valuable both for explaining and for influencing behavior.

COGNITIVE INTERPRETATION OF CLASSICAL CONDITIONING

One of these theories is in what might seem an unlikely topic within learning: classical conditioning. Robert Rescorla (b. 1940) of the University of Pennsylvania has analyzed Pavlovian conditioning, not as attaching responses to conditioned stimuli, but as teaching animals or people that the conditioned stimulus is a warning signal that the unconditioned stimulus is coming. What is learned is an expectancy that when the conditioned stimulus comes, the unconditioned stimulus will follow. This is a way of talking about conditioning that Tolman would like, but, as stated simply here, it should also sound fine to Pavlov. However, when we look more closely at what Rescorla is saying, we can see that he has rather complicated ideas about what is learned.

In a typical conditioning experiment, there are a number of trials in which the conditioned stimulus is followed by the unconditioned stimulus, which in turn produces the unconditioned response. As a result, the conditioned stimulus comes to elicit the conditioned response. Typically, the more of these paired trials there are, the greater the conditioning. The standard connectionist interpretation has been that each paired trial increases the strength of a connection between the conditioned stimulus and the unconditioned response. When this connection becomes strong enough for the conditioned stimulus to elicit the response, it is then called the conditioned response.

An alternative, cognitive interpretation would be that each time the conditioned stimulus is followed by the unconditioned stimulus, an expectation is strengthened: the expectation that whenever the conditioned stimulus comes, the unconditioned stimulus will quickly follow. As a result, when the conditioned stimulus appears, the learner reacts in a way that prepares for the unconditioned stimulus. Whereas in the connectionist interpretation, what was strengthened was a connection between a stimulus and a response, in this cognitive interpretation what is strengthened is a cognition relating two stimuli to one another.

Rescorla accepts this latter interpretation, as did Tolman, but he goes further. For Rescorla, it is not enough to substitute an expectation about two stimuli for a connection between a stimulus and a response. He also rejects the idea that there is a gradual buildup of strength as the number of paired trials increases. Instead, he asks us to do something that sounds odd in a conditioning study, though Krechevsky may have prepared us for it: to look at the learner (human or animal) as being like a scientist testing a hypothesis.

Think of the learner as trying to predict when the unconditioned response will occur, in order to be prepared for it when it comes without wasting effort in preparing for it when it's not coming. A prediction that it will occur is indicated by the learner's making the conditioned response, and a prediction that it will not occur is indicated by not making the response. How does the learner decide which to predict at any given moment? Since the conditioned stimulus is the only basis for deciding, the learner needs to find out the relation between it and the unconditioned stimulus. This relationship is called the *contingency* between the two stimuli (just as Skinner talked about the contingency between a response and a reinforcer). Specifically, is the unconditioned stimulus more likely to occur when the conditioned stimulus has just been presented than when it has not? If it is more likely, then there is a contingency. In that case, how much more likely is it? That will indicate the degree of the contingency.

Contingencies themselves are characteristics of the environment; they are there whether a learner notices them or not. However, Rescorla is interested in the cognitions that learners form about the contingencies. These cognitions are intervening variables, states of the organism that Rescorla infers are there. Regarding these cognitions about contingencies, the human or animal subject in a classical conditioning experiment is in the same situation as either the scientists or the amateur weather prophets who were discussed in Chapter 2. Like them, the experimental subject is trying to figure out a law specifying when the unconditioned stimulus will occur, based on a possible contingency between it and the conditioned stimulus.

For the learner trying to find out about this contingency, the important evidence is not how *often* the conditioned and unconditioned stimulus have been paired, but how *consistently*. If the conditioned stimulus is always followed by the unconditioned stimulus, but the unconditioned stimulus never comes at any other time, the contingency is perfect. As a result, prediction can also be perfect, and the cognition that there is a contingency will soon be strongly learned. That, says Rescorla, is what happens in ordinary acquisition in a conditioning experiment.

How can we decide whether this interpretation of conditioning is any better than others? The clearest test case would be to compare two groups of subjects that both receive the same number of paired trials. However, one of the groups also often receives the unconditioned stimulus at times when the conditioned stimulus has not been presented, so that they get the unconditioned stimulus without any warning. If conditioning is a matter of building up a connection between a stimulus and a response, then the two groups should show equally strong conditioning, since they had the same number of paired trials to build up the connection. The extra unpaired unconditioned stimuli that one group experienced would not make any difference.

Suppose, however, that what is important is the contingency between the two stimuli. No matter how often the two stimuli have occurred together, their contingency is still weak if the unconditioned stimulus occurs often without the conditioned stimulus. If this is not obvious, think again of the weather example from Chapter 2, that a red sky in the morning predicts bad weather. No matter how often the red sky is followed by bad weather, the red sky is still useless for predicting bad weather if bad weather is equally likely to come after any other color of sky. Rescorla would therefore predict that conditioning would be weaker in the group with the extra unconditioned stimuli, and that is what he has found. This line of research and several others bearing on this interpretation of classical conditioning are presented in Rescorla (1988).

COGNITIVE BEHAVIORAL THERAPY

As we saw in Chapter 7, Skinner's form of behaviorism led to a vigorous movement in the treatment of behavioral problems, both in educational and in psychotherapeutic settings. Under the name of behavior modification, it is a straightforward application of operant principles. When used in therapeutic settings, it comes under the heading of behavioral therapy. However, it is not the only type of procedure that goes under that name. Whereas behavior modification involves the shaping of operant behavior, other forms of behavioral therapy are more closely related to what Skinner would call respondent behavior, and its modification by techniques related to Pavlovian conditioning.

Of these latter forms of behavioral therapy, the best known is *systematic desensitization*, first developed by Joseph Wolpe (b. 1915). Systematic desensitization (Wolpe, 1958) is a way of getting rid of fears by imagining the feared object while remaining very relaxed. To use this method, a person must first do two things. One is to make up a list of feared situations, in order from least feared to most feared. For a person with a fear of snakes, the least feared item on the list might be seeing the word "snake" in a book, and the most feared might be having a large boa constrictor wrap itself around the person's body. The other thing is to learn to relax thoroughly, which is not as easy as one might think. Given these necessary preparations, the person can begin the desensitization by imagining the least feared item, while at the same time relaxing thoroughly. He or she can continue doing this until fear is no longer felt at imagining that least feared item. The person can then repeat the process with the second least feared item, and so on until even the originally most feared item no longer gives rise to any fear.

To go through the entire list of items until there is no further fear can be fairly time consuming, but it is still brief compared to many other forms of psychotherapy. There is no guarantee that becoming unafraid to imagine an event will mean that one is also unafraid to have the event actually happen, but often this is not very important. The goal is rarely to turn a snake-phobic person into a professional snake handler; often it is enough if the person can hike in an area where there are snakes without being in a constant state of terror. On that hike the person will quite likely never encounter a snake, but if the encounter does take place, it would probably be just as wise to move out of its way anyhow. Systematic desensitization has indeed been found to be among the more effective forms of therapy (Smith, Glass, & Miller, 1980).

How should systematic desensitization be interpreted theoretically? Remembering Watson & Raynor's study of Little Albert (discussed on p. 33), we might think of the process as one of extinction, presenting the feared object as a conditioned stimulus without any unconditioned stimulus. However, given the importance of relaxation in systematic desensitization, it seems more appropriate to interpret it in Guthrie's terms. The goal of the therapy is to change the person's response to the feared object from the tension of fear to relaxation. Systematic desensitization is a way of doing this that includes elements both of Guthrie's method of incompatible stimuli (the relaxation) and of his method of thresholds (gradually going up the hierarchy).

To some people the most interesting thing about systematic desensitization is that the whole method uses only imagined versions of the feared object, never any actual ones. To Watson, who vigorously rejected the notion of mental images, this would probably have seemed ridiculous. Other behaviorists would have been more accepting of it, treating images as stimuli produced by one's own responses of imagining, but it still seems out of place in traditional behaviorist theory. It may be seen as the first step in a long process of combining behavioral therapy with cognitive psychology. The result of this combining is known as *cognitive behavioral therapy*. A number of versions of cognitive behavioral therapy (as well as other kinds of behavioral therapy) are discussed in Schwartz (1982).

Much of cognitive behavioral therapy involves not images but rather the things that people say to themselves. (Watson, with his references to subvocal speech, would probably be less bothered by this approach than by the images we have already considered.) One simple and fairly behavioral example is a technique known as *thought stopping* (also developed by Wolpe, 1973). This technique is useful for people who tend to obsess and ruminate about their problems, which may take the form of criticizing themselves harshly for their inadequacies, nursing resentments against other people for their inconsiderate behaviors, wallowing in self-pity, or other such exaggerated and largely useless thoughts. Once the person realizes that he or she is pursuing these thoughts far beyond anything that could be useful, it makes sense to try to stop them. One cannot, of course, just decide not to think about something and have those thoughts stop immediately and completely. (There is a story that alchemists knew the technique for turning lead into gold, but that the final step involved staring at the lead for an hour without ever thinking of the left eye of a camel, and no one ever succeeded in doing that.) Nevertheless, a person can often learn to recognize quickly when he or she is doing this kind of obsessive thinking, which had become so automatic the person was barely aware of doing it, and to respond to that recognition with the thought *Stop that.* This thought-stopping technique can often greatly reduce the rumination, even though not eliminating it completely.

Other forms of behavior cognitive therapy make use of more elaborate forms of self-instruction. One person who has done extensive work on the instructions that people give to themselves is Donald Meichenbaum (b. 1940) of the University of Waterloo (Meichenbaum, 1977). He notes that as young children are acquiring language, they often use self-instructions to guide their own behavior. Children who talk to themselves while playing are not merely providing a commentary on what they are doing but also guiding their own behavior. This is especially noteworthy if they are carrying out a complicated task, such as building with blocks or dressing a doll. Likewise, one of the signs of a developing conscience is a child's admonishing him- or herself what to do or not do, sometimes in the exact words an adult has used toward the child. Meichenbaum notes that children who suffer from attention deficit/hyperactivity disorder are less likely to use such self-instructions, and suggests that training in the use of self-instructions should be particularly helpful to these children. However, he sees other children (and adults) as also often behaving inappropriately for much the same reason as do the children with attention deficit/hyperactivity disorder: they do not stop, look, and self-instruct before they act.

Meichenbaum and his collaborators have trained children to use self-instructions to deal with a variety of problems, from taking tests to dealing with social situations to managing stress. They have used a five-step training technique to shape the sort of self-instructional behavior that they consider normal for adults. First, the experimenter does a task in front of the child while telling him- or herself aloud what to look for, how to proceed, and in general to be careful and think before acting. Second, the child does the same task with instructions from the experimenter similar to those that the experimenter gave to him- or herself. Third, the child does the task and is told to keep saying during the task what he or she is trying to accomplish, looking for, and planning to do. Fourth, this out-loud commentary is replaced with whispered self-instructions. Finally, the child is told just to think the self-instructions, as an effective adult problem-solver might (Meichenbaum, 1977).

If the purpose of this training is to make the child more effective in achieving a particular goal, such as solving "story problems" in math or making more successful social overtures to other children, the above training sequence may be enough. If, instead, it is to make a generally overimpulsive child better able to think ahead before he or she acts, training on a variety of problems would presumably be necessary. In any case, the child would be acquiring useful skills for solving problems that were significant in his or her life.

If we look at the way the training is done, we see ample evidence of its behavioral origins in such Skinnerian ideas as shaping and fading, as well as in related Guthrian techniques. At the same time, we see the increasing cognitive emphasis, focusing not on such simple self-instructions as with thought stopping, but on more elaborate self-instructions that guide the person through a complex task, helping the person to focus on the appropiate stimuli, organize the most useful responses, and minimize distractions. In this chapter section, we have thus moved from behavioral therapy with a slight cognitive leaning to genuine cognitive behavioral therapy.

Meichenbaum's approach is only one among several that have focused on the things we say to ourselves and the effects they have on us. Meichenbaum himself focuses more on the benefits of the things we say to ourselves. Then in explaining maladaptive behavior, he notes the absence of useful self-instructions, and his idea of therapy is to train people to use such self-instructions. Other psychologists focus more on the harmful effects of certain kinds of self-talk, and in the process become even more cognitive in their explanations and recommendations. It is to one of these theorists that we turn next.

EXPLANATORY STYLES

A more elaborate analysis of the things we say to ourselves is concerned with how we interpret our failures and other troubles. Martin Seligman (b. 1942), at the University of Pennsylvania, has suggested (along with many collaborators) that our explanations vary in three ways. First, do we attribute the outcomes to ourselves (*internal*) or to someone or something else (*external*)? Second, do we explain them by something very broad, such as "everyone has it in for me" or "I'm stupid," or to something narrower, such as "Harry opposes me because he sees me as a competitor" or "I have trouble remembering faces"? Seligman calls the broad explanations *global* and the narrow ones *specific*. Third, do we attribute outcomes to factors that change readily, such as "I had a headache that afternoon," or to factors that tend to stay the same for long periods, such as "I never have much pep"? Explanations in terms of factors that change readily are called *unstable*, and those in terms of more persisting ones are called *stable*.

For each of these three pairs of explanations, we can make a prediction as to which will make a person feel worse about the bad things that happen to him or her. First, it feels worse to be responsible for your own troubles (internal) than to be able to blame them on someone else (external). Second, if you believe that the causes of your troubles are global, then you would reasonably expect to have trouble in many areas of life, since the same cause would operate in all of them. If, instead, you believe that the causes are specific, then there is no reason to expect the problem to extend beyond that particular issue. For example, if you think your application to a country club was turned down because people in general have it in for you, you can expect many other rejections in all sorts of situations. However, if you think it was turned down because Harry resents you as a competitor, there is no reason to think you will have trouble in other situations where Harry is not involved. The global attribution would therefore be much more discouraging than the specific.

Similarly, if your explanations for bad outcomes are by stable causes, you expect these causes to go on producing bad outcomes far into the future, whereas if your attributions are to unstable causes, it is just as likely that things will improve quickly. Suppose, for example, that you played basketball today and realized you were playing quite badly. If you decided that this poor performance was because of never having any pep, then you would expect to continue doing badly in the future. However, if you attribute the poor playing to a headache, you would expect next time to play well, or at least adequately. You would therefore feel better if your explanations were unstable than if they were stable.

The advantages of a specific explanatory style over a global one and of an unstable explanatory style over a stable one are clear. For one thing, if you attribute bad outcomes to specific and to unstable causes, there is more hope for other situations and other occasions, and hence more reason to try for better outcomes next time. For another, explanations by specific and by unstable causes result in more satisfying feelings. If you believe that the causes of your troubles are specific and unstable, you will feel better about yourself or better about the world (depending on whether these explanations are also internal or external) than if you believe those causes are global and stable.

Whether internal or external explanations are better is less clear. Although internal ones tend to make one feel worse about this particular trouble, since it is one's own fault, one might also feel more hopeful about the future, since the outcome is more under one's own control. We will see more about the benefits of internal attributions later in this chapter. However, Seligman and his co-workers have focused more on the disadvantages of internal attributions. Part of the justification for doing so is that they often treat the combination of internal, global, and stable attributions as a single composite explanatory style. If people use mostly global and stable explanations for their troubles, they won't feel that there is much they can do about them, so feeling that they are internal makes them feel worse about themselves without giving them any extra hope.

These ideas have led Seligman and other researchers to make and test a number of predictions about differences between people who typically use internal, global, and stable explanations of bad events (called collectively a pessimistic explanatory style) and people who typically use external, specific, and unstable explanations (called an optimistic explanatory style). These are summarized, along with the basic theory, in Buchanan and Seligman (1995), and in a less technical form in Peterson, Maier, and Seligman (1993). One prediction is that those who use the pessimistic type of explanation will be more likely to become depressed. By now there is a lot of evidence that they are more likely to *be* depressed, but it is unclear whether the explanations cause the depression or vice versa. The few studies that have looked at explanatory style at one time and used it to predict depression at a later time have obtained weak or mixed results, so the issue remains somewhat in doubt.

Another line of prediction is that those with an optimistic explanatory style will be less likely to be seriously discouraged by setbacks and therefore more likely to go on working efficiently in spite of those setbacks than will people with a pessimistic explanatory style. The "optimists" would therefore be expected to get better grades in school, be less likely to drop out of schools or training programs, and have higher productivity on the job than the "pessimists." All of these predictions have been to some extent confirmed. However, the results are quite variable both from one study to another and from one aspect of optimism or pessimism to another, so it is too soon to conclude that we should admit students to college or hire them for jobs on the basis of their explanatory styles.

Perhaps the most surprising findings to come out of Seligman's thinking are those related to physical health. College students with pessimistic explanatory styles have more colds and flu in the next month and year than those with positive styles. Men who showed optimistic explanatory styles at age 25 also showed better overall health at age 45 than those with pessimistic styles (on a scale that had "deceased" at the unhealthy extreme!). Among men who had already survived one heart attack, death rate from further heart attacks over the subsequent eight years was higher for those with pessimistic than with optimistic explanatory styles. Though these findings show the same sorts of complexities as those in the previous two paragraphs, together they indicate some link between the things we say to ourselves and our physical health, a link for which there are also other lines of evidence. To the "person in the street," these findings may seem like remarkable evidence that the mind influences the body, but to a behaviorist they would be evidence that "the mind" is just a sloppy way of talking about some of the things the body does.

THE STRUCTURE OF LEARNING

The use of programmed instruction began as an attempt to apply such Skinnerian principles as immediate reinforcement and the gradual shaping of responses to complex verbal situations in education. However, as more programs were written and the more and less successful ones compared, it became evident that there is a lot more to programming than eliciting and reinforcing responses. Programs need to be constructed in ways that clarify the logical structure of the material. What needs to be learned are not merely particular responses, but a structure of principles from which particular responses can be derived. Programs are successful to the extent that they are organized so as to clarify this structure for the learner.

The importance of the structure of material applies not only to the writing of teaching-machine programs but also to such related topics as industrial and military training. We mentioned in Chapter 9, in looking at the beginnings of the cognitive revolution, the conclusion that Robert Gagné reached about the importance of the structure of material to be learned. The kind of analysis to which this led him has come to be widely accepted as a central aspect of cognitive psychology.

When one analyzes a complex task into its components, as Gagné recommended, one finds a hierarchical structure. The final task can be broken down into various component items of knowledge or skill, each of which can then be broken down into subcomponents, and so forth. Gagné (1962a) provides a further analysis of this hierarchical structure in an educational setting, where the focus is on knowledge rather than on manual skills or mechanical operations. Suppose we ask what knowledge a person must already have in order to perform a certain task, given only instructions. The answer will be mastery of some other tasks that are simpler and more general. For example, one can tell algebra students that the way to solve two simultaneous linear equations is to use one equation to get a value for one of the unknowns and then substitute that value in the other equation. To act on this instruction, the students must know both how to solve a single linear equation and how to substitute one value for another in an equation. If the learners do not have these two items of knowledge at their disposal, they will not achieve the final performance of solving the simultaneous equations, even if the instructions are clear and they attend carefully. If they do have both items of knowledge available, they will quite possibly be able to act on the instructions and carry out the task, but they may not; the instructions could be inadequate to bridge the gap between the components and the final task.

Each of the two components, in turn, depends on others. Solving a single equation, for example, depends on knowing that a term can be moved from one side of the equation to another with a change of sign, that both sides can be multiplied by the same factor, and so forth. These component items of knowledge are necessary, but not always sufficient, to solve a single linear equation. Thus the final performance is at the apex of a pyramid of component items of knowledge.

Given such a hierarchical arrangement of knowledge, in which a performance can be achieved only by those who have already mastered its components, it is clear why Gagné considers task analysis the key to effective teaching. To teach any task, one must at a minimum ensure that all the necessary components are learned, which may in turn require teaching *their* components. When the components are mastered, simple instructions may be enough to obtain the final performance. Often, however, simple instructions are not enough; some more complex presentation may be needed to bridge the gap, to get the components put together in the proper way. Such a presentation should make clear what performance is required, focus attention on the necessary components, identify crucial stimuli, and otherwise point the learner in the right direction. These are what a good teaching program does, in addition to simply providing information, as it moves the learner up the hierarchy to higher and higher levels of knowledge.

Gagné's views have implications beyond either schooling or applied training: they indicate the way in which our whole structure of knowledge and skills is gradually built up throughout life. Early in life, simple items are acquired, such as the skill to grasp an object in the hand and the knowledge that objects still exist even when they are out of sight. Such items form the components for the next higher level, such as knowledge about the ways in which various objects can or cannot be changed, or skills in performing such manipulations of objects. The learning of spoken language, and afterward of written language, mathematics, and other symbolic systems, makes possible many additional levels of learning, so that the hierarchies of knowledge for an educated adult are extremely complex. This interpretation of development, though arrived at differently, fits well with Piaget's.

Given the complexity of structure in so much of the material there is to be learned, there is a constant danger of not seeing the forest for the trees, of failing to note the structure and thus missing the most important aspect of what one is attempting to learn. Helping learners to avoid this mistake is one of the chief concerns of psychologists who apply their knowledge of learning to education.

One such psychologist is David Ausubel (b. 1918). Ausubel's approach is called *assimilation theory,* since it argues that most learning, especially in adulthood but in childhood as well, consists of assimilating new experience into one's existing cognitive structure. It follows from this view that the essence of good teaching is to present new material in such a way that it can be readily assimilated. One device for accomplishing this is an *advance organizer.* An advance organizer is a preview of coming material, but a special kind of preview. Often previews are like summaries, except placed at the beginning of a presentation instead of the end. (This fits the old approach of "Tell them what you're going to tell them, and then tell them, and then tell them what you've told them.") An advance organizer, however, is more abstract, general, and inclusive than that. It "tells them what you're going to tell them" in a way that is specially designed to create a bridge from what the learner already knows to what is to be learned next. It provides an overview of where the coming material fits in the learner's whole cognitive structure, and an "ideational scaffolding" for that new material (Ausubel, Novak, & Hanesian, 1978). It is thus perhaps the most cognitive of the various ideas we have considered in this chapter.

Ausubel's advance organizers help to solve the problem that Gagné raises of making the transition from the necessary components to the final performance. Ausubel's focus on assimilation also sounds much like Piaget's. In addition, Gagné's analysis of hierarchical structure is reflected in Anderson's ACT theory, though that aspect of the theory was not emphasized when we looked at it in Chapter 10. It is interesting that these and other cognitive approaches have all converged on this idea about cognitive organization. The idea of hierarchies is not inherently a cognitive idea, for connectionists likewise assume that simple habits get organized into complex skills, but the idea is currently more associated with cognitive thinking. Whether connectionist, cognitive, or a mixture of both, the idea of hierarchical organization is important in the study of learning, thinking, and human development.

BANDURA'S SOCIAL COGNITIVE THEORY

Another respect in which theorists in the connectionist tradition have moved in a cognitive direction involves the things that people learn from other people. In the early days of connectionist theory, such learning was downplayed in favor of learning by doing. One conspicuous exception, however, was a book by Neal Miller and John Dollard (written before their book on personality and psychotherapy) called *Social Learning and Imitation* (Miller & Dollard 1941). Although this book pointed to the importance of social learning, it did so in a thoroughly behaviorist way. Many of the stimuli that influence our behavior are those from other people, and one way we can respond to these stimuli is to model our behavior after someone else's. If we are reinforced for imitating others, say Miller and Dollard, we will continue to imitate them, and if we are reinforced for imitating some people but reinforced for doing the opposite of what other people do, we will learn the discrimination and follow that pattern.

Later theorists have gone well beyond Miller and Dollard's simple behaviorist view of imitation. Of the various contributors to this resurgence of interest in imitation, probably the most influential has been Albert Bandura (b. 1925) of Stanford University. He and Richard Walters collaborated on a book called *Social Learning and Personality Development,* in which they presented their views, not only on imitation, but on a range of related topics (Bandura & Walters, 1963). Their one small book, in fact, covered much of the same range of topics, including social learning processes, personality development, and psychotherapy, that Miller and Dollard covered in the two books on which they collaborated.

An Analysis of Modeling

As regards imitation, Bandura and Walters start at about the point where Miller and Dollard stopped. The form of imitation that Miller and Dollard analyzed in detail was like a simple version of follow-the-leader. They showed that rats could learn to follow (or not follow) other rats in a T-maze, and that children could learn to make (or not make) the same response that an adult or another child made. The responses the rats or the children made were ones that they would have made in that situation anyway; all the leader did was to provide a cue as to which of two responses would be reinforced. Certainly humans, probably monkeys, and perhaps various other species can learn by imitation in considerably more complicated ways than that. People can learn how to perform some fairly elaborate sequence of operations by observing someone else doing it and then modeling their own behavior after what they have observed. Whether or not they can acquire completely new responses by imitation is largely a matter of definition, but they can surely learn to arrange simple responses in a complex sequence purely by observing and imitating someone else.

Consider how hard it would be to learn to drive a car if every step in the process had to be shaped by Skinnerian procedures. Reinforcing the learner for each successive approximation to the final correct use of each of the controls would not only be maddeningly slow; it would also give little assurance that the learner would survive the training course, considering how a person would be likely to drive who had achieved only a first approximation to mastery of the steering wheel and the brake. The fact that a learner can observe and imitate an experienced driver greatly increases both the speed of learning and the chance of living to the end of the course.

You may feel that this example ignores the importance of language. A person can learn a lot about how to drive a car by observation, but that person can also learn a lot by being told how to work the controls and what sorts of precautions to take. You might guess that certain aspects of driving could be better acquired by watching and others by listening, while a combination of both might be better still. Bandura and Walters do not worry much about this distinction. They are really concerned with a concept even more general than imitation: *modeling*. When behavior is modeled after someone else's, that someone else may be called the model, and the whole process referred to as modeling. Modeling thus includes not only simple imitation of one person by another, but also those more pervasive processes (often called identification) by which a person tries to be the same kind of person as another. Given this broader concept, the model need not be a particular real person whom one observes. He or she may, instead, be a character in history or fiction or a generalized ideal person whom one has only heard described. When we think in terms of modeling behavior after that of some real, imaginary, or hypothetical person, the distinction between learning by observing and learning by being told becomes less important. We may still ask which will work better in a given case, but both are examples of modeling and hence, in a broad sense, of imitation.

The example of learning to drive a car refers to the acquisition of at least relatively new responses. Considering all the skills and social behaviors that people acquire from one another, such acquisition of new responses is certainly a very important kind of imitation. However, it is only one of three processes of imitation that Bandura and Walters consider. The second involves the inhibition or disinhibition of already learned responses. In other words, the person has already learned to make a response, but he or she learns by observing other people whether or not to make a given response under a given set of conditions. In the case of *inhibition*, the person learns from observing someone else not to make the response that he or she otherwise very likely would have made. Teachers hope that such inhibition by observation will take place when they reprimand a student for being noisy in class—that other students will thereby learn not to be noisy either. As with every other hope in education, the process often does not work that way, but it works often enough to illustrate that observational learning of inhibition is a real process. *Disinhibition* refers to the case in which a person has already both learned how to make a response and learned not to make it in a given situation, but now observes someone else making the response and proceeds to do so also. The inhibited response has been disinhibited through a process of imitation. Just as the inhibitory effects of imitation were illustrated by what teachers hope will happen, the disinhibitory effects may be illustrated by what they fear may happen after they have trained a class to be quiet. One student making a commotion may have a disinhibitory effect, inducing the rest of the class to abandon its inhibitions and join in rowdy noisemaking.

The third way in which imitation can operate is by eliciting an already learned response. Such *elicitation* is particularly noteworthy in children, though common enough in adults; as soon as one person starts to do something, several other people want to do the same thing, even though they had given the possibility no thought until that moment. This tendency can be a nuisance if the resources for that one activity are limited (only one set of crayons for a dozen children who suddenly want to color), but a benefit if the activity is one that requires a number of people for best results, as with group games and team sports.

It is not always easy to tell whether a given case of imitation is elicitation or disinhibition, since both involve an increased tendency to perform an already learned response when someone else is observed to be doing it. In principle, however, the two processes are distinctly different. In elicitation the sight of the model creates a positive desire to perform the activity, whereas in disinhibition the desire is already active and all that is needed is some indication that the desire can safely be indulged.

Both the second process of imitation (inhibition and disinhibition) and the third (elicitation) depend at least in part on the consequences of the activity to the model. If the model is punished for whatever was done, the result is likely to be inhibition, and the chance of the model's being imitated goes down. If there is no obvious consequence, good or bad, the model may be imitated either through disinhibition or through elicitation, but the chance of imitation is greater if the model is conspicuously rewarded for the behavior. In effect, reward or punishment of the model acts much like reward or punishment of the observer, in that we tend to imitate those we see rewarded and refrain from imitating those we see punished. This process by which consequences to the model influence the behavior of the observer is often called *vicarious reinforcement.*

Although vicarious reinforcement is important for the second and third kinds of imitation, it seems not to be very important for the acquisition of new responses. That is, an observer learns what it was that the model did, and becomes able to imitate it irrespective of reinforcement to the model. What reinforcement to the model does is to influence whether the observer will show what he or she has learned about the model's behavior. Studies have shown that even when children do not spontaneously imitate a model, they can still imitate the model with a good deal of accuracy if specifically asked to do so. Studies have also shown that whether or not the children spontaneously imitate the model depends considerably (though by no means entirely) on the reinforcement or punishment that the model received.

Much of the research carried out by Bandura and Walters dealt with the imitation of aggressive behavior. Both were concerned with the problems posed by aggression, and Bandura in particular worried about the extent to which aggressive models on television might contribute to aggressive behavior by children who watched television. Research by Bandura and others has amply demonstrated that children learn the aggressive responses they observe and that in many cases their subsequent play is influenced into more aggressive forms by what they have observed. This change in behavior involves the learning of new responses, the disinhibition of old ones, and probably the elicitation of old ones without disinhibition.

It is less clear to what extent observing aggression on television induces viewers to engage later in real-life aggression. As with so many practical applications of psychology, speculation goes well beyond data, and there is plenty of room to argue both sides of the case. However, the weight of evidence suggests that there is at least some real effect (e.g., Eron et al. 1972).

Observational Learning

Walters died not long after their book was published, but Bandura has continued to work and write on modeling and its implications and applications. In doing so, he has dealt increasingly with the "how" and "why" of modeling (Bandura 1971). With regard to the "how," his interpretations are quite cognitive. The main thing that goes on in modeling is learning by observation. The observer sees what the model does, notes what the consequences to the model are, remembers what has been learned, makes various inferences from it, and either then or later takes account of it in his or her own behavior. What is learned is not responses in the connectionist sense, but knowledge about responses and their consequences. On this matter, therefore, Bandura is clearly with Tolman rather than with Guthrie, Hull, or Skinner. Indeed, he suggests that instrumental conditioning might best be viewed as observational learning about the consequences of our own actions, just as we may learn from observing others.

How is learning by observation achieved? Bandura points to four necessary components: attention, retention, production, and motivation. *Attention* indicates that we do not automatically learn everything to which we are exposed. We notice events selectively, both in obvious physical ways, such as what things we look at, and in various subtler ways. *Retention* indicates that what we learn doesn't have any practical effect unless we remember it long enough to do something about it. *Production* is perhaps more challenging, since anyone who has either given or received coaching in a skill knows that observing someone else's behavior does not automatically convey the ability to imitate it accurately. How is that ability acquired?

In some cases, says Bandura, we have already mastered all the components of a performance, so all we need to learn from observation is when to do them. If this is not the case, so that we need to acquire the component skills themselves, the learning is harder, but there are a number of ways it can be achieved. A coach can help by guiding us through the performance with a mixture of talking, demonstration, and moving our bodies through the proper motions. However, polished skill also requires that we try making the responses and receive sensory feedback from our own responses. Thus Bandura admits that there is no perfect substitute for practice when it comes to the production of a new skill, even though he also insists that practice per se is only a limited part of human learning.

Whereas these three factors determine how much observational learning will occur, the fourth, *motivation*, determines whether observational learning of someone's behavior will lead us to imitate that someone. For Miller and Dollard, this factor meant that we imitate because we are reinforced for imitating, and can also learn not to imitate under those conditions where imitation is not reinforced. Bandura rejects this view, which is too connectionist to fit in his more cognitive theory. However, for many practical purposes, his own interpretation amounts to much the same thing as theirs. We model our behavior after that of others when we expect to be rewarded for doing so, and one factor that leads us to expect reward is having been rewarded before under similar conditions.

What makes this view different from the simple reinforcement interpretation is that it also allows for other factors to influence our expectations. We may expect that imitating someone in a particular situation will lead to reward because we have been told that it will, or because we see other people similar to ourselves being rewarded for such imitation. Each of these sources of information, including our own direct experience of reinforcement, gives some indication of whether imitation will be rewarded on this particular occasion. However, none of them is infallible. We make a judgment on the basis of any or all of them, and imitate or not accordingly. Depending on the outcome, our confidence in that source of information will go up or down, which in turn will affect our tendency to imitate different people under various future conditions.

We do not need to assume that people are always aware of what goes into these decisions as to whether or not to imitate. If a child in one of Bandura's experiments were asked why he or she imitated the model, the child's answer would probably be no more informative than "I felt like it" or "It looked like a fun thing to do." Nevertheless, there is evidence that the likelihood of imitation depends on reward to the model, reward to the child, the apparent power and status of the model, and other motivational variables. Such cases of what looks like automatic imitation resulting from reinforcement obscure the difference between Bandura's interpretation and Miller and Dollard's, but the difference is still real, and typical of the differences between connectionist and cognitive views.

Like many theorists, Bandura has gradually increased the scope of his theorizing, spreading out from the study of modeling to consider a wide variety of other topics. His most recent book, *Social Foundations of Thought and Action* (Bandura 1986), deals not only with general principles of learning and modeling but also with development, judgment, self-regulation, and social processes—a considerable part of the subject matter of psychology.

Some Special Topics

Two of the topics Bandura has studied have received particular attention. One, as already mentioned, is aggression (Bandura 1973). He has little use for interpretations of aggression as either an innate human drive or an automatic reaction to frustration. Instead, he emphasizes aggression as a way of obtaining rewards that might have been obtained in other ways. One way of reducing aggression, therefore, is to teach people more socially desirable ways of getting what they want. Moreover, as we might guess, Bandura considers modeling an important factor encouraging people to behave aggressively. On the controversial question of whether violence on television tends to increase violence in real life, he is strongly on the "yes, it does" side. If we want less aggression, we should show fewer aggressive models, particularly fewer successfully aggressive ones, and more models who achieve their goals effectively in nonaggressive ways.

The other topic is what Bandura refers to as *self-efficacy*—a person's sense of his or her ability to deal effectively with the environment (Bandura 1982). An application in which Bandura has been particularly interested is the treatment of phobias. Whereas many psychologists, including Dollard and Miller, focus on reducing the person's fear of the feared object, Bandura focuses on increasing the person's self-efficacy with regard to it. In other words, the key question is not how afraid the person is but how able he or she feels to deal with the fear and with the object—that is, the person's self-efficacy. Bandura has shown that after phobic people have gone through training designed to reduce their fear of snakes, for example, their judgment of how close they will be able to approach a different species of snake is a better predictor of how close they actually will come than is a measure of fear based on their behavior during therapy (Bandura, Adams, & Beyer 1977).

Another application of self-efficacy is to social activism. Among people who are unhappy with the status quo, which ones will take action to try to change it? Bandura cites evidence from several sources showing that it is those people with higher self-efficacy who are most likely to take such action. Presumably they are the ones who believe that their own actions are likely to make a difference, and who therefore are willing to make the necessary effort and sacrifice, whereas those with low self-efficacy feel that the chances of success are not enough to be worth it.

Assuming that we want to increase someone's self-efficacy, how might we go about it? As you might easily guess, an approach that Bandura particularly recommends is modeling, and he has obtained a good deal of evidence as to what kinds work best. Suppose, for example, that a therapist tried to increase a snake-phobic person's willingness to approach and handle a snake by showing someone else doing so. We might at first guess that this would work best if the model handled the snake fearlessly. Actually, however, it works better if the model at first shows fear of the snake but gradually overcomes that fear and begins to handle the snake (Meichenbaum 1971). This is, of course, what we would expect if we think of the modeling, not as reducing fear of the snake, but as increasing the person's sense of efficacy in dealing with it.

Bandura has been a prolific writer on a number of topics, and his approach has become quite widely known under the title of *social learning theory*. Under that name, it occupied an intermediate position between cognitive positions like Tolman's on the one hand and connectionist positions like those of Miller and Dollard and Skinner on the other. Recently, however, it has become more fully cognitive, as noted above, and been renamed *social cognitive theory*. Though it is still not quite as cognitive as, for example, Piaget's, it represents a long move in a cognitive direction from its connectionist beginnings.

Chapter
13

Issues in Motivation

Why do we want what we want, seek what we seek, avoid what we avoid? Why are we sometimes desperate to obtain some immediate goal (such as air if we're smothering or a drug fix if we're addicted), sometimes calmly sampling from among life's little pleasures, and sometimes working with intense concentration toward long-term life goals? These are questions of motivation, and to many people they are the most central issues in psychology. Attempts to answer them are part of nearly all the major theories of learning, since these topics are not only important but also closely related to the processes of learning. However, there have also been a number of contributions to the analysis of motivation that were not closely associated with any of the major theories we have considered. In this chapter we will examine some of them.

INTERPRETATIONS OF DRIVE AND REINFORCEMENT

One topic on which there have been important recent developments is the nature of reinforcement. No theorist questions that the effects of our actions influence whether we will repeat these actions (which is the basic principle of reinforcement), but theorists disagree widely on how this influence should be interpreted and even on whether "reinforcement" is an appropriate way of thinking about it. Hull was the only early reinforcement theorist who dealt explicitly and in detail with one central question: What do all reinforcers have in common that makes them reinforcing? His answer was that all reinforcers reduce the strength of a drive. Given Hull's great influence in his day, the drive-reduction interpretation of reinforcement thus became a baseline with which more recent answers to the question may be compared.

New Descriptions of Drives

We will consider three trends in the interpretation of reinforcement, two that work within a drive-reduction framework and one that does not. Within the drive-reduction framework, there has been a concentration on what drives are innate. In the past, connectionist psychologists like Hull who used the concept of drive have tended to treat as primary, or innate, only a few drives (such as hunger, thirst, sex, and pain) that are clearly physiological. What of more complex motivational tendencies such as pride, ambition, and affection, which have little apparent physiological basis? They were generally regarded by connectionist theorists as the result of complex learning processes, including the acquisition of learned drives. However, to support this belief the connectionist theorists had to make assumptions about the learning of motives that are extremely difficult to support by experiments. Although Miller was quite successful in demonstrating a learned drive of fear, other learned drives that are predicted by theory have proved very difficult to demonstrate in the laboratory. As a result, there has been increasing interest in the possibility that there may be far more primary drives than have previously been recognized.

One such drive (or perhaps category of drives) that has received much attention is that which is satisfied by new experience. It is known variously as a drive of curiosity or exploration or manipulation or novelty seeking. Its existence is supported by many lines of evidence. Harlow, Harlow, and Meyer (1950) showed that monkeys would work to unfasten a clasp device over and over again, even though neither food, escape, nor any other obvious reward was given for doing so. Butler (1953) showed that monkeys in a closed cage would press a lever to open a window so they could look out. If the monkeys were kept in the closed cage for several hours before the lever was made available, they would press more (indicating higher drive following deprivation). If the lever no longer opened the window, their rate of pressing would drop (indicating extinction). Such novelty-seeking behavior is found not only in monkeys, which have long been famous for their curiosity, but also in rats. Montgomery and Welker have made extensive studies of rats exploring new places and of the responses they will learn in order to be able to do such exploring. These and other related studies are discussed by Berlyne (1960) and by Welker (1961).

A second kind of drive that has been investigated is satisfied by activity. This is different from the kind of drive we have just discussed in that the activity does not have to produce any novel stimulation. Such activity occurs when a rat runs in an activity wheel, which is a sort of voluntary treadmill, a fancier version of the running wheels found in many pet rodents' cages. A rat in such a wheel can, if it chooses, get exercise by running, but no exploration is involved, since the wheel just goes around without getting anywhere. Kagan and Berkun (1954) have shown that a chance to run in such a wheel will reinforce lever pressing, and Hill (1956) has shown that rats do more running in the wheel when they have been deprived of activity for a long time.

A third kind of drive has been referred to as contact comfort. It was first analyzed in detail, as were many interesting phenomena, by Harry F. Harlow

(1905–1981) at the University of Wisconsin. Contact comfort is a drive that is satisfied by certain kinds of physical contact. Harlow (1958) originally studied it by rearing baby monkeys with *surrogate mothers*, wire models that gave milk like real mothers. He found that monkeys not only preferred a "mother" covered with terry cloth to one made of bare wire, but ran to the terry cloth "mother" when frightened. They did so even if the wire "mother" supplied milk and the cloth "mother" did not. These and other findings in his experiments suggested to Harlow that contact comfort, exemplified by the baby monkeys' attraction to the cloth surrogate mother, is an important factor in personality development. It may well play a major part in personality development, not only in the attachment of infants to their mothers, but also in other aspects of love, in sexual behavior, and in the development of social relationships.

The importance of these various drives is not simply in the recognition that people and animals seek new experience, activity, and pleasant sensations of touch. All these tendencies have long been known. Rather, their importance is in the recognition, supported by experimental evidence, that they may well be just as much a part of our innate, biological nature as hunger, sex, or pain. This recognition does not by any means answer all our questions about why we seek companionship, achievement, or glory. (Why it doesn't is discussed in Hill, 1968.) Nevertheless, it helps to bridge the gap between the drives usually employed in laboratory studies of learning and the motives we all recognize in ourselves and others.

Optimal Arousal

The second trend involves a modification of drive theory—the theory of *optimal arousal*. Different versions of this theory have been presented by several writers; one good collection of ideas about it is Berlyne and Madsen (1973). The optimal-arousal theory holds that reinforcement consists not necessarily of a decrease in drive but rather a change in drive toward some optimal level. The term *arousal* is preferred to *drive* in discussing this interpretation, so as to avoid confusion with more conventional drive theory. If the present level of arousal is higher than the optimal level, a decrease will be reinforcing, as in the ordinary drive interpretation. However, if the present level is below the optimum, an increase rather than a decrease will be reinforcing. When the level of arousal is exactly at the optimum, reinforcement is presumably not possible for the moment. However, both the level and the optimum are constantly changing, so any such limitation is quite temporary.

Optimal-arousal theory allows for the often observed fact that people frequently seek more stimulation rather than less. Conventional drive interpretations, such as Dollard and Miller's (1950), have not been very successful in explaining such behaviors as riding on roller coasters, reading exciting stories, or just complaining of boredom and expressing a wish that something would happen to break the monotony. Since optimal-arousal theory states that increases as well as decreases in arousal can be reinforcing, it has less trouble with such occurrences. However, the recognition that either kind of change in arousal, up or down, can sometimes be reinforcing carries with it a responsibility to indicate when one will be reinforcing and when the other. This responsibility in turn requires knowing a lot about the determinants both of the present level of arousal and of the optimal level.

One additional assumption (or postulate, in Hull's terms) about the relationship between stimulation and arousal represents a start toward making the theory more specific. This assumption states that the level of arousal is an increasing function of the intensity, the complexity, and the novelty of the stimulation. In other words, more intense stimuli, more complex ones, and more novel ones are more arousing than those that are weaker, simpler, or more familiar. This assumption, along with the one we have already mentioned—that moderate levels of arousal are more reinforcing than either high or low levels—forms the basis of optimal-arousal theory.

Several predictions follow from these two assumptions. Moderate stimuli should be reinforcing as compared with either weak or intense stimuli. Stimuli that are somewhat different from those we are used to should be preferred both to thoroughly familiar ones (which would be judged uninteresting) and to highly unfamiliar ones (which would be judged incomprehensible). Stimuli that are moderately complex should prove more reinforcing than those that are either dully simple or overwhelmingly complex. When more than one aspect of the stimulus varies, the higher the stimulus is on intensity, novelty, or complexity, the lower the optimal value of the other variables should be. Thus a highly novel stimulus should be more reinforcing if it is mild and simple, whereas among very familiar stimuli the more intense and complex ones should be preferred.

The assumption that arousal is an increasing function of intensity, novelty, and complexity fits in well with a concept that has been quite popular among theorists in Russia—the *orienting reflex*. Although the term implies that individuals tend to orient themselves toward stimuli as they appear, what is actually measured in the orienting reflex is primarily the general arousal produced by a stimulus. The greater the galvanic skin response, the change in heart rate, or the increase in muscle tension produced by a stimulus, the greater the orienting reflex to that stimulus is considered to be. Measures of central-nervous-system activity, such as the electroencephalogram (EEG), also give indications of the strength of the orienting reflex. The orienting reflex is greater for more intense stimuli than for milder ones and shows some tendency to be greater for more complex stimuli than for simpler ones. If the same stimulus is presented repeatedly (thus making it more familiar), the orienting reflex progressively decreases. However, it can be restored a good part of the way to its original strength in either of two ways—by changing it in some way or by just waiting for a while—either of which has the effect of making it more novel. Thus the orienting reflex serves as evidence that the level of arousal is affected by various aspects of stimuli in the way that optimal-arousal theory says it should be.

You may have noted that optimal-arousal theory attempts to deal with some of the same phenomena that drive theory has tried to deal with by postulating such drives as exploration and activity. To say that there are drives that can be reduced by exploring new things or by becoming more active is to say that sometimes an increase in stimulation produces a decrease in drive. Thus both drive theory and optimal-arousal theory are getting away from the older version of drive theory—particularly closely associated with Hull—that what is reinforcing is a reduction in the level of stimulation. The newer drive theory makes the shift by looking at each drive separately without worrying about whether it conforms to any general notion about drives as states of high stimulation. Optimal-arousal theory, however, keeps the idea of an overall level of arousal that is closely related to reinforcement, but broadens its interpretation of just what the relationship to reinforcement is.

RESPONSES AS REINFORCERS

The third trend in the interpretation of reinforcement, outside the drive-reduction framework, relates reinforcement to the learner's own responses to a goal. Reinforcement depends not on what happens to the individual (drive reduction, e.g.) but on what the individual does. This wording sounds like something Guthrie might say—and indeed, one of the psychologists who developed this idea, Fred Sheffield at Yale (b. 1914), drew his inspiration from Guthrie. Sheffield maintained that the essential factor in reinforcement is the learner's behavior in relation to a goal object, rather than any form of drive reduction. Will a response that leads to some goal object be reinforced by the goal object and learned? This depends, says Sheffield, on what the individual does after obtaining the goal object. Food, for example, is reinforcing if one eats it, water if one drinks it, and a maze if one explores it, but not if one doesn't do these things. It is thus our own activity of eating, drinking, or exploring that provides the reinforcement, so as to reinforce whatever response brought us to the food, the water, or the maze.

Sheffield did several experiments to support this position. For the most part, however, they were inconclusive. He showed, for example, that drinking a saccharine solution is reinforcing for rats, even though saccharine is completely nonnutritive (Sheffield & Roby 1950). This finding certainly argues against the view that all reinforcers involve reduction in a body need, since saccharine does nothing to reduce the body's need for food. The study does not show, however, that the drinking activity was what produced the reinforcement. One could just as well say that the sweet taste of saccharine is the critical reinforcing factor.

Sheffield's point of view can be elaborated by dividing responses into two categories. On the one hand are those responses that lead to rewards and are reinforced by those rewards. Since these responses are instrumental to obtaining rewards, they are called *instrumental responses*. On the other hand are responses that are directed more specifically toward certain rewards rather than others. In the case of food rewards, these include not only such obvious responses as chewing and swallowing, but also such related behaviors as the raccoon's "washing" of its food. These are called *consummatory responses*.

Whereas the behaviors by which animals obtain food are fairly variable and subject to learning, the consummatory responses are much more stereotyped and less subject to learning. All sorts of motivated behavior sequences end with

consummatory responses: not only eating but also drinking, copulation, elimination, and various forms of exploration and play. It is the opportunity to engage in
these species-specific consummatory responses that serves to reinforce the
whole chain of instrumental behavior leading to them.

Because the consummatory responses often involve consuming a reward, as
when one eats food, one might imagine that the word consummatory is derived
from the word "consume." Actually, however, it refers to the consummation of a
sequence of acts, that is, bringing them to an appropriate end, or fulfillment. We
are closer to the derivation of the term "consummatory response" when we think,
not of eating as consuming food, but of sex as consummating a marriage.

This extension of Sheffield's theory has been developed in considerable detail
by Glickman and Schiff (1967). It has the advantages both of making Sheffield's
ideas more specific and of basing them to a greater degree in biology. However, the
division into instrumental and consummatory is not very clearcut. If a cat lies in
wait for prey, then sees a mouse and stalks it in typical catlike fashion, then catch-
es it and plays with it for awhile, then kills it with a quick bite to the neck, and finally eats it, at just what point has this typically feline sequence of behavior moved
from instrumental to consummatory? Perhaps a further refinement of Sheffield's
idea is needed.

Premack's More General Version

A more general formulation of the idea that responses are reinforcing has been
presented by David Premack (b. 1925), currently at the University of Pennsylvania. He simply states that of any two responses, the one that occurs more often
when both are available can reinforce the one that occurs less often, but not vice
versa. This relationship is illustrated by an experiment with children (Premack
1959). The children were given an opportunity to engage in two activities, eating
candy and playing a pinball machine. Some did one of these two more often, some
the other. Premack then arranged the apparatus so that for half the children the
candy dispenser would work only if the child first operated the pinball machine. To
the children who preferred playing, the new arrangement made little difference—
they just went on happily playing the machine. To the children who preferred eating to playing, however, this change did make a difference—their rate of playing
went up, indicating that candy was reinforcing the playing. So far this is a familiar
relationship—food reinforcing an instrumental activity—in this case, playing pinball. For the other half of the children, the arrangement was reversed, so that the
pinball machine would work only if the child first took candy from the dispenser.
To the children who preferred candy, this change made no difference. The children who preferred playing, however, took more candy under this arrangement
than before. In this case, playing reinforced eating.

In this experiment, for any one child only one of the two activities could function as a reinforcer. This is not, however, a necessary restriction. For example,
Premack (1962) also studied the reinforcement relationships between running and
drinking in rats. If a rat has spent a day without water, but with continuous access

to an activity wheel, it will run for the reinforcement of a chance to drink, as we would expect. If, instead, the wheel is locked so that the rat cannot run unless it first drinks, this relationship will have no effect on how much the rat drinks—running will not reinforce drinking. So far, this is a familiar relationship.

However, the situation can be reversed by having the same rat live for a day with water always available but with no chance to run. Now the tendency to run will be high and to drink will be low. Consequently, running can be used to reinforce drinking—if the rat has to drink in order to unlock the wheel and run, its drinking will increase. But requiring the rat to run in order to be able to drink will now have no effect on the amount of running. Thus the same animal can be in either a state where drinking reinforces running or a state where running reinforces drinking, and in each case the reverse does not apply. All that is necessary to change the animal from one state to the other is to do something (in this case, deprive it of drinking or of running) that will change its relative tendency to engage in these two activities.

In a conventional schoolroom, where one of the most difficult demands on pupils is to sit still for long periods of time, we would expect from Premack's analysis that it would often be possible to use access to the playground as a reinforcer for a certain amount of quiet work, but rarely possible to do the reverse. However, in a strenuous program of physical education, it might be possible to reinforce a student's putting forth his or her last ounce of athletic effort by rewarding the student with the chance to sit quietly and read. This latter arrangement would of course be expected to work better for the less athletic and more bookish students. Both individual differences and situational differences determine what activities can reinforce what other activities for a given individual at a given time.

In Premack's interpretation, then, there is no special class of consummatory responses that act as reinforcers. Any kind of response can reinforce any other kind of response, says Premack. All that is necessary is for the reinforcing response to be one that the learner makes more frequently than the response being reinforced. Actually, the relationship is more complex than that. We must consider not only whether, for example, a rat chooses to spend more time running or drinking, but also how much drinking it has to do to earn a given amount of running, or vice versa. Under some such "work requirements," the less frequent activity could actually reinforce the more frequent activity (Timberlake & Allison 1974). Consider, for example, a boy whose free choice would be to spend four times as many hours playing baseball as painting fences. We might (inspired by Tom Sawyer) make fence painting a scarce opportunity that had to be earned: eight hours of baseball playing for every hour of fence painting. Under those conditions, the boy would probably do even more baseball playing than otherwise, reinforced by the less frequent activity, fence painting. This leads us to a more general statement of Premack's principle: in order for one kind of response (such as painting) to reinforce another (such as playing), opportunities for the one doing the reinforcing (here, painting) must be scarcer relative to what the person would freely choose than are opportunities for the one being reinforced.

Behavioral Regulation

With these ideas, the view of reinforcement as response becomes less a theory of reinforcement and more a theory of behavioral regulation. For every possible activity there is an amount of time that the individual will freely choose to spend doing it. This amount of time is called the *bliss point*. The higher the bliss point, the more a person likes or values that activity. The bliss points of different activities thus provide an objective scale of liking or of value.

If it were possible for us to perform every activity exactly at its bliss point, we would be in a sort of Garden of Eden (Allison 1979). However, in the real world this is rarely possible. In order to do something we want to do, we typically first have to do something else we like less, whether it is as minor as walking upstairs or as major as working enough to earn thousands of dollars. More generally, in order to maintain the bliss point of one activity, we have to do either more or less than the bliss point of some other activity.

One way of dealing with this necessity is by doing more of the less preferred activity than you would like to, that is, more than its bliss point. For some children, this might mean doing more studying than they would prefer to, in order to be allowed to watch as much television as they would like. Since they are doing more studying than their bliss point for studying in order to keep television watching close to its bliss point, this means that television (the more preferred activity) is reinforcing homework (the less preferred).

Alternatively, one can deal with the problem by doing less of the more preferred activity—giving up some television time in order not to have to do so much studying to earn the televison watching. This is the kind of solution about which someone might say, "This is such fun that I'd like to do it more, but I have to go to so much trouble to get the chance that it wouldn't be worth it."

The most common outcome is neither of these two possibilities alone, but a combination of both. You do more of the less preferred activity (which is thus being reinforced) and also do less of the more preferred activity, which has become too "expensive" to do at its bliss point. The particular combination of the two that is chosen represents the best possible compromise (from the individual's point of view) between maintaining the bliss point of one activity and maintaining the bliss point of the other. This is a complex process of behavior regulation, and various mathematical models have been developed to describe it (e.g., Hanson & Timberlake 1983). These models can become rather complicated, especially when more than two activities are considered, and we will not explore them here.

Psychologists have noted that there is some similarity between these models of behavior regulation, typically studied with rats, and the kinds of models developed by economists. Suppose a rat's bliss point involves eating six pellets of food per minute and pressing a lever once per minute, but the rat is required to press the lever five times for every pellet. A psychologist would say that in that situation eating will reinforce lever pressing, while the contingency between lever pressing and eating will also reduce the rate of eating. An economist, commenting on the same situation, might say that the rat must buy the food at a price of five presses per pellet. One could then ask how the amount the rat "buys" varies with the "price" (in economists' terms, how elastic the demand curve is), and what difference it makes how hungry the rat is, how good the food tastes, and how available other kinds of food are. Mathematical models developed by psychologists to describe what rats do in such situations turn out to agree well with models developed by economists to describe the behavior of human consumers as prices change. This and other convergences suggest that the models deal correctly with important general aspects of behavioral regulation (Allison 1983).

This way of looking at behavior and the effects of reinforcement suggests that much of life consists of trying to maintain as nearly as possible the bliss points of many different activities. We do more of some activities and less of others as necessary, but keep departures from all the bliss points as small as possible. The bliss-point view of behavior sounds surprisingly like another that came originally from a quite different source. It is to this related view that we now turn.

CYBERNETICS

At least since the Industrial Revolution, some theorists have thought of animals and sometimes even people as just glorified machines. Until quite recently, however, it has been evident that the emphasis in that suggestion would have to be on "glorified," since no machine could come close to the performance of humans or even of the higher animals. Now the suggestion is beginning to look more realistic, though it is still far from accurate. Two characteristics have seemed to separate humans and at least some animals on the one hand from machines on the other: intelligence and purpose. We have already seen how computers can be programmed to behave in seemingly quite intelligent ways. As for purpose, there are various devices, called control mechanisms or servomechanisms, that show at least rudimentary forms of purpose. The study of such mechanisms is called *control theory* or *cybernetics.*

The term *cybernetics* was coined by Norbert Wiener (1948). The word is derived from the Greek for "steersman," since it is concerned with devices that keep some operation, like the sailing of a ship, on its proper course. In order to keep an operation on course, it is necessary to compensate for any deviation in either direction. If a ship drifts off course, either to port or to starboard, the helmsman must move the rudder the proper amount and direction to bring the ship back on course. This illustration presents the general concept of *negative feedback.* Negative feedback involves adjustments in a system to keep it in a steady state by compensating for any deflections from that state.

Negative Feedback

The concepts of cybernetics emerged from the branch of engineering concerned with control mechanisms. Such mechanisms operate by negative feedback. The thermostat is a simple familiar example. The purpose of a thermostat is to regulate a particular variable, temperature. In the terminology of control systems, temperature is the *controlled quantity*. At any given time the thermostat is set to maintain the temperature in a room at a given constant level, the *set point*. When the room temperature drops below the set point, the thermostat turns on the furnace so that the temperature will rise. Then when the temperature rises above the set point, the thermostat turns the furnace off and lets the temperature fall. In such a system, the output (a change in temperature) is fed back to the thermostat as input—hence the term *feedback*. The effect of the feedback is to produce a change in the opposite direction (warmer if it is too cool, cooler if it is too warm), which is why it is called negative feedback. Thus negative in this case does not imply anything bad; on the contrary, negative feedback is the stabilizing factor that permits systems to keep operating effectively.

When people perform any skilled act, they are constantly guided by sensations from their muscles, usually also from their eyes, and often from other sources. These sensations warn them whenever they are starting to make a mistake and thus enable them to return to the proper procedure. This response often happens so quickly and automatically that they are unaware of it, but it occurs nonetheless. This behavior is an example of negative feedback, with the output being fed back to control the operation and keep it on course.

A similar process operates in the body's physiological regulation. Body temperature, blood sugar level, alkalinity of the blood, and a great variety of other physiological variables must be maintained within some range in order for the body to function properly. They are, then, controlled quantities, and the optimal level for each of them is its set point. Negative feedback operates at the physiological level to correct deviations either up or down from the set point. These automatic regulatory processes are known collectively as *homeostasis*.

To maintain all these physiological controlled quantities close to their set points over long periods of time, it is not enough to have homeostatic mechanisms at the physiological level. To make homeostasis possible, we must eat, drink, and in most environments also move around, change clothes, and engage in many other activities. When we discuss these more molar activities, we are clearly in the realm of motivation. Just as there is a set point for level of blood sugar at a given time, so is there also a set point for amount of food intake over a period of time. We are aware of deviations from this set point—sometimes being hungry, at other times uncomfortably stuffed—and eat or stop eating to correct them. Over a period of time this negative feedback is often remarkably effective in maintaining the set point. When people eat whatever amount they wish, neither dieting nor under social pressure to eat more than they want, their weight often stays quite stable for months or even years. It may not be the weight they would most like to be at, but it is the level that their free food consumption maintains, and therefore a set point.

As we noted earlier in this chapter, hunger is only one of many drives or motives that have been observed, even in animals. Among humans there is an even greater variety. For a great many of them, the most desirable level is neither the maximum nor the minimum possible, but somewhere in between. We want a certain amount, but not too much, of exercise and rest and company and privacy and adventure and security. Each of these motives, then, can be considered a controlled quantity.

When we get too little of any controlled quantity, we seek more, and when we get too much, we try to cut down. When optimal-arousal theory says that this is true of general arousal, a cybernetic theory of motivation agrees, but adds that it is also true of most of the things we desire.

When we proceed to more complex purposive behaviors, the same principle applies. A student going through college may discover that he or she is getting failing grades. If the discovery results in the student's working harder and thus receiving better grades, this affords an example of negative feedback. In the unlikely event that the student studies so hard as to affect his or her health, the student can cut down on studying. In both cases the student discovers a deviation from his or her progress through college, one that threatens the success of his or her education, and corrects the deviation so as to continue to progress toward the degree.

The Place of Cybernetics in Learning Theory

Cybernetics as the answer to questions discussed in the two previous sections of this chapter is clear. Reinforcement is a change in a controlled quantity, bringing it closer to its set point. All the theories of reinforcement we have discussed so far can be incorporated within this framework. Drives, for example, involve controlled quantities with low set points. Thus, our set point for pain is very low, so it is nearly always a reduction in pain rather than an increase that brings that particular controlled quantity closer to its set point. The theory of optimal arousal reflects the fact that the set point for general arousal is typically neither very high nor very low, so decreases from high to medium arousal and increases from low to medium are both reinforcing. The basis of behavioral regulation is the rate at which we make any given response when free to respond as much or as little as we like. That rate is the set point for that response, and we do what we have to in order to keep the rate of responding as close as possible to its set point. If the response is restricted to a rate below its set point, any other response that moves it up toward its set point will be reinforced. Cybernetics is thus a very broad theory of motivation and reinforcement.

The great strength of feedback theory in psychology is the range of topics to which it applies. It is a method of analysis that applies to units as small as a flick of the hand or as large as a person's aim in life. It shows that the coordination of a movement, the pursuit of a goal, the regulation of a physiological function, and the operation of a motive can be viewed as basically the same thing: maintenance of a set point through the process of negative feedback. Moreover, the various levels at which this process operates are interrelated. For example, a coordinated movement, which has set points for speed and direction, may be the means of bringing some other controlled quantity back to its set point (as by getting a glass of water to the mouth and thus reducing thirst). It is possible to think of all our activities as arranged in a hierarchy, interrelated in such a way that maintaining the set point of each one serves to correct a deviation from the set point of the next higher one. This idea is too complicated and speculative to pursue here, but the interested reader can find discussions of it in Powers (1973).

The great weakness of feedback theory in psychology, at least for the purposes of this book, is that it is not a theory of learning. It tells us how a system operates but not how its operation changes as a result of learning. Presumably one learns what techniques are successful in bringing any given controlled quantity back toward its set point, but cybernetics tells us nothing about how that learning occurs. Thus, although it is a theory of motivated behavior within which learning can be studied, cybernetics is still tangential to the study of learning itself.

OPPONENT-PROCESS THEORY

During the 1950s and 1960s, Richard L. Solomon (1918–1995), whose last position was at the University of Pennsylvania, was involved in various experiments that involved giving electric shocks to dogs. His initial interest was in how the dogs learned a response that permitted them to avoid the shock, but later he became increasingly interested in the dogs' emotional responses to the shocks, including the response to shocks that could not be avoided. He and his collaborators observed that when dogs were first exposed to electric shocks, they appeared terrified by the experience. For a few minutes after the shocks were over, the dogs acted unfriendly and stealthy, before returning to their more typical active, friendly behavior. After a number of days of being shocked, their reactions were considerably different. The reaction to the shocks was much less extreme, more one of anxiety or annoyance than terror. More striking was the change in behavior just after the shocks ended: the dogs were even more active and friendly than usual; they seemed to be expressing their joy that the shock was over.

At about the time Solomon was making these observations, he learned about a study of skydivers (Epstein 1967) and noticed a marked resemblance between their reactions and those of the dogs. Before their first few jumps, the skydivers were highly anxious, and afterward they experienced first a sort of emotionally drained numbness and then a few minutes of pleasant liveliness. After a number of jumps, their reactions were quite different. Before the jump their arousal was in the form of nervous eagerness rather than anxiety, and afterward they spent a couple of hours in a state of exhilaration. For both dogs and skydivers, one thing remained the same: the period just after the frightening experience was (not surprisingly) more pleasant than just before the experience. The whole level, however, had changed, from frightened before and fairly unemotional after to less emotional before and pleasantly excited afterward.

Thinking about these changes in the ways dogs and people react to situations that are originally frightening, Solomon wondered whether there might be similar changes in an experience that was originally pleasant. A striking example came to mind: morphine addiction. Early in the addict's experience with morphine (before becoming an addict), the initial reaction to taking the drug is highly pleasant, whereas the effect of its wearing off is fairly neutral. After many exposures, the person (whom we can now call an addict) gets less pleasure from the administration of the drug, but finds its wearing off very unpleasant (withdrawal symptoms).

Though the directions are reversed, the kinds of changes are the same as with the dogs and the skydivers: the emotional reaction at the beginning of the experience becomes weaker, whereas at the end of the experience there is an opposite reaction that gets larger and larger.

The Theory

Eventually Solomon and J. D. Corbit collected a number of such examples and stated a theory to explain them (Solomon & Corbit 1974) known as the *opponent-process* theory. First, this is a *hedonic* theory; that is, it refers to pleasure and displeasure. Second, it might be summarized by saying that for every feeling there is an opposite (but not exactly equal) reaction. The original feeling and the opposite reaction are the opponent processes that give the theory its name. Third, the opposite reaction increases with repeated exposures, producing the changes noted in the examples above. Thus there are opponent processes that counteract both pleasure and displeasure, weakly so at first, but more and more strongly with repeated presentations of the pleasant or unpleasant experience.

Figure 13.1 makes these ideas more explicit. The graphs in panel A of the figure show what happens when a pleasant stimulus (such as an addictive drug) is first presented. When the stimulus is presented (top), the immediate effect is hedonically positive, as shown in the middle graph. This positive (pleasant) effect (called the a process) increases rapidly to a maximum, remains at that high level as

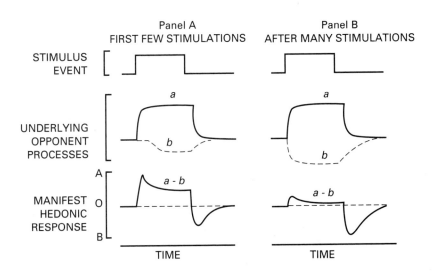

Figure 13.1   Hedonic opponent processes. Panels A and B each show the time that a stimulus is on (top section), the a process with its opponent b process (middle section), and the resulting manifest hedonic reaction (bottom section). From Solomon (1980). Copyright © 1980 by the American Psychological Association. Adapted by permission of the author.

long as the stimulus is on, and then drops rapidly back to zero when the stimulus is turned off. (In the case of a drug, the "stimulus on" period is the time that the drug remains active in the body.) This simple sequence of the *a* process is represented by the solid line. Shortly after the stimulus goes on, its opponent *b* process also begins, as represented by the broken line. Compared with the *a* process, the *b* process not only begins later but also increases more slowly and to a lower level. When the stimulus goes off, the *b* process again lags behind the *a* process: it continues for a short time after the stimulus is gone and then drops slowly toward zero. Since the *b* process tends to counteract the *a* process, we can determine the net effect of combining them by adding them algebraically (i.e., taking account of sign), as shown in the bottom graph. As long as the stimulus is on, the *a* is much stronger, so the *b* process has only a slight counteracting effect. However, since the *b* process is still going on after the *a* process has returned to zero, the net effect at the end will be negative. Thus the ending of a pleasant experience is not just neutral but slightly unpleasant.

Panel B of the graph shows the situation for the same stimulus after it has been presented many times. The *a* remains the same, but the *b* process has now increased in strength. Thus when we combine the two there is still a pleasant period just after the stimulus goes on and an unpleasant period just after the stimulus goes off, but the relative sizes of these two are much different than before. Whereas at first the initial pleasure was strong and the displeasure at the end mild, now it is just the reverse. As for the period in between, while the stimulus remains on, whereas before it was quite pleasant (though not as much as the initial few moments), now it is barely pleasant at all. The *b* process has not completely counteracted the *a* process during that period of time, but it has come very close to doing so.

If we were graphing an unpleasant primary process, as with the shocked dogs or the skydivers, we would get exactly the same graphs except that the up and down directions would be reversed. The *a* process would now be in the negative direction and the *b* process in the positive direction, but the *b* process would still lag behind the *a*. Moreover, the *b* process would still increase with repeated presentations of the stimulus until it almost but not quite counteracted the unpleasant *a* process.

Some Implications

The most interesting examples of opponent processes are not necessarily the most practical on which to do research. One that lends itself well to quantitative research is *imprinting* in ducklings. The attachment of ducklings to their mother appears to be learned rather than innate, and the process by which it is learned is called imprinting (Lorenz 1952). What most students of imprinting have studied is the duckling's response of following the mother, which can be considered to involve a pleasant *a* process. Solomon and his collaborators chose instead to study the distress calls that the duckling makes when separated from the mother—the opponent *b* process. The number of distress cries in the first minute after separation from the mother makes a good quantitative measure of the strength of the *b* process. In one study (Hoffman et al. 1974) ducklings received 12 exposures of 30 seconds each to the mother with intervals of separation between. For different groups of ducklings, the lengths of the separation periods were different. When these intervals were 1 minute each, the number of distress calls increased from one interval to the next. This change indicates that, as the theory predicts, repeated presentations were strengthening the b process. Where the separation intervals were 5 minutes long, however, no such increase occurred. This difference led the researchers to conclude that repetition increases the strength of the b process only if the repetitions are close enough together. How close is close enough would vary from one situation to another, but for any particular b process there would be a *critical delay duration,* the period within which the stimulus must be presented again in order for the repetition to strengthen the b process. With intervals between presentations that are longer than the critical delay duration, the increase in strength of the b process would not occur.

It should be noted that the increase with repetition in the b process, provided the repetitions come within the critical delay duration, results only from the fact that they occur. This is not a matter of conditioning or even of learning, as that term is often used. Nothing else has to be paired with the b process in order to produce the change. It is the repetition of the b process itself that strengthens it, as in the repeated use of a muscle. Of all the forms of learning we have considered so far, the only one resembling it in this respect is the habituation of the orienting reflex. This kind of change resulting simply from exposure, has, however, received increasing attention relative to more traditional changes through conditioning (e.g., Hill 1978).

Why should there be such opponent processes? We may note that b processes, by counteracting a processes, tend to move hedonic states back toward zero. Thus neither pleasure nor displeasure is able to become very powerful without being counteracted by negative feedback. This tendency would suggest that affective neutrality is a more adaptive state than either strong pleasure or strong displeasure. Perhaps either kind of strong affective state is too much of a strain on the organism, and homeostasis must be restored to keep us from being emotionally worn out. In any case, opponent-process theory resembles traditional drive theory in one respect: both regard a reduction in arousal as the standard tendency of the motivational system.

Although the b process can thus be seen as a negative feedback mechanism correcting a deviation from a set point of affective neutrality, it is not a very efficient one. It undercorrects while the stimulus is on and then overcorrects after the stimulus goes off, pushing the controlled quantity in the opposite direction. As the b process becomes stronger, its undercorrection during the stimulus decreases, but its overcorrection at the end increases. Using the steersman analogy from cybernetics, it is as though the boat is constantly buffeted by strong and rapidly shifting currents, so that the steersman can never completely compensate for them while they are flowing, but then shoots off in the other direction when the current for which he was correcting suddenly stops. Presumably it would be a wild ride indeed if the steersman were not there to exert at least some degree of control.

At a more philosophical level, the theory suggests that the pursuit of pleasure is bound to be less successful than one might hope, since a pleasant a process not only often carries an unpleasant b process along with it but also keeps strengthening that b process. However, the theory also suggests that life's misfortunes are not as bad as they might be, since so many unpleasant a processes have opponent b processes that not only blunt the displeasure but provide a "sweet aftertaste." (Neither Solomon nor anyone else claims to know just how many a processes have opponent b processes strong enough to be important, only that a great many of them do.) As Solomon (1980) comments, it is a puritan's theory. Ralph Waldo Emerson would probably feel that it captures much of the spirit of his essay on compensation.

Chapter
14

Heredity, Evolution, and Learning

Development refers not only to the changes within an individual from conception to death, but also to the changes in a lineage over generations—in other words, evolution. Biologists and physical anthropologists have taken a strong interest in these evolutionary changes, but psychologists have for the most part been little interested in them. Though learning theorists have done research on a variety of species, they have seldom focused on the differences between species, differences that are products of evolution. Rather, they have been mainly interested in the similarities between species, with the differences commonly being dismissed as inconvenient irrelevancies.

Skinner's attitude may be taken as representative. He recognizes that species differ in their responsiveness to different stimuli (e.g., dogs are color-blind, while pigeons have excellent color vision); in the responses they can easily make (e.g., grasping by monkeys but not by dolphins); and in the reinforcers that affect their behavior (e.g., raw worms as positive reinforcers for robins but not for humans). To study learning in different species effectively, therefore, it is necessary to find the right stimuli, responses, and reinforcers for each species. When that is done, however, different species will react to the same independent variable in the same way. A thirsty rat pressing a lever for drops of water, a hungry pigeon pecking a key for access to a hopper of grain, and a human pulling a vending-machine-type plunger for chewing gum will show the same reactions to their schedules of reinforcement. Put all three on a fixed-ratio 5, for example, and their response patterns will be indistinguishable.

This view that the basic laws of learning are the same for different species has been a fundamental tenet of most connectionist learning theories and some cognitive ones. It serves to justify the fact that out of all the species in the world, learning theorists have made greatest use of rats; moderate use of pigeons, monkeys, dogs, and humans; and only slight use of all the rest. It also serves to justify applications of learning theory based largely on rats or pigeons to complex human clinical and social issues, as in the publications of Skinner and of Dollard and Miller. Without this assumption, learning theory would be a substantially different enterprise.

Along with this assumption has gone another: that stimuli, responses, and reinforcers can be paired up in any way, and all ways are equally effective. In other words, how much one learns from a given series of experiences depends on the distinctiveness of the stimuli, the ease of making the required responses, and the effectiveness of the reinforcers, but it does not depend on which stimuli are used with which reinforcers to teach which responses. For example, if lever pressing and jumping are equally easy responses to learn, and if food and escape from shock are equally powerful reinforcers, it does not matter whether the lever pressing is reinforced with food and the jumping with escape from shock or vice versa; either will be learned equally well. This assumption makes it possible to state laws of learning in general terms, referring only to stimuli, responses, and reinforcers, without having to specify what particular ones are to be paired.

SPECIES-SPECIFIC BEHAVIOR

Although the two assumptions above have until recently been basic articles of faith for many if not most learning theorists, evidence has by now been gradually accumulating for a third of a century that they are not altogether valid. Perhaps the first widely noticed sign that all was not well with the assumptions was an article by Keller and Marian Breland. This husband-wife team had been leaders in the use of Skinnerian techniques of animal training, preparing animals to perform on television, at fairs, and in many kinds of exhibits. As such, they were dedicated believers in the power of reinforcement. To their surprise, however, they found their animals sometimes behaving in ways that seemed quite un-Skinnerian. For example, a raccoon that was supposed to put two coins in a slot machine in exchange for food would instead keep rubbing the coins together—as in the raccoon's familiar "food washing" pattern. A pig in a similar situation would drop the coins and root for them in the ground in typical pig fashion. The common problem was that the food-related consummatory responses characteristic of a species often interfered with the response that the experimenter was trying to shape with food reinforcement. Parodying Skinner's book *The Behavior of Organisms* (1938), the Brelands said that they were observing the "misbehavior of organisms" (Breland & Breland 1961).

The "misbehavior" that the Brelands observed consisted of the responses that animals typically make in the presence of food. They are not learned food-getting responses, but innate responses that tend to occur when food is present or is anticipated. Since they vary from species to species, but are relatively fixed and stereotyped for the members of any given species, they are known as *species-specific responses*. Though there are many kinds of species-specific responses, those connected with food are among the most conspicuous to psychologists, since psychologists so often use food as a reinforcer. Since the psychologist arbitrarily selects some response to reinforce, there is always the chance that species-specific responses relevant to the reinforcer will interfere with the animal's making that response.

Species-specific responses do not always interfere with learning, however. In some cases they may make learning easier. Consider, for example, that Skinnerian favorite, a pigeon reinforced with food for pecking a lighted key on the wall of its cage. To Skinner it is obvious that the pigeon pecks because it is reinforced for pecking. However, we can show that things are not always as obvious as they seem. Suppose we vary the experiment by leaving the key dark most of the time, but every now and then lighting it briefly, followed immediately by presenting food. Since the light is always followed by the food, we might expect some form of classical conditioning to occur but we would not expect any operant behavior to be learned, since the food comes regardless of what the pigeon does. Nevertheless, pigeons exposed to this series of events show an increasing tendency to peck the key whenever the light goes on. Skinner might call the pecking a superstition, since anything the pigeon does is followed by food, but the interesting thing is that what pigeons almost universally come to do is that one response—pecking. This process of acquisition, in which pigeons come to peck the lighted key even though there is no systematic connection between the pecking and the food, is called *autoshaping* (Brown & Jenkins 1968).

Once we know that autoshaping will occur, we see the traditional learning to peck a key in a new way. Why do pigeons learn so readily to peck a key when they are reinforced with food? Perhaps it is not so much because pecking is reinforced as because food and a conspicuously peckable target (the key) occur close together. This possibility is strengthened by the fact that autoshaping can occur even when pecking *prevents* the food from appearing on that trial. With that arrangement, pecking is never reinforced; in fact it is punished by loss of food. Nevertheless, most pigeons peck the key often enough under these conditions to lose a substantial proportion of the reinforcers they could have obtained by simply waiting without pecking (Williams & Williams 1969). Apparently, in the presence of food, pecking at the most conspicuous object in the vicinity is a species-specific behavior of pigeons—fortunately so, for this is exactly the behavior that the experimenter wants the pigeon to learn. So, whereas the Brelands kept finding that species-specific behaviors were interfering with what they wanted to teach their animals, here species-specific behavior makes the learning exceptionally easy.

Not all species-specific behaviors involve reward situations. There are also species-specific responses to danger—responses that an organism makes under conditions of pain or fear. In general, such responses to danger involve either fleeing, freezing, or in some cases fighting, but the detailed form they take varies considerably with the species. They are the responses that members of the species tend to make automatically, without the need for any special learning, when confronted with indications of danger.

Just as with species-specific responses to reward, those to danger can either facilitate or interfere with new learning. If an animal can escape or avoid shock by doing something that resembles its species-specific fleeing or freezing behavior, that response will be learned very quickly. If, on the other hand, it can escape or avoid the shock only by doing something very different from its innate reactions to danger, that response will be quite difficult to learn. Bolles (1970) has shown that a number of findings about the way rats learn to escape and to avoid shock, ranging from responses that are often learned in one trial to responses that are nearly impossible for a rat to learn as a way of dealing with shock, can be explained by noting how similar a given response is to the species-specific behavior in situations of danger.

A similar example of a species-specific response giving rise to rapid learning is seen in the experiment by Guthrie and Horton (1946) that was mentioned in Chapter 4. The cats in that study escaped from a puzzle box by bending a flexible pole in the middle of the box. A large proportion of the cats made this response in a stereotyped way, by rubbing their sides against it, rather than moving it in the many other ways that would have been possible. Guthrie saw this stereotyping as evidence that they continued to make the response in whatever way they had made it before. (To Skinner it might be an example of superstition.) It now appears, however, that the cats were actually making a species-specific "greeting" response. Normally cats will rub up against people in that way as a form of greeting. When in the box they cannot rub against people, so they rub against what is available—the pole. The response need not produce escape from the box, or food, or any other obvious reinforcer. However, if there are no humans in the room, the cats do not make the response. This combination of facts suggests that the rubbing was not acquired, as Guthrie believed, by being the last thing done in the situation, but rather that it was an innate species-specific social reaction (Moore & Stuttard 1979).

PREPAREDNESS

What we have seen so far of the misbehavior of organisms is to some degree only an extension of what was already known: that some responses are easier to learn than others, and those that are easiest for one species may be quite different from those that are easiest for another species. It is, however, a considerable extension. Whether a given response is easy or hard for a given individual to learn depends not only on whether the individual is pigeon, pig, or person, but also on the relevant drives and reinforcers. It is not simply that pecking is an easy and natural response for a pigeon, but that it is particularly natural for a hungry pigeon in an environment where there is or has been food. We thus see foreshadowed a new kind of specificity—that certain responses may be easy to learn for one reinforcer but not for another. And indeed that suspicion is quite correct, for pigeons are almost as bad at learning to peck a key to avoid shock as they are good at learning to peck to get food.

Moreover, it turns out that the relationship between responses and reinforcers is only part of the issue. Not only are certain responses easy to learn for some reinforcers and hard for others, but certain stimuli are effective cues for some responses but not for others. One example is what happens when sounds are used as discriminative stimuli for dogs. If the discrimination to be learned is whether to turn right or left for reinforcement, it works well to have a tone coming from above the dog as the cue to turn right and a tone from below the dog as the cue to turn left. If the tones come from the same place, with a high-pitched tone signaling that the food is on the right and a low-pitched tone signaling that it is on the left, learning is much more difficult. Suppose, instead, that the discrimination is whether to go get the food or to stay still and wait for food to come. In that case just the opposite relationship applies. It is easy for the dog to learn that a high-pitched tone means "go" and a low-pitched tone means "stay," but hard to learn that a tone coming from above means "go" and one coming from below means "stay." In short, location of the tone is a good cue for location of the food, and pitch of the tone is a good cue as to whether going for the food will be reinforced, but not vice versa (Lawicka 1964).

So far we have seen that the specific pairing is important both for stimuli with responses and for responses with reinforcers. How about the pairing of stimuli with reinforcers? This too turns out to be important, particularly with negative reinforcers. Suppose you want to teach a rat not to drink a certain liquid by following the drinking with some unpleasant consequence. You might (like many psychologists) use electric shock as the unpleasant consequence. Or you might instead make the rat sick, which can be done by (among other ways) subjecting it to a heavy dose of X rays. Garcia and Koelling (1966) compared these two methods, but they also varied the characteristics of the liquid. In one case what made it distinctive was its sweet taste, in the other case the fact that it was accompanied by a light and a noise. By now you may be able to guess the outcome, even though it came as a surprise to a great many psychologists. If drinking was followed by shock, the rats learned to avoid lighted and noisy liquid, but not to avoid sweet liquid. If drinking was followed by illness, they learned to avoid sweet liquid but not liquid accompanied by light and noise. In this case, therefore, whether or not punishment would lead the rat to avoid a stimulus depended not merely on what the stimulus was and on what negative reinforcer was used as a punisher, but also on which pairing of the two was used.

Martin Seligman, whose work on explanatory styles we considered in Chapter 12, has also taken an interest in the above findings. He concluded that any given organism may be *prepared, unprepared,* or *contraprepared* to learn any particular response to any particular stimulus for any particular reinforcer. Prepared responses are especially easy to learn because they reflect species-specific tendencies; pigeons pecking a lighted key for food are an example. Contraprepared responses are exceptionally difficult to learn because they run counter to species-specific tendencies, as with dogs using the pitch of a tone as the cue for a left-right discrimination. Unprepared responses are those that are neither prepared nor contraprepared, those that can be learned with moderate effort, such as lever-pressing for food by a rat. Learning theorists have tended to think of all responses as unprepared, as neutral with regard to stimuli and reinforcers, capable of being learned but with no special advantage. It is this assumption that Seligman (1970) rejects.

We implied above that preparedness is a characteristic of the species—that learning a particular combination of stimulus, response, and reinforcer may have a different degree of preparedness for one species than for another. There is some evidence to support this prediction, too. For example, we noted above that rats did not learn to avoid a liquid on the basis of its appearance if drinking the liquid was followed by illness, even though they did when drinking was followed by electric shock. Quail, however, for which vision is more important in seeking food, *will* learn to avoid the appearance of a liquid that has been followed by illness (Wilcoxon, Dragoin, & Kral 1971).

Do humans, like rats, pigs, and pigeons, have species-specific tendencies? Humans sometimes seem to be so adaptable, capable of such varied learning, that we might suspect they lack such tendencies. One striking piece of evidence to the contrary is the existence of language. Although many species communicate with sound, and chimps have been taught to carry on conversations in sign language (Gardner & Gardner 1969, 1980; Linden 1974), no species except *Homo sapiens* (so far as we know) uses vocal sound as the basis of a complex, grammatical language. Most humans, by the age of 3 and usually without any deliberate training, have learned to speak in sentences, with an extensive vocabulary, and make reasonably correct use of a complexity of grammatical rules that they would be quite unable to explain. In fact, children under the age of 3 often use the rules more consistently than do adults. For example, they may follow the general rule for plurals by saying "two mans" or the general rule for past tenses by saying "bunny runned away," rather than using the correct irregular forms "men" and "ran." The use of vocal language thus appears to be an example of human species-specific behavior, and the learning of regular grammatical rules a form of prepared behavior.

IMPLICATIONS FOR LEARNING THEORY

At first glance, the notions of species-specific behavior and preparedness seem rather disconcerting for learning theory. The great beauty of learning theory has seemed to be that it offered some hope of reducing all the complexities of learning (and possibly motivation, thinking, or perception as well) to a manageable list of general laws. These laws would not depend on the particular stimuli, responses, and reinforcers being learned or on the species being studied. Thus experiments on rats pressing levers would be relevant to the training of seeing-eye dogs, and experiments on pigeons pecking keys would be relevant to humans working on a production line. But if the laws of learning depend on what particular stimulus, response, or reinforcer are being paired, and for what species, can there be any such generality? Must the simplicity and generality of theory that psychologists of learning have sought be replaced by a bewildering complexity of highly specific laws?

Although the recent findings we have discussed are discouraging for the more optimistic hopes of learning theorists, they are by no means disastrous. For one thing, the degree of generality of any given law is a matter to be determined by research. It remains to be seen how many of the laws of learning are specific to the stimulus, response, reinforcer, and species, versus how many have the degree of generality for which learning theorists hope.

For another thing, it has always been the role of theory to organize laws in some more general way. Perhaps the situation now seems confused only because we have no good way to predict what particular combinations of stimuli, responses, and reinforcers will be easily learned by which species. What is needed is a theory that can tell us under what conditions a response is prepared, unprepared, or contraprepared. Finding the right bases of classification for independent and dependent variables and finding intervening variables to link them meaningfully is what theories are all about. The task of learning theory may be even more challenging than had previously been realized, but that does not mean that theorists cannot rise to the challenge. If the world of variables and laws relevant to learning seems to be in a state of confusion, there is all the more need for theories to bring order out of that confusion.

Moreover, there is already a basis for starting to find that order. Species-specific behavior and preparedness are part of the biological heritage of a given species. This heritage is by no means random. The characteristics of any species have come about through the process of evolution, according to the principle of natural selection. Presumably, therefore, the characteristics of any species are those that have helped that species to survive. If we want to find order in the patterns of learning, we need to ask what patterns are likely to have had survival value in the environment where the ancestors of a given species lived.

Let us consider the case of a rat learning what to avoid in its environment. (For the present purpose it does not matter whether we assume it is learning a habit of avoidance or a cognition about what is dangerous.) If it gets sick, it is probably because of something it ate, and the best way of recognizing that food again is by taste or smell. Whether the dangerous food was in a place that was light or dark or noisy or quiet probably had nothing to do with whether the food would make it sick. It would therefore be to the rat's advantage to learn to avoid any food that tasted like what it ate before it became ill, but it would not be to the rat's advantage to avoid eating in places that looked or sounded like the place where it ate the tainted food. Suppose, however, that it suffered an injury. In that case, the taste or smell of anything it ate just before would probably be irrelevant, but what the place looked or sounded like would be much more likely to serve as a warning of traps or predators or other dangers. It would thus be to its advantage to avoid places that looked or sounded like the place where it was hurt, but of no advantage to avoid foods that tasted like what it ate before it was hurt. The reader will note that this is exactly the learning pattern that Garcia and Koelling (1966) found.

For other species, what it is most adaptive for the individual to learn might be different. A bird preparing to swoop down and capture its dinner cannot afford to follow the rat's strategy of carefully tasting a bit of food to see if it has the same flavor as something that once made the animal sick. The bird is much better off deciding on the basis of what it can see whether to snap up an insect that may or may not be edible. One would predict, therefore, that when a bird eats something that makes it sick, the bird will learn to avoid other foods that look the same, to a much greater extent than do rats. As already noted for quail, that is what has been found.

To find such evidence that organisms learn in ways that are adaptive for their lifestyle, we do not need to compare organisms as different as rats and quail.

Cowan (1977) studied a different form of avoidance learning—the tendency to avoid an unfamiliar object that suddenly appears in a familiar place. He compared this kind of learning among several kinds of rats. Some were lab rats, whose ancestors had lived in lab rat colonies for numerous generations. Others were members of the same species, but their recent ancestors were wild rats, living close to humans in houses and alleys, but not domesticated. A third group were members of two different species of rat, one living in the desert and the other in the forest, but both far from humans.

All three of these kinds of rats were kept in a maze until they were familiar with it, at which point two white aluminum cubes were put in one of the arms. One of the three kinds of rat showed a strong tendency to avoid that arm for all of the next day; the other two did not. Which of the three might we expect it to be?

If we simply try to guess which group would be most distinctive from the others in general, we would probably predict that it would be the desert and forest rats, since they were of different species from the others. They were also the ones whose ancestors had lived for the shortest time in captivity; indeed, some of these rat subjects had themselves been born in the wild. If, instead, we focus on wildness versus domestication, we might expect the lab rats to be most distinctive from the others, since their ancestors had been domesticated by humans for many generations. Both of these predictions, however, would be wrong.

If we ask for what kind of rat such an avoidance response would be adaptive, we might predict instead that the most cautious around the new objects would be the wild rats whose ancestors had lived near humans but had not been domesticated by them. Why? One of the great risks their ancestors faced was being trapped by humans, and only those rats that avoided the risk at least long enough to have offspring ever got to pass their genes on to subsequent generations. Since a rat trap generally appears as an unfamiliar object in a familiar place, rats that avoided such objects would be the ones most likely to become ancestors and to pass that form of caution on to their descendents. As predicted, it was this group that avoided the unfamiliar objects in the familiar maze. Again, therefore, we see an example of differences in the pattern of learning (or, in this case, motivated behavior resulting from learning of familiarity) that fit predictions from the principle of evolutionary adaptation.

More on the Concept of Adaptation

Organic evolution and learning have a good deal in common, at least if one takes a reinforcement view of learning. In natural selection, which is the basis of evolution, those behaviors (as well as structures) that work for a species are passed on to subsequent generations. In learning, those behaviors that work for an individual are continued by that individual. In learning, the mechanism is reinforcement of some behaviors and not of others. In evolution the mechanism is selective survival and procreation: those organisms that tend to behave in certain ways because of their genes are more likely to survive and pass those genes on to their offspring. In spite of their differences, both natural selection and learning are adaptive mechanisms that increase the effectiveness of organisms in dealing with their environment.

Given that both processes are forms of adaptation to the environment, it remains only to look at their connection. The capacity to learn in certain ways is one of the characteristics that increases (or decreases) through evolution. To put it another way, natural selection determines the ways in which learning will evolve in a given species. In trying to predict an organism's preparedness for given patterns of stimuli, responses, and reinforcers, it therefore seems reasonable to ask, "What pattern would be most likely to have survival value in the environment in which this species evolved?" What this means is that a theory of learning is most likely to be complete and accurate if it is a theory of evolution as well—or, most generally, a theory of overall adaptation to the environment.

THE PLACE OF HEREDITY IN BEHAVIOR

No one questions that heredity is important in determining our behavior. If human beings inherited hands without an opposable thumb, or inherited nervous systems that were not capable of acquiring language, our behavior would be greatly different, and civilization as we know it would never have appeared. What is controversial is the particular ways in which heredity expresses its importance.

Shared Heredity: Sociobiology

One controversial question is the extent to which our common heredity as human beings sets limits on what we can learn, or at least biases us to learn certain things much more readily than others. Such biases might involve either such cognitive matters as finding language easier to learn than math or such emotional matters as finding it easier to condition a fear of snakes than a fear of flowers. The main thrust of this chapter has been that such constraints on learning are more widespread than earlier learning theorists recognized. Though learning has enormous effects on how we think and feel, what we do, indeed what we are, it has those effects within the framework of our shared biological humanness.

Some of the theorists who focus on this aspect of heredity and on its relation to evolution are known as *sociobiologists* (a term coined by Wilson, 1975). Sociobiologists analyze human social behavior (and that of other species) in terms of adaptive inherited mechanisms. Whereas learning theorists look at how adaptations are acquired by learning within an individual's life, sociobiologists look at those adaptations that have been acquired over a time scale of many generations by a different process, that of biological evolution.

For this evolutionary analysis, adaptation is a matter of passing on one's genes to future generations, so that those genes become more frequent over successive generations. In this evolutionary sense, a well-adapted individual is one who has many surviving offspring, not necessarily one who is strong or intelligent or economically successful or socially dominant. Any trait that tends to result in many surviving offspring is adaptive, whether it works by keeping the individual alive long enough to have children, or by giving the individual more chances to have children, or by keeping those children alive and healthy. In analyzing how these adaptive traits work, sociobiologists talk in terms of *strategies*. These are usually not strategies in the sense of deliberate plans, but just things that certain animals or people tend to do that typically result in their having more offspring that survive.

Though some of the sociobiologists' examples involve careful studies of the behavior of birds or of insects, those pertaining to humans are often presented in casual, anecdotal ways. This casualness, like Guthrie's style of discussing learning, tends both to make them more interesting and to leave the impression that sociobiologists perhaps care more about being clever and 'relevant' than about being scientific.

As an example, consider a girl who asks her brother to do her a favor, one that will require some minor sacrifice on the brother's part. He refuses. She appeals to their mother, who tells the brother that he ought to be more generous to his sister. He feels that their mother's reaction is unfair—"Why should I make a sacrifice for *her?*" However, on a different occasion he unhesitatingly goes to a good deal of effort to support his sister in a conflict with someone outside the family. Why does each of these three people show the particular attitudes about family cooperation that he or she does?

Though the particular favor the sister wants is trivial, sociobiologists ask us to analyze these little incidents as though the brother's sacrifices for his sister—both the sacrifice he objected to making and the one he made gladly—would be of major importance to both their lives. Suppose that the favor the sister wanted were a huge one, which might affect both his and her survival or chance of having children. We can then think of his making the sacrifice for her as reducing his biological adaptation but increasing hers. Looking at the little family drama in this somewhat melodramatic way, can we explain the characters' attitudes?

The key to the three characters' attitudes is their degree of genetic relationship. Since the brother and sister share half of their genes, if she is more successful in passing on her genes to the next generation, this means that her brother's genes are being passed on, too, though to only half as great a degree. It is therefore to his advantage to help her as long as it does not harm him. Indeed, it is still to his advantage to help her even if it does harm him, provided it helps her more than twice as much as it harms him. This explains why he was quick to support her interests against an outsider. However, a sacrifice that helps her less than twice as much as it harms him is to his disadvantage, so he refuses to do it.

What of their mother? Her chance of passing her genes on to future generations depends equally on both of her children. Therefore, any sacrifice the brother makes for his sister is beneficial to the mother, as long as it helps his sister more than it harms him. She, therefore, urges a greater degree of generosity to his sister than seems fair to him.

To sociobiologists, this sort of analysis helps us to see the genetic, adaptive basis of many of our attitudes and behaviors, revealing the profound significance of what seems at first glance a trivial family disagreement. To critics of sociobiology, however, it seems silly to jump so glibly from a precise calculation based on number of surviving offspring to trivial favors that a brother may or may not do for his sister. The sociobiologist would reply to the critic that we do not actually make these calculations, but we are programmed by our genes to behave as if we did make them, in small matters as well as in the large matters where they are most obviously appropriate. The critic would then reply that these behaviors depend so much on social and cultural learning that the sociobiologist's genetic analysis misses the main point, and the sociobiologist would reply in turn that social and cultural learning are themselves influenced by our shared human genes. The argument could go on and on, but at least the example shows how assumptions about our shared human nature can be used to make predictions about our social attitudes and behavior.

Heredity and Individual Differences

The other question about the role of heredity deals with individual differences: How much do the differences among individuals depend on their genes? Since this is a book on learning, what little we have considered about individual differences has focused on how they are learned, on how we acquire the habits, cognitions, or emotional reactions that make us unique individuals. However, these learned differences are only part of the story. Differences among individuals also depend on differences in their genes, and the relative importance of genes and of learning in determining the differences among people has long been a major controversy in psychology.

For perhaps a half century, beginning in the 1920s, learning was regarded as the major determining factor in individual differences. To a considerable degree, this emphasis reflected the influence of behaviorism, with its enthusiasm for the improvability of human behavior and society. However, it also reflected at least two other influences. One of these was cultural anthropology. As anthropologists studied the world's many cultures closely (rather than just calling some "primitive" and others "advanced"), they discovered great differences among these cultures both in the details of behavior and in the broad systems of beliefs and values. Moreover, it became increasingly clear that these cultural differences were learned: they reflected the demands of the environment and the history of cultural contact rather than the biological ancestries of the people in any given culture. The other influence was psychoanalysis, which focused on the ways that different childhood experiences might have profound effects on adult personality. The combined effect of behaviorism, cultural anthropology, and psychoanalysis (however much they might disagree about other things) was to advance the belief that differences among human beings result largely from differences in their experiences.

Although the influence of learning was emphasized, the importance of heredity in individual differences was not completely ignored. Even Watson admitted that inherited physical differences had *some* effect on behavior. More recently, these genetic factors have received increased attention. Evidence has accumulated that genetic factors are major contributors to individual differences in abilities, personality characteristics, sexual orientation, even vocational preferences. Research has suggested as a convenient (though of course very rough) rule of thumb that half of the variation among people in a variety of personal characteristics is due to differences in their genes, and half to all environmental factors combined (Bouchard, 1994).

To the extent that this view is correct, there is no clear victory for either a hereditary or an environmental interpretation. However, this view still represents a disappointment to those who hoped to use learning as a highroad to human perfectability, just as does the emphasis on species-specific characteristics that can be modified only with great difficulty by learning. In some ways, it is even more of a disappointment to such hopes than appears at first glance. When we say that only half of the variation among individuals is environmental, we are including not only learning experiences but also such other environmental influences as nutrition and exposure to diseases. This means that all learning experiences combined, whether systematic (like parental teaching of their values) or accidental (like being a crime victim), account for less than half of the variation in behavior among individual human beings.

However, there is another aspect to the conclusion that also needs to be kept in mind. To a great extent, the influence of the genes is mediated by learning experiences. For example, if someone inherits a high aptitude for sports, that person is more likely to seek out opportunities to participate in sports, and is also likely to be treated differently by other people than if he or she lacked this aptitude. These different behaviors mean, in turn, that the person will have a different set of learning experiences, and hence will learn somewhat different things from what other people learn. Since the fact that this person had these particular learning experiences depended originally on his or her genes, they are included in the hereditary part of the influences on the person's development. Nevertheless, they involve learning, and environmental factors could have affected the outcome (Bouchard, Lykken, McGue, Segal, & Tellegen, 1990).

How might environmental factors have changed the outcome? Consider, as a related example, all the ways in which people who inherit good looks (as defined by their culture) tend to have different experiences from people who are considered physically unattractive. Such differences may range from being more talked to by strangers as children to having more dates as teenagers to finding it easier to get jobs dealing with the public to being suspected of a lack of intellectual depth. If the attractive and unattractive people grow up with different degrees of self-confidence or social dominance or seriousness, these differences will be treated by researchers as results of their different genes, even though differences in learning were crucially involved.

Moreover, suppose that these children had grown up in a different culture, where the standards of physical beauty were different. The same genetic differences that gave them different appearances would have had quite different outcomes, since other people's reactions to them would have been so different from what those reactions actually were. If the standards of beauty were opposite to what they are in our culture (if, e.g., they grew up in one of those cultures where fatness is as valued as thinness is for us), the two children's learned traits might also have been opposite to what they were in our culture. If, instead, it had been a culture in which physical attractiveness was of less interest to people, the attractive and unattractive children might have grown up much more alike. The effects of differences in heredity are thus greatly modified by the particular learning environment in which one lives.

The above discussion of genetic factors in the development of individual differences points in the same direction as our earlier discussion of genetic species-specific factors. Both show that the effects of learning are more complex than were previously realized, and cannot be studied thoroughly without also considering heredity. However, they leave unchanged the conclusion that learning is of crucial importance to individual differences, to social structure, and to our very humanness.

Chapter
15

Learning Theory Past, Present, and Future

*I*n any survey of an area of knowledge, such as that attempted in this book, there is a great danger that the reader will come away with a kaleidoscope of impressions—some, we may hope, interesting and enlightening—but with no overall picture of the field. To a cognitive theorist, at least, such an outcome would seem most regrettable. In hopes of avoiding this, let us consider what the various interpretations we have examined can contribute to our understanding of learning.

ISSUES ON WHICH LEARNING THEORIES DIVIDE

The theories we have considered in this book can be grouped according to the ways they answer certain basic questions, including questions about both the nature of learning and the process of theory building (Hillner 1978). The answers to these questions indicate not the details of the theory but in broad outline what it tries to do and how it tries to do it. Eight such questions (differing somewhat from Hillner's) are given below.

Eight Controversial Questions

The first question a learning theorist needs to answer is whether or not to use intervening variables. Tolman, who introduced the idea of intervening variables into psychology, and Hull, who developed the most elaborate system, are the two theorists who have given the most emphatically positive answers to this question. Skinner, with his rejection of theories of learning, has given the clearest negative answer. Most theorists have included elements in their theories that could reasonably be called intervening variables, but often without labeling them as such. The most common answer to this question might therefore be given as "yes, but. . ."

The second question is whether the intervening variables, or whatever else plays a similar role in the theory, should be connectionist or cognitive. This is the question that has caused more argument than any other in the history of learning theory, and around which more than any other this book has been organized. For about three quarters of the history of the field, connectionist theories were dominant and set the tone of the field.

More recently, cognitive approaches have come to dominate the scene, a change dramatic enough to be called the cognitive revolution. Various attempts have been made to combine the best features of both, though usually with a noticeable leaning one way or the other. Among these, the new connectionism of network models derives cognitive behavior from connectionist assumptions in quite sophisticated ways. There is now widespread agreement that some behavior seems superficially to fit better with connectionist interpretations and other behavior better with cognitive ones, but the disagreement goes on as to what type of intervening variable works best overall.

The third question deals with reinforcement: Is reinforcement a basic and central principle of learning, or is it a sloppy way of talking about certain phenomena that could more appropriately be explained in other ways? Thorndike, Hull, and Skinner have been among the strongest supporters of the former answer, and Watson and Guthrie the strongest supporters of the latter. Cognitive theorists have tended to prefer the latter interpretation, though for reasons quite different from Watson's and Guthrie's, and without putting as much emphasis on the issue. As a result, the cognitive revolution has included a rejection of reinforcement as an automatic stamping in of response tendencies. However, the empirical law that reinforcement typically increases the tendency to make a response is still generally accepted, however one chooses to interpret it.

The fourth question, not as strongly argued but nonetheless significant, is whether learning should be analyzed at a molar or a molecular level. All theorists work at least partly at the molar level, that is, at the level of everyday acts, but they differ as to whether these acts should be explained by analysis at a more molecular level. Though Tolman was most explicit about staying at the molar level, the majority of the theorists we have considered also took a predominantly molar position. One striking exception was Guthrie, who saw the learning of molar acts as resulting from a more basic kind of learning at the molecular level, a conditioning of tiny elements that combine to produce the molar acts.

The fifth question is whether the theory should be presented formally or casually. The majority of the earlier systems were closer to the casual end of the scale: even when there was the suggestion of a strong logical structure to the theory (as, e.g., with Guthrie), it was not worked out with the formal trappings of logic and philosophy of science. Hull, in contrast, did have those formal trappings; he presented the logical structure of his theory explicitly. Tolman was fairly formal at times, but had trouble sticking to any one particular structure. More recently, a number of mathematical model builders have been formal. Computer approaches have had to be formal in the sense of giving precise instructions to the computer, since that is the only kind computers respond to (understand?). It is not always clear how to relate these formal computer programs to more general formulations about the nature of learning, but Anderson is among those who have made a strong effort to do so.

The sixth question is one of breadth: How wide a range of topics should a theory try to deal with? There is some tendency for those theories that answer the fifth question in favor of formality to answer this one in favor of narrowness. Almost inevitably, the more formally a theory is stated, the more rigorous and precise it will have to be, which in turn makes it harder for the theory to deal effectively with a wide range of topics. A more casually stated theory, however, can deal with a wider range of topics with less danger of being caught in inconsistencies or ambiguities. Nevertheless, a theory that would combine formal precision with great breadth is such a desirable goal that its challenge has continued to lure theorists. Hull tried hard to achieve such a theory, and while part of his failure can be attributed to his invalidism and premature death, part of it also reflects the enormous difficulty of the challenge. Though Hull's impressive failure may have led a number of other theorists to stick to narrower theories, some have continued to try to combine formal rigor with breadth. Anderson is an example.

The seventh question is how much emphasis to give to the innate aspects of behavior and to the biological constraints on learning. This has been a major issue for considerably less than half the history of learning theory, and for most of the theories we have considered the answer has been "not much emphasis." American learning theory, from Watson and Thorndike on, has emphasized the acquired over the innate; although Watson's rejection of hereditary factors was extreme, it nevertheless set the tone for the field. Increasingly, however, theorists are considering this issue. The importance of biological factors in learning is being increasingly recognized, even among Skinnerians. The question is how far those concessions should go. Are we now in a phase that overemphasizes the innate, as the earlier phase probably overestimated the acquired, or are we only beginning to discover the actual extent of biological constraints on learning and behavior? It is a question for which theorists have only recently begun to stand up and be counted.

Finally, there is the question of practicality. Is a theory of learning a creation of the laboratory and the armchair, an intellectual exercise in understanding the world, or is it a device for dealing with and perhaps changing that world? Though at times theorists have demanded the right to do pure science, undistracted by any pressures toward practical usefulness, that attitude has been distinctly the exception. The question is not so much whether theories of learning should be useful but rather who should do the applying. Some theorists, like Thorndike and Skinner, have jumped directly into applications. Others, like Dollard and Miller and Tolman, have written about possible applications but played relatively little part in putting them into practice. Still others, like Hull, have been themselves pure scientists but had substantial influence on others of a more applied bent. Even these examples are debatable; the distinction is a hard one to maintain, given the generally applied nature of American learning theory.

Positions of the Right, Left, and Center

Although all of the above issues have to some extent divided learning theories, the two that dominated much of the history of the field were the second and third, as can be inferred from the table of contents of this book. If we look at the positions various theorists took on these two issues, we can see the history of American learning theory through the greater part of the twentieth century as consisting of a mainstream that dominated the field, withstood challenges from different directions, incorporated some of those challenges within the mainstream, and continued on its way. This is the connectionist-reinforcement tradition that began with Thorndike, reached its greatest theoretical flowering in Hull, and has more recently been dominated by Skinner. It may seem odd to group Hull and Skinner together in this way, given the sharp disagreements between them about both theory construction and research technique—especially since Skinner is not a connectionist in the narrow sense of talking about habits or stimulus-response bonds as something inside the organism. Nevertheless, they stand together in contrast to two other traditions that have challenged the mainstream.

Perhaps it would be best at this point to change the metaphor to a political one and speak of the mainstream instead as a party of the center. Its basic principle is that what is learned is the tendency to make various responses, and that an essential feature in that learning is reinforcement. This party of the center was challenged both from the right and from the left by smaller though vocal parties. The party of the right agreed enthusiastically with the center that what was learned was responses, and focused even more consistently than the center on the stimulus-response bond as the unit of learning. It disagreed with the center, however, in rejecting the central role of reinforcement in favor of simple contiguity as the basic principle of learning. It is the most mechanistic of the approaches, and it focuses particularly on the importance of practice and of learning by doing. The outstanding figures in this party of the right were Watson and Guthrie. Its challenge to the center was thus most dominant in the earlier part of the century, though its influence continues to be felt.

The challenge from the left, in contrast, has to a considerable degree ignored the reinforcement issue and instead concentrated on rejecting the idea that responses are what is learned. Instead, they argue that we learn knowledge, beliefs, expectancies, understanding—in other words, cognitions. Among actual learning theorists, the outstanding early exponent of this position was Tolman. Although Tolman himself never succeeded in founding a school of psychology, his point of view remained influential. For a number of years the dominant theme in learning theory was the attempt by the center to incorporate cognitive ideas like Tolman's into its theories while still maintaining a basically connectionist orientation. Then the cognitive approach became increasingly strong and took over the central position, pushing the former center off to the right.

What is the present situation? Although the old right no longer represents a strong position, in a limited sense it made its point. Few theorists now regard reinforcement in the Thorndikian way, as stamping in stimulus-response bonds. Rather, the majority see learning as taking place by contiguity, as the right claimed, and reinforcement as affecting only the performance of what has already been learned. However, this learning by contiguity is seen as involving contiguity of stimuli with other stimuli more than contiguity of stimuli with responses. This view therefore contains more of Tolman and later cognitive theorists than of Guthrie or Watson. The old right has thus left its most distinctive influence within current cognitive theory, the last place its supporters would have expected. It is an irony that Tolman would have enjoyed.

Indeed, the main question is how far the former left, in becoming the center, has crowded the former center off to the right. Some would argue that it has done so completely, and that the former center is not only crowded off to the side but moribund—a relic of interest only to antiquarians. Others would argue that the former center, though much less influential than in the past, is still competing with the former left, now the center, on nearly equal terms.

The argument focuses partly on Skinner's place in the current scene. On the one hand, he more than anyone else represents learning theory to those outside the field. This is ironic, in view of his claim not to be a theorist, yet it is just as an exemplar of the traditional ideals of learning theory—straightforward, wide-ranging, practical—that Skinner has his greatest influence. He does not represent the psychology of learning as a whole, which is now too cognitive for his taste, but the traditional connectionist-reinforcement mainstream of learning theory, a direct descendent of Thorndike. Does he represent the last flickering popularization of a dying tradition, or does he represent those aspects of learning theory that will have the most lasting influence on psychology and on other fields?

The argument also focuses partly on interpretations of the new connectionism of network models and parallel distributed processing. To its supporters, this approach combines the best features of other approaches and resolves the disagreements between the older connectionist and cognitive positions. It demonstrates, they claim, that learning distributed through many specific connections can combine to produce a quite gestaltish cognitive outcome. Its opponents claim, however, that it has serious problems and so far represents much more of high hopes than of real achievement. With this approach, as with the Skinnerian, only time will tell.

CRITERIA FOR AN IDEAL THEORY

The arguments among theorists of learning are not as strident as they were in the "golden age" of learning theory, when Hull traded barbs with Guthrie on the right and Tolman on the left, while Skinner in effect said, "A plague on all your houses." More of the theorizing is in the form of models for predicting a narrower range of phenomena, with each theorist trying to see how far a given model can go in predicting data. Thus the person who developed a model may also be the one who reveals its inadequacies, as suggested in the title of an article by Frank Restle (1966): "Run Structure and Probability Learning: Disproof of Restle's Model."

Nevertheless, more general disagreements do remain, and we can reasonably ask to what extent the questions raised in the previous section can now be resolved. To put it another way, can we now see what the criteria for an ideal theory of learning would be?

The ideal kind of theory toward which the most ambitious theorists strive is much like the ideal that Hull set up but failed to realize: formal, precise, internally consistent, yet at the same time broad enough to cover the whole range of topics in learning and motivation. It would have postulates and theorems and would be so constructed that it could be changed to deal with new evidence as one or another theorem failed to be confirmed by experiments. Given this combination of breadth and precision, it inevitably would be useful in the solution of practical problems.

This ideal theory would undoubtedly include intervening variables, and being a formal theory it would be quite explicit about what they were. These intervening variables would be much more cognitive than those of the earlier theories of the center; they would deal with beliefs and the evidence on which they are based, with the calculation of contingencies between events, with the incorporation of new experience into schemas, with both logical and illogical thinking. The theory would thus have a very cognitive sound—not only more so than any of the connectionist theories we have considered, but perhaps even more so than some of the cognitive ones. However, there would be postulates linking the cognitions both to behavior and to the processes by which cognitions are acquired and changed, thus making the theory behavioristic in the very broad sense of that term. So, while its format would be most like Hull's, its content would be more like Tolman's. It might be quite close to Anderson's ACT.

Such a cognitive theory would be less disturbing to connectionist theorists than would be the case if we were not familiar with computers. Since the computer, which is physically a connectionist device, can be programmed to behave in such cognitive ways, a connectionist theorist might argue that he was right all along, that this is really a connectionist theory that deals effectively with the behaviors, including internal ones, of reasoning, imagining, seeking explanations of past events, and making plans for future actions. It could thus be considered either an updating of Tolman or an extreme modification of connectionist theory to incorporate cognitive findings. It might turn out to be much like the new connectionist network theories currently being developed—but that remains to be seen.

Moreover, the theory would need to be somewhat connectionist in another sense. It would have to explain not only our knowledge and understanding but also the responses we make automatically without thinking and the skills we are able to perform without being able to explain just how we do them. Even Tolman (1949) conceded that there is noncognitive learning of what he called motor patterns. Again the computer analogy is helpful, since computers can just as easily be programmed to make certain specific responses under certain conditions as to behave in more cognitive ways. So, while the details of the theory would be very complex, there should be no problem for the theorist in having some of those details appear straightforwardly connectionist and others highly cognitive.

The complexity of the theory would be of a developmental sort. In other words, it would explain how humans and animals get programmed to function in the way they do. The word "programmed," of course, reflects again the computer analogy. A computer system consists basically of certain "hardware," which are the computer itself and its peripheral attachments, as pieces of machinery. These are comparable to the physique, perceptual and learning capacities, and innate motivational tendencies of an organism. To be useful, the computer system must also have "software," the programs that determine what it will do. Whereas computer programs are written by people, the programs of people and animals are developed through experience. Learning can thus be regarded as the process that corresponds to program writing. We might say either that a computer is like an animal that has been carefully trained, or that an animal (or person) is like a computer with a very open-ended program that in effect keeps rewriting itself on the basis of its experience. Again, the new connectionist network models may have a lot to offer here.

The hardware, of course, corresponds to those species-specific characteristics that set constraints on behavior and learning. Some computers can do jobs that others cannot. Of two that can both do a job, one can often do it faster than the other, or the procedure that is fastest for one computer to do may be different from that which is fastest for the other. These are the same sorts of differences that are found among species of animals, and to a lesser extent among individuals within a species. However, in humans and animals, unlike computers, they represent hereditary differences developed through natural selection over many generations. They are the constraints within which learning has to work, but within which it can still produce enormous individual differences in behavior depending on differences in experience.

The results of this long-term programming would have a hierarchical structure, as suggested by Gagné and numerous other people. As indicated above, the hierarchy would include both knowledge that can be expressed in words or other symbols and skills that to a considerable degree cannot, as noted by Anderson. These skills would very likely be analyzed in cybernetic terms, with each unit of skill in the hierarchy dependent on lower-level units that would serve to maintain the set point of the higher-level unit. The process by which all of these hierarchies would develop would be one of accommodation, as described by Piaget, in which the structure would gradually change in response to experiences that were inconsistent with it. However, in most cases these accommodations would not be simply changes but rather the incorporation of less adequate patterns of skill and understanding into higher-level patterns that would include their good points while at the same time improving on them. Though this process includes the possibility of mistaken or maladaptive learning, such as that discussed by Dollard and Miller, for the most part it would involve a continuing increase both in complexity and in effectiveness.

How would reinforcement and motivation be treated? This may be the hardest question for which to provide even the outline of an answer. On the one hand, as we have noted, there is fairly wide support for the view that much learning depends only on contiguity, without the need for reinforcement. This includes not only learning by doing but also learning by observation, as emphasized particularly by Bandura. In this view, we acquire knowledge and skills by a mixture of observation and practice. Among the things we learn are what activities toward what objects are rewarding or punishing. We then use our knowledge and skills to obtain access to the rewards and to avoid the punishments.

On the other hand, there seem clearly to be some cases that do not fit this interpretation. When we gradually master a skill without being able to explain completely what we are now doing differently, the best explanation seems to be that the precise responses that work are being acquired and those that don't work are dropping out. Though Guthrie would say that "work" means "change the situation into something else," most people would insist that it means "change the situation into something *better*." This latter meaning sounds like traditional Thorndikian reinforcement: stamping in the rewarded stimulus-response bonds. So, although the simple, old-fashioned notion of reinforcement is a good deal less popular than it used to be, it doesn't look as though we can entirely get rid of it.

Perhaps the ideas of cybernetics can help here. They suggest that all the stimuli Skinner would call positive reinforcers are signals that a deviation is being corrected, that one is moving closer to a set point. With higher-level set points, we can describe accurately what is happening, and in those cases we may speak of the set point as an incentive toward which behavior is directed. With lower-level set points we are only hazily able to describe what is happening, or perhaps not at all able, making the term *incentive* seem inappropriate. However, what is actually going on is the same at all levels: a set point, deviations from it, behavior that serves to reduce the deviations, and "reinforcement" by getting closer to the set point. The principles are the same; only the degree of our conscious awareness is different. This is one direction from which a resolution of the question about reinforcement might eventually come. It would be ironic if cybernetics, which has very little to say directly about learning, should nevertheless provide the answer to such a persistent issue in learning theory as the nature and significance of reinforcement.

For a complete theory, a number of other topics would also need to be considered. One is perception: How do we convert the physical energy that stimulates our sense receptors into perceptions of objects and events? Of the theorists we have considered, only the gestaltists put much emphasis on this question, and they were only secondarily interested in learning. Another topic is attention. Though theorists differ as to whether it is possible to learn about something without paying any attention to it, we can at least say with confidence that one usually learns more about something to which one is paying attention than about something to which one is not. Bandura discusses this issue, but again most of the theorists we have considered largely ignored it. A third topic is memory: What determines how well we retain what we have learned? This issue has come up a number of times in this book, but it has not been a really central issue for any of the theorists we have considered. During the history of psychology, research and theory on memory have to a substantial degree gone on separately from research and theory on learning. In recent years cognitive psychology has changed from being one possible approach to the study of learning to being a separate field of study, focusing much more on perception, attention, memory, and other aspects of information processing. Though a complete theory needs to incorporate these topics, just as it needs to consider the physiology and biochemistry of our nervous systems, they are topics that would have taken this book too far afield.

THE PRESENT-DAY VALUE OF LEARNING THEORIES

Whatever form the theory of the future may take, most of us have to make the best of the theories we have today. Granted that all of them fall short of the ideals we have set for a truly adequate theory, what use can we make of them? For the most part, whatever exact predictions they make are applicable only to carefully controlled laboratory conditions. They can rarely predict directly to the complex, uncontrolled conditions of everyday life. Even with the most precise of scientific theories, engineers are needed who can use their ingenuity and experience to apply the theory to practical ends. Since theories of learning are not among the most precise, this "psychological engineering" is perhaps even more challenging than in other areas of science. Such "engineering" enters into many jobs, from animal training to psychological warfare, but above all it is the province of the educator.

Hilgard (1964) has argued that a single category of behavioral engineers or applied psychologists, in contrast to pure research psychologists, is much too simple. He suggests that we can distinguish six steps along the scale from the "purest" of researchers on learning at one extreme to the "purest" of educational appliers at the other. The first three steps all fall under the heading of "pure-science research," but vary in the extent to which the learners and the learned materials resemble those in ordinary educational practice. The remaining three steps, which he groups under "technological research and development," are of more specific interest here. These are step 4—"research conducted in special laboratory classrooms, with selected teachers"; step 5—"a tryout of the results of prior research in a 'normal' classroom with a typical teacher"; and step 6—"developmental steps related to advocacy and adoption" (1964, p. 409). Here the research and development proceed from asking "Will it work under the best of conditions?" in step 4, to "Will it work under typical conditions?" in step 5, to "Will it be generally adopted by educators?" in step 6.

The applied psychology of learning is important not only as a way of putting theories to practical use but also as a way of improving theories. Along with their other contributions, applied studies help to determine the limitations of theories. If a theory based on laboratory data is used to make predictions to an applied situation, and the predictions are not confirmed, this event shows that the theory is not appropriate for that situation. It may still, however, be a perfectly good theory for predicting in other situations. In addition, applied studies reveal new laws that may then be used in the modification of old theories or the construction of new ones. For example, as we noted earlier, Gagné developed his ideas about the hierarchical organization of tasks largely as a result of an unsuccessful attempt to apply more traditional laws of learning to the problems of military training. The ideas about learning that emerged from that applied work served as the basis for new theoretical developments in the pure psychology of learning.

For most of us, the various learning theories have two chief values. One is in providing us with a vocabulary and a conceptual framework for interpreting the examples of learning that we observe. These are valuable for anyone who is alert to the world. The other, closely related, is in suggesting where to look for solutions to practical problems. The theories do not give us solutions, but they do direct our attention to those variables that are crucial in finding solutions.

Let us consider the ways in which various theoretical interpreters do these two things for us. Guthrie directs our attention to the importance of practicing the particular responses to be learned under the particular conditions in which they will be used, and also to the value of practicing them under varied conditions if they are to be firmly established and lasting. Skinner advises us always to find out what reinforces a given act, so that we can present that reinforcer if we want the act to occur or remove it if we want to extinguish the act. Dollard and Miller warn us to consider the drives that may be learned in a situation and may then serve as the basis of new, often undesired, learning. Wertheimer and Köhler point out the importance of arranging learning situations so as to foster real, creative understanding rather than blind rote memorization. Bandura reminds us how much of our learning involves observation of other people's behavior and its outcomes. Piaget and Gagné emphasize the extent to which present learning develops out of earlier learning. Tolman, Hull, and Anderson offer many of these same suggestions in more technical form. All of these suggestions require ingenuity if they are to be put to practical use. Each, however, serves to emphasize some aspect of the learning process that we would be wise to consider. Thus each serves both to enrich our understanding of the learning situations we observe and to help us find solutions to the practical learning problems with which we have to deal. Although many theorists aspire to make a greater contribution than this, and to some extent succeed in doing so, this contribution alone is enough to make their theories invaluable to the study of learning.

Summary List of Theorists

Most of the theorists discussed in the text are listed here in the order in which they are considered. With each theorist are one or more key terms or summary comments particularly connected with that person.

Ivan P. Pavlov (1849–1936) Classical conditioning; excitation; inhibition.

John B. Watson (1878–1958) Founder of behaviorism; laws of frequency and recency.

Edward L. Thorndike (1874–1949) Law of effect; satisfiers and annoyers; cats in a puzzle box.

Edwin R. Guthrie (1886–1959) Single principle of learning by contiguity of a stimulus and a movement; maintaining stimuli; movement-produced stimuli; three methods of changing habits.

Clark L. Hull (1884–1952) Postulates and theorems; $_sE_R = {_s}H_R \times D \times K$.

Neal E. Miller (b. 1909) and John Dollard (1900–1980) Learned drives; imitation; personality; psychotherapy.

B. F. Skinner (1904–1990) Rejection of intervening variables; emphasis on reinforcement; respondent and operant behavior; shaping; behavior modification and other applications.

Max Wertheimer (1880–1943) Founder of gestalt psychology; emphasis on insight in education.

Wolfgang Köhler (1887–1967) Gestalt psychologist; research on problem solving in chimpanzees.

Jean Piaget (1896–1980) Development of schemas; accommodation and assimilation; four stages of development; conservation.

Edward C. Tolman (1886–1959) Purposive behaviorism; originator of intervening variables in psychology; sign-gestalt expectations; cognitive maps; latent learning.

John R. Anderson (b. 1947) ACT theory; declarative and procedural knowledge.

Terrence J. Sejnowski (b. 1947) Network models; NETtalk.

Robert A. Rescorla (b. 1940) Cognitive aspects of classical conditioning.

Joseph Wolpe (b. 1915) Systematic desensitization.

Donald Meichenbaum (b. 1940) Cognitive behavioral therapy; self-instructions.

Martin E. P. Seligman (b. 1942) Explanatory styles; biological constraints on learning; species-specific behavior; preparedness.

Robert M. Gagné (b. 1916) Development of hierarchical organization.

Albert Bandura (b. 1925) Imitation; modeling; self-efficacy; social cognitive theory.

David Premack (b. 1925) Response interpretation of reinforcement; reversibility of reinforcement relationship.

Norbert Wiener (1894–1964) Cybernetics; negative feedback.

Richard L. Solomon (1918–1995) Opponent-process theory of motivation.

Glossary

***a* process** *(Solomon)*   The hedonic effect produced immediately by a stimulus, lasting as long as the stimulus lasts.

accommodation *(Piaget)*   A change in a schema to incorporate new experience.

advance organizer *(Ausubel)*   A kind of general preview, designed to help a learner assimilate new material into an existing cognitive structure.

assimilation *(Piaget)*   Interpretation of new experiences in terms of an existing schema.

autoshaping   The learning of what appears to be an instrumental response (such as key pecking in pigeons) through the procedures of classical rather than instrumental conditioning.

***b* process** *(Solomon)*   The hedonic opponent process that lags behind and serves to counteract an *a* process.

behavior modification *(Skinner)*   The process of changing behavior in practical situations, such as education or psychotherapy, by appropriately changing the contingencies of reinforcement.

behavioral contrast *(Skinner)*   A higher rate of responding on a given schedule of reinforcement if it alternates with another schedule that provides fewer reinforcers.

behaviorism   Any learning theory that focuses on observable behaviors and the stimuli that control them, especially the early one propounded by J. B. Watson.

bliss point   The amount of time an individual would spend on an activity if there were no requirements or restrictions.

chain *(Skinner)*   A series of responses, leading to a reinforcer, that comes to function much like a single operant.

cognition   A belief (including expectancies, items of knowledge, and the like).

cognitive   Explaining behavior and learning in terms of cognitions.

cognitive behavioral therapy   Psychotherapy that attempts to modify behavior by first modifying thoughts, feelings, or self-instructions.

cognitive map *(Tolman)*   A cognition about where various things are located.

cognitive revolution   The historic change, largely during the 1960s and early 1970s, in which cognitive interpretations became more widely accepted than connectionist ones.

conditioned stimulus   See *conditioning, classical.*

conditioning, classical   A form of learning in which two stimuli are presented together and the response originally elicited by one of them, the unconditioned stimulus, comes to be elicited also by the other, the conditioned stimulus.

connectionism   The view that learning is the forming and changing of connections, now especially those interpretations based on models of neural networks.

connectionist   Dealing with the connections between stimuli and responses, especially as assumed to represent connections in the nervous system.

conservation *(Piaget)*   A person's understanding that certain characteristics of things, such as their length or number, remain the same when other characteristics are changed.

consummatory response *(Sheffield)*   A response that consummates and reinforces prior instrumental responses.

contiguity   The occurrence of two or more events together.

contingency *(Rescorla)*   Tendency for certain kinds of events, such as stimuli or reinforcers, to occur together more than would be expected by chance.

contingencies of reinforcement *(Skinner)*   Specific relationships of reinforcers to the responses and stimuli that precede them; determinants of when reinforcement occurs.

continuity position *(Hull and others)*   The interpretation that the process of learning a discrimination takes place gradually and continuously, opposed to *noncontinuity position*.

contraprepared *(Seligman)*   Especially difficult to learn; applied to a response in relation to particular stimuli or reinforcers with which that response is hard to learn.

controlled quantity *(cybernetics)*   A variable maintained at a set point by the operation of negative feedback.

critical delay duration *(Solomon)*   The longest delay between successive presentations of a stimulus that will still permit the b process to increase with repetition.

cue   A stimulus that serves to guide behavior.

cybernetics *(Wiener)*   The study of control mechanisms.

D *(Hull)*   Abbreviation for *drive*.

declarative knowledge *(Anderson)*   Knowledge in the form of propositions about what is true; "knowing that" (as opposed to *procedural knowledge*).

demand *(Tolman)*   A motive or desire for a given goal object.

discrimination   Learning to make different responses to similar stimuli.

disinhibition   Removal of inhibition.

drive   An aroused state that motivates action in an organism, and the reduction of which often functions as a reinforcer.

excitation *(Pavlov and others)*   The activation of a response tendency, as opposed to *inhibition*.

excitatory potential *(Hull)*   The strength of the tendency for a given response to occur.

experiment   A research study in which one or more independent variables are manipulated and the effects on one or more dependent variables are measured.

explanatory style *(Seligman)*   Tendency to explain events, particularly one's own bad experiences, as due either to internal, global, and stable factors or to external, specific, and unstable factors.

extinction   A weakening of the tendency to make a response when the response is not followed by a reinforcer.

fading *(Skinner)*   Gradually removing a prompt, so that the behavior supported by the prompt still continues.

feedback *(cybernetics)*   The process by which the effects of a response control that response.

negative The form of feedback that compensates for deviations so as to maintain a steady state.

fixed-interval schedule *(Skinner)* An arrangement in which reinforcement becomes available after a fixed period of time since the previous reinforcement.

fixed-ratio schedule *(Skinner)* An arrangement in which reinforcement becomes available after a given number of responses since the previous reinforcement.

fixed-time schedule *(Skinner)* A schedule of reinforcement in which reinforcers are delivered at a fixed rate regardless of what the individual does.

generalization The tendency for a response to occur to a new stimulus that is similar to one present during original learning.

genes The units of heredity.

gestalt A form or pattern perceived as a whole.

habit A learned tendency for a certain stimulus to elicit a certain response.

habit strength *(Hull)* The strength of the bond connecting a stimulus with a response.

hedonic Pertaining to pleasure and displeasure.

hierarchy A set of items categorized as being at different levels, which are commonly levels of generality.

homeostasis The process by which various physiological processes are regulated automatically at set points.

hypothesis A working assumption or tentative explanation or glorified guess. Believed by Krechevsky to occur in animal as well as human discrimination learning.

hypothesizing Assuming for theoretical purposes that something is true although it has not been shown to be definitely true.

imprinting The formation of attachments early in life, especially attachments of young birds to their parents.

incentive motivation *(Hull)* The strength of the tendency to approach a given goal object.

inhibition Suppression of a response by any active process within the organism (cf., various kinds of inhibition).

insight A sudden understanding of the solution to a problem.

irradiation *(Pavlov)* A spreading out of excitation or inhibition on the surface of the cortex.

K *(Hull)* Abbreviation for *incentive motivation.*

key A disk that when pressed closes an electrical circuit to activate a recording and/or reinforcing device, especially one designed to be pecked by pigeons.

knowledge compilation *(Anderson)* The process of converting declarative knowledge into effective procedural knowledge.

latent learning *(Tolman)* Learning that is not immediately evident in behavior.

law of effect *(Thorndike and other reinforcement theorists)* The principle that a tendency to make a response depends on the reinforcing consequences of making it.

law of exercise *(Thorndike)* The principle that simply making a response to a stimulus increases the likelihood that one will do so again; regarded as a much weaker principle than the law of effect.

law of frequency *(Watson)* The principle that the more often one has made a certain response to a particular stimulus, the more likely one is to do so again.

law of recency *(Watson and Guthrie)* The principle that the more recently one has made a certain response to a particular stimulus, the more likely one is to do so again.

law, scientific A statement about the conditions under which certain kinds of events occur.

learning curve A graph showing how much has been learned at each stage of practice.

maintaining stimuli *(Guthrie)*   Strong stimuli that keep an organism active; their removal contributes to learning.

mand *(Skinner)*   An utterance that instructs someone to do something.

manipulandum   A device that an organism can manipulate.

modeling *(Bandura)*   Trying to make oneself more like someone else (the model), either in specific behavior (equaling imitation) or in more general characteristics.

molar *(esp. Tolman)*   Analyzed at the level of everyday acts, as opposed to molecular.

molecular *(esp. Guthrie)*   Analyzed in terms of small units, such as stimulus elements or muscle contractions, as opposed to molar.

movement-produced stimuli *(Guthrie)*   Stimuli produced by one's own responses that serve to direct further behavior.

noncontinuity position *(Krechevsky and other cognitive theorists)*   The interpretation that discrimination learning takes place discontinuously, as the learner tests one hypothesis after another, learning at each stage only whether or not the current hypothesis is correct.

operant *(Skinner)*   A unit of behavior emitted by the organism without being elicited by a specific stimulus, as opposed to *respondent*.

orienting reflex   An aroused reaction to a novel stimulus.

oscillation *(Hull)*   Momentary random fluctuations in excitatory potential.

parallel (distributed) processing   Carrying out different mental or computer operations at the same time in different parts of a system, rather than one at a time.

phobia   An exaggerated fear.

postulates *(Hull)*   The basic statements in a theory, that are assumed to be true without proof and then used to deduce theorems.

prepared *(Seligman)*   Especially easy to learn; applied to a response in relation to particular stimuli or reinforcers that go well with it for rapid learning.

procedural knowledge *(Anderson)*   The ability to carry out procedures; "knowing how" (as opposed to *declarative knowledge*).

production theory (or system) *(Anderson)*   A theory of how knowledge gives rise to behavior.

program   A series of instructions, as for a computer or for a student using a teaching machine.

prompt *(Skinner)*   Any stimulus that makes a given operant more likely to occur.

psychotics   People who are mentally ill.

reinforcement   The strengthening of the tendency to make a response that occurs when the response is followed by a reinforcer.

> **continuous**   Occurring after every response.
>
> **intermittent**   Occurring after only some of the responses, according to any schedule of reinforcement.
>
> **vicarious**   Resulting from reinforcement to someone else (the model) rather than to the learner.

reinforcer   One of a class of events that, when they follow a response, increase the tendency for that response to occur.

> **conditioned**   One that is effective because of previous pairing with a primary reinforcer.
>
> **negative**   One whose removal strengthens the tendency for the response to occur.
>
> **positive**   (Understood when neither positive nor negative is specified.) One whose presentation strengthens the tendency for the response to occur.
>
> **primary**   One that is effective without prior learning.

respondent *(Skinner)*   A response elicited by a specific stimulus, as opposed to *operant*.

response Any item of behavior (usually analyzed in relation to a stimulus).

    consummatory One that consummates and reinforces instrumental responses.

    instrumental One that leads toward a goal.

scalloping *(Skinner)* A pattern of response, typical of fixed-interval schedules, in which the rate is lowest immediately after reinforcement and then gradually increases.

schedule of reinforcement *(Skinner)* The relationship of responses emitted to reinforcers received; the systematic pattern according to which reinforcers are delivered.

schema *(Piaget and others)* A fairly generalized cognition; an element of cognitive structure.

self-efficacy *(Bandura)* A person's sense of being able to deal effectively with the environment.

$_sE_R$ *(Hull)* Abbreviation for excitatory potential.

set point *(cybernetics)* The particular level at which a controlled quantity is maintained by negative feedback.

shaping *(Skinner)* Teaching a novel response by reinforcing closer and closer approximations to that behavior.

$_sH_R$ *(Hull)* Abbreviation for habit strength, an intervening variable.

Skinner box An experimental chamber in which an organism can be placed for measuring the rate at which some operant occurs under various conditions.

sociobiology *(Wilson)* The study of the genetic, evolutionary basis of social behavior.

species-specific behavior Behavior particularly characteristic of a given species of animal that will tend to appear in that species under a wide variety of conditions and without any special training.

spontaneous recovery The tendency for a response that has been extinguished to recover in strength with the passage of time without further training.

stimulus Any input of energy to the organism that tends to affect behavior.

stimulus control *(Skinner)* The capacity of a stimulus to determine whether and when a particular operant will occur.

subject A person or animal studied in an experiment.

systematic desensitization *(Wolpe)* A therapy for phobias, in which a person imagines feared objects while completely relaxed, gradually working up a hierarchy from least to most feared.

tact *(Skinner)* An utterance that conveys information, as opposed to *mand*.

theorem *(esp. Hull)* A statement deduced logically from a set of postulates.

theory A systematic way of describing and analyzing regularities in the way events occur, organizing scientific laws in a broader framework.

threshold The weakest stimulus that will elicit a response, either an external stimulus or an impulse within a network.

token economy *(Skinner)* A form of behavior modification in which the desired behavior is reinforced with some form of symbolic reward (functioning as a conditioned reinforcer) that can be traded for primary reinforcers.

variable A characteristic that can vary from one situation to another.

    dependent One that changes in response to changes in other (independent) variables.

    independent One whose changes produce or predict changes in other (dependent) variables.

    intervening Concepts hypothesized by a theorist to explain the connection between independent and dependent variables.

variable-interval schedule *(Skinner)* An arrangement in which reinforcement becomes available after a predetermined time since the previous reinforcement, a time that varies randomly with a specified average.

variable-ratio schedule *(Skinner)*   An arrangement in which reinforcement follows a predetermined number of responses since the previous reinforcement, a number which varies randomly with a specified average.

References

Allison, J. 1979. Demand economics and experimental psychology. *Behavioral Science* 24: 403–415.

———. 1983. *Behavioral economics*. New York: Praeger.

Anderson, J. R. 1982. Acquisition of cognitive skill. *Psychological Review* 89: 369–406.

———. 1983. *The architecture of cognition*. Cambridge, MA: Harvard University Press.

———. 1987. Skill acquisition: Compilation of weak-method problem solutions. *Psychological Review* 94: 192–210.

———. 1993. *Rules of the mind*. Hillsdale, NJ: Erlbaum.

Anderson, J. R., Boyle, C. F., & Reiser, B. J. 1985. Intelligent tutoring systems. *Science* 228: 456–462.

Atkinson, R. C. 1974. Teaching children to read using a computer. *American Psychologist* 29: 169–178.

Ausubel, D. P., Novak, J. D., & Hanesian, H. 1978. *Educational psychology: A cognitive view,* 2nd ed. New York: Holt, Rinehart & Winston.

Bandura, A., ed. 1971. *Psychological modeling: Conflicting theories*. Chicago: Aldine-Atherton.

———. 1973. *Aggression*. Englewood Cliffs, NJ: Prentice-Hall.

———. 1977. *Social learning theory*. Englewood Cliffs, NJ: Prentice-Hall.

———. 1982. Self-efficacy mechanism in human agency. *American Psychologist* 37: 122–147.

———. 1986. *Social foundations of thought and action: A social cognitive theory*. Englewood Cliffs, NJ: Prentice–Hall.

Bandura, A., Adams, N. E., & Beyer, J. 1977. Cognitive processes mediating behavioral change. *Journal of Personality and Social Psychology* 35: 125–139.

Bandura, A., & Walters, R. H. 1963. *Social learning and personality development*. New York: Holt, Rinehart and Winston.

Bazerman, M. H., & Neale, M. A. 1992. *Negotiating rationally*. New York: Free Press.

Bechtel, W., & Abrahamsen, A. 1991. *Connectionism and the mind: An introduction to parallel processing in networks.* Cambridge, MA: Blackwell.

Bekhterev, V. M. 1994. *Collective reflexology,* ed. L. H. Strickland. Trans. by E. Lockwood. New York: Nova Science Publishers.

Berlyne, D. E. 1960. *Conflict, arousal, and curiosity.* New York: McGraw-Hill.

Berlyne, D. E., & Madsen, K. B., eds. 1973. *Pleasure, reward, preference: Their nature, determinants, and role in behavior.* New York: Academic Press.

Bolles, R. C. 1970. Species-specific defense reactions and avoidance learning. *Psychological Review* 77: 32–48.

Boneau, C. A. 1974. Paradigm regained? Cognitive behaviorism restated. *American Psychologist* 29: 297–309.

Bouchard, T. J., Jr. 1994. Genes, environment, and personality. *Science,* 264: 1700–1701.

Breland, K., & Breland, M. 1961. The misbehavior of organisms. *American Psychologist* 16: 681–684.

Brooks, R. A. 1991. New approaches to robotics. *Science* 253: 1227–1232.

Brown, P. L., & Jenkins, H. M. 1968. Auto-shaping of the pigeon's key peck. *Journal of the Experimental Analysis of Behavior* 11: 1–8.

Buchanan, G. McC., & Seligman, M. E. P., eds. 1995. Explanatory style. Hillsdale, NJ: Erlbaum.

Buxton, C. E. 1940. Latent learning and the goal gradient hypothesis. *Contributions to Psychological Theory* 2: 6.

Campbell, D. T., & Krantz, D. L. Tolman's failure as a tribal leader: An essay in the social psychology of science. Paper read at 82nd annual convention of the American Psychological Association, 1 September 1974, New Orleans. Mimeographed.

Chambers, J. A., & Sprecher, J. W. 1983. *Computer-assisted instruction: Its use in the classroom.* Englewood Cliffs, NJ: Prentice-Hall.

Chomsky, N. 1959. Review of Skinner's "Verbal behavior." *Language* 35: 26–58.

Cowan, P. E. 1977. Neophobia and neophilia: New-object and new-place reactions of three Rattus species. *Journal of Comparative and Physiological Psychology* 91: 63–71.

Cowan, P. A., Langer, J., Heavenrich, J., & Nathanson, M. 1969. Social learning and Piaget's cognitive theory of moral development. *Journal of Personality and Social Psychology* 11: 261–274.

Dollard, J. C., & Miller, N. E. 1950. *Personality and psychotherapy.* New York: McGraw-Hill.

Elms, A. C. 1981. Skinner's dark year and *Walden Two. American Psychologist* 36: 470–479.

Epstein, S. 1967. Toward a unified theory of anxiety. In *Progress in experimental personality research,* vol. 4, ed. B. A. Maher. New York: Academic Press.

Ernst, G., & Newell, A. 1969. *GPS: A case study in generality and problem solving.* New York: Academic Press.

Eron, L. D., Huesmann, L. R., Lefkowitz, M. M., & Walder, L. O. 1972. Does television violence cause aggression? *American Psychologist* 27: 253–263.

Estes, W. K. 1959. The statistical approach to learning theory. In *Psychology: A study of a science,* vol. 2, ed. S. Koch. New York: McGraw-Hill.

Faber, S. (1995). We're number 2. *Discover* 16: 103.

Feigenbaum, E. A., & Feldman, J., eds. 1963. *Computers and thought.* New York: McGraw-Hill.

Ferster, C. B., & Skinner, B. F. 1957. *Schedules of reinforcement.* New York: Appleton-Century-Crofts.

Flavell, J. H. 1963. *The developmental psychology of Jean Piaget.* New York: Van Nostrand.

Frey, P. 1983. *Chess skill in man and machine,* 2nd ed. New York: Springer-Verlag.

Gagné, R. M. 1962a. The acquisition of knowledge. *Psychological Review* 69: 355–365.

————. 1962b. Military training and principles of learning. *American Psychologist* 17: 83–91.

Garcia, J., & Koelling, R. 1966. Relation of cue to consequence in avoidance learning. *Psychonomic Science* 4: 123–124.

Gardner, B. T., & Gardner, R. A. 1980. Two comparative psychologists look at language acquisition. In *Children's language,* vol. 2, ed. K. E. Nelson. New York: Halsted.

Gardner, R. A., & Gardner, B. T. 1969. Teaching sign language to a chimpanzee. *Science* 165: 664–672.

Glaser, R. 1990. The reemergence of learning theory within instructional research. *American Psychologist* 45: 29–39.

Glickman, S. E., & Schiff, B. B. 1967. A biological theory of reinforcement. *Psychological Review* 74: 81–109.

Godden, D., & Baddeley, A. D. 1975. Context-dependent memory in two natural environments: On land and under water. *British Journal of Psychology* 66: 325–331.

Greenspoon, J. 1955. The reinforcing effect of two spoken sounds on the frequency of two responses. *American Journal of Psychology* 68: 409–416.

Guthrie, E. R. 1960. *The psychology of learning,* rev. ed. Gloucester, MA: Smith.

Guthrie, E. R., & Horton, G. P. 1946. *Cats in a puzzle box.* New York: Rinehart.

Hanson, H. M. 1959. Effects of discrimination training on stimulus generalization. *Journal of Experimental Psychology* 58: 321–334.

Hanson, S. J., & Timberlake, W. 1983. Regulation during challenge: A general model of learned performance under schedule constraint. *Psychological Review* 90: 261–282.

Harlow, H. F. 1958. The nature of love. *American Psychologist* 18: 673–685.

Harlow, H. F., Harlow, M. K., & Meyer, D. R. 1950. Learning motivated by a manipulation drive. *Journal of Experimental Psychology* 40: 228–234.

Hart, B. M., Allen, K. E., Buell, J. S., Harris, F. R., & Wolf, M. M. 1964. Effects of social reinforcement on operant crying. *Journal of Experimental Child Psychology* 1: 145–153.

Hebb, D. O. 1949. *The organization of behavior.* New York: Wiley.

Heppenheimer, T. A. 1988. Nerves of silicon. *Discover* 9 (2): 70–79.

Hilgard, E. R. 1964. A perspective on the relationship between learning theory and educational practices. In *Theories of learning and instruction. Sixty-third yearbook of the National Society for the Study of Education, Part I,* ed. E. R. Hilgard. Chicago: University of Chicago Press.

Hilgard, E. R., & Marquis, D. G. 1940. *Conditioning and learning.* New York: Appleton-Century-Crofts.

Hill, W. F. 1956. Activity as an autonomous drive. *Journal of Comparative and Physiological Psychology* 49: 15–19.

———. 1968. Sources of evaluative reinforcement. *Psychological Bulletin* 69: 132–146.

———. 1978. Effects of mere exposure on preferences in nonhuman mammals. *Psychological Bulletin* 85: 1177–1198.

Hillner, K. P. 1978. *Psychology of Learning: A conceptual analysis.* New York: Pergamon.

Hoffman, H. S., Eiserer, L. A., Ratner, A. M., & Pickering, V. L. 1974. Development of distress vocalization during withdrawal of an imprinting stimulus. *Journal of Comparative and Physiological Psychology* 86: 563–568.

Hull, C. L. 1943. *Principles of behavior.* New York: Appleton-Century-Crofts.

———. 1952. *A behavior system.* New Haven: Yale University Press.

Huxley, A. L. 1932. *Brave new world.* London: Chatto & Windus.

Kagan, J., & Berkun, M. 1954. The reward value of running activity. *Journal of Comparative and Physiological Psychology* 47: 108.

Kazdin, A. E. 1994. *Behavior modification in applied settings,* 5th ed. Chicago: Dorsey.

Kinkade, K. 1973. *A Walden Two experiment: The first five years of Twin Oaks Community.* New York: Morrow.

Kohlberg, L. 1964. The development of moral character and ideology. In *Review of child developmental research,* M. L. Hoffman & L. W. Hoffman, Vol. 1. New York: Russell Sage.

Köhler, W. 1925. *The mentality of apes,* trans. from 2nd rev. ed. by Ella Winter. New York: Harcourt Brace Jovanovich.

Komar, I. 1983. *Living the dream: A documentary study of the Twin Oaks community.* Norwood, PA: Norwood.

Krechevsky, I. (1932). "Hypotheses" in rats. *Psychological Review* 39: 516–532.

Lawicka, W. 1964. The role of stimuli modality in successive discrimination and differentiation learning. *Bulletin of the Polish Academy of Sciences* 12: 35–38.

Levine, M. (1970). Human discrimination learning: The subset sampling assumption. *Psychological Bulletin* 74: 397–404.

Linden, E. 1974. *Apes, men, and language.* New York: Saturday Review Press, E. P. Dutton.

Lorenz, K. Z. 1952. *King Solomon's ring.* New York: Crowell.

Meichenbaum, D. H. 1971. Examination of model characteristics in reducing avoidance behavior. *Journal of Personality and Social Psychology* 17: 298–307.

Meichenbaum, D. H. 1977. *Cognitive behavior modification: An integrative approach.* New York: Plenum.

Miller, G. A., Galanter, E., & Pribram, K. H. 1960. *Plans and the structure of behavior.* New York: Holt.

Miller, N. E. 1963. Some reflections on the law of effect produce a new alternative to drive reduction. In *Nebraska symposium on motivation,* vol. 11, ed. M. R. Jones. Lincoln: University of Nebraska Press.

Miller, N. E., & Dollard, J. C. 1941. *Social learning and imitation.* New Haven: Yale University Press.

Moore, B. R., & Stuttard, S. 1979. Dr. Guthrie and *Felis domesticus:* On tripping over the cat. *Science* 205: 1031–1033.

Neisser, U. 1967. *Cognitive psychology.* New York: Appleton-Century-Crofts.

Orwell, G. 1949. *1984.* New York: Harcourt Brace Jovanovich.

Osgood, C. E. (1953). *Method and theory in experimental psychololgy.* New York: Oxford University Press.

Pavlov, I. P. 1960. *Conditioned reflexes,* trans. and ed. by G. V. Anrep. New York: Dover (orig. trans. Oxford University Press, 1927).

Peterson, C., Maier, S. F., & Seligman, M. E. P. 1993. *Learned helplessness: A theory for the age of personal control.* New York: Oxford University Press.

Phillips, J. L., Jr. 1981. Piaget's theory: A primer. San Francisco: Freeman.

Piaget, J. 1926. *The language and thought of the child,* trans. by M. Worden. New York: Harcourt Brace Jovanovich.

————. 1932. *The moral development of the child.* New York: Harcourt Brace Jovanovich.

Powers, W. T. 1973. *Behavior: The control of perception.* Chicago: Aldine.

Premack, D. 1959. Toward empirical behavior laws: I. Positive reinforcement. *Psychological Review* 66: 219–233.

————. 1962. Reversibility of the reinforcement relation. *Science* 136: 255–257.

Razran, G. 1961. The observable unconscious and the inferable conscious in current Soviet psychophysiology: Interoceptive conditioning, semantic conditioning, and the orienting reflex. *Psychological Review* 68: 81–147.

Rescorla, R. A. 1988. Pavlovian conditioning: It's not what you think. *American Psychologist* 43: 151–160.

Restle, F. 1966. Run structure and probability learning: Disproof of Restle's model. *Journal of Experimental Psychology* 72: 382–389.

Rosenfeld, H. M., & Baer, D. M. 1969. Unnoticed verbal conditioning of an aware experimenter by a more aware subject: The double-agent effect. *Psychological Review* 76: 425–432.

Schank, R. C., & Abelson, R., 1977. *Scripts, plans, goals, and understanding.* Hillsdale, NJ: Erlbaum.

Schwartz, A. 1982. *The behavior therapies: Theories and application.* New York: Free Press.

Sechenov, I. M. 1965. *Reflexes of the brain,* ed. G. Gibbons; trans. by S. Belsky. Cambridge, MA: MIT Press.

Sejnowski, T. J., & Rosenberg, C. R. 1987. Parallel networks that learn to pronounce English text. *Complex Systems,* 1, 145–168.

Seligman, M. E. P. 1970. On the generality of the laws of learning. *Psychological Review* 77: 406–418.

Seligman, M. E. P., & Johnston, J. C. 1973. A cognitive theory of avoidance learning. In *Contemporary approaches to conditioning and learning,* eds. F. J. McGuigan & D. B. Lumsden. Washington, D.C.: V. H. Winston.

Seward, J. P. 1942. An experimental study of Guthrie's theory of reinforcement. *Journal of Experimental Psychology* 30: 247–256.

Sheffield, F. D., & Roby, T. B. 1950. Reward value of a nonnutritive sweet taste. *Journal of Comparative and Physiological Psychology* 43: 471–481.

Simon, H. A., & Newell, A. 1971. Human problem solving: The state of the theory in 1970. *American Psychologist* 26: 145–159.

Skinner, B. F. 1938. *The behavior of organisms: An experimental analysis.* New York: Appleton-Century-Crofts.

———. 1948. *Walden Two.* New York: Macmillan.

———. 1953. *Science and human behavior.* New York: Macmillan.

———. 1957a. The experimental analysis of behavior. *American Scientist* 45: 343–371.

———. 1957b. *Verbal behavior.* New York: Appleton-Century-Crofts.

———. 1958. Reinforcement today. *American Psychologist* 13: 94–99.

———. 1968. *The technology of teaching.* New York: Appleton-Century-Crofts.

———. 1971. *Beyond freedom and dignity.* New York: Knopf.

———. 1979. *The shaping of a behaviorist: Part two of an autobiography.* New York: Knopf.

Smith, K. U., & Smith, M. F. 1966. *Cybernetic principles of learning and educational design.* New York: Holt, Rinehart & Winston.

Smith, M. L., Glass, G. V., & Miller, T. I. 1980. *The benefits of psychotherapy.* Baltimore: Johns Hopkins Press.

Solomon, R. L. 1980. The opponent-process theory of acquired motivation: The costs of pleasure and the benefits of pain. *American Psychologist* 35: 691–712.

Solomon, R. L., & Corbit, J. D. 1974. An opponent-process theory of motivation: I. Temporal dynamics of affect. *Psychological Review* 81: 119–145.

Spielberger, C. D., & DeNike, L. D. 1966. Descriptive behaviorism versus cognitive theory in verbal operant conditioning. *Psychological Review* 73: 306–326.

Stanfill, C., & Waltz, D. 1986. Toward memory-based reasoning. *Communications of the ACM* 29: 1213–1228.

Sullivan, E. V. 1967. The acquisition of conservation of substance through film-mediated models. In *Recent research on the acquisition of conservation of substance,* eds. D. W. Brison & E. V. Sullivan. Education Monograph. Toronto: Ontario Institute for Studies in Education.

Terrace, H. S. 1963. Discrimination learning with and without "errors." *Journal of the Experimental Analysis of Behavior* 6: 1–27.

———. 1971. Escape from S—. *Learning and Motivation* 2: 148–163.

Thorndike, E. L. 1898. Animal intelligence: An experimental study of the associative processes in animals. *Psychological Review Monograph Supplements* 2, no. 8.

———. 1913. *The psychology of learning.* New York: Teachers College, Columbia University.

Timberlake, W., & Allison, J. 1974. Response deprivation: An empirical approach to instrumental performance. *Psychological Review* 81: 146–164.

Thorndike, E. L. (1935). The psychology of wants, interests, and attitudes. New York: Appleton-Century-Crofts.

Tolman, E. C. 1932. *Purposive behavior in animals and men.* New York: Appleton-Century-Crofts.

11

———. 1938. The determinants of behavior at a choice point. *Psychological Review* 45: 1–41.

———. 1942. *Drives toward war.* New York: Appleton-Century-Crofts.

———. 1959. Principles of purposive behavior. In *Psychology: A study of a science*, vol. 2, ed. S. Koch. New York: McGraw-Hill.

Tolman, E. C., Ritchie, B. F., & Kalish, D. 1946. Studies in spatial learning: I. Orientation and the shortcut. *Journal of Experimental Psychology* 36: 13–24.

Verplanck, W. S. 1955. The control of the content of conversation: Reinforcement of statements of opinion. *Journal of Abnormal and Social Psychology* 51: 668–676.

Waldrop, M. M. 1988a. Toward a unified theory of cognition. *Science* 241: 27–29.

———. 1988b. Soar: A unified theory of cognition? *Science* 241: 296–298.

Walter, W. G. 1953. *The living brain.* New York: Norton.

Watson, J. B. 1913. Psychology as the behaviorist views it. *Psychological Review* 20: 158–177.

———. 1930. *Behaviorism,* rev. ed. Chicago: University of Chicago Press. (6th printing, 1966.)

Welker, W. I. 1961. An analysis of exploratory and play behavior in animals. In *Functions of varied experience*, eds. D. W. Fiske & S. R. Maddi. Homewood, Ill.: Dorsey.

Wertheimer, M. 1945. *Productive thinking.* New York: Harper & Row.

Wiener, N. 1948. *Cybernetics.* New York: Wiley.

Wilcoxon, H. C., Dragoin, W. B., & Kral, P. A. 1971. Illness-induced aversions in rat and quail: Relative salience of visual and gustatory cues. *Science* 171: 826–828.

Williams, D. R., & Williams, H. 1969. Auto-maintenance in the pigeon: Sustained pecking despite contingent nonreinforcement. *Journal of the Experimental Analysis of Behavior* 12: 511–520.

Wilson, E. O. 1975. *Sociobiology.* Cambridge, MA: Harvard University Press.

Wolpe, J. 1958. *Psychotherapy by reciprocal inhibition.* Stanford, CA: Stanford University Press.

——— 1973. *The practice of behavior therapy,* 2nd ed. New York: Pergamon.

Woodworth, R. S., & Schlosberg, H. (1954). *Experimental psychology.* Rev. ed. New York: Holt, Rinehart & Winston.

SUPPLEMENTAL REFERENCES

Readers wanting to study more thoroughly the topics covered in this book may find the following references helpful.

Bower, G. H., & Hilgard, E. R. 1981. *Theories of learning,* 5th ed. Englewood Cliffs, NJ: Prentice-Hall. The standard secondary reference on theories of learning through the 1970s, providing both authoritative descriptions and critical evaluations. The chapters vary in ease of reading; some are rather technical.

Koch, S., ed. 1959. *Psychology: A study of a science,* Vol. 2. New York: McGraw-Hill. A collection of 12 readings on various learning theories, most of them written by the theorists themselves. The study, of which this volume forms a part, emphasizes certain topics in the philosophy of science, with the result that the distinctive styles of some of the authors are partly lost. In addition, it was published before a number of the developments discussed in the present book had occurred. However, this is the most complete source book available for the classic learning theories.

Mazur, J. E. 1994. *Learning and behavior,* 3rd ed. Englewood Cliffs, NJ: Prentice-Hall. A presentation of current psychology of learning organized by topics rather than by theories and with a good deal of experimental data on numerous issues that concern psychologists of learning.

Index